Hitler's Inferno:
Eight Personal
Histories
from the Holocaust

Vera Schiff

ISBN (paper): 0-974-92701-5

The map of the camps on page 6 and the photographs not courtesy of the author, are from *The Holocaust*, by Gerhard Schoenberner, translated by Susan Sweet and published by Hurtig Publishers Ltd., Edmonton, Canada. The photograph on page 292 is by Obozu Zaglady.

Library of Congress Control Number 2002108904

First Edition
First Printing 2002

Introduction

Hitler's Inferno is an anthology, describing the unique fates of several relatives and friends of the author. The book joins an impressive library of Holocaust literature attempting to bring the reader some understanding of the terrible days of Nazi rule.

Much has been said and written about those times, but *Hitler's Inferno* offers in some ways new and different insights. The author was either a relative or a personal friend of the men and women described. Although all hailed from Czechoslovakia, the war took them to many different camps, which are described in some detail. Some of the camps were practically unknown, like Maly Trostinec, a death camp in Belarus. Others are more notorious, but it is the day-to-day life of these human beings in inhuman conditions that casts a new light on the unique attempts at survival by those destined to die.

Many feel that they have learned much about those times, and there is no doubt in my mind that this is the case. Still I believe that there is no better way to gain insight into the physical and emotional anguish of the victims than by following the footsteps of those who walked the path. While the Nazi concentration camps shared many basic features, there were also marked differences from one to another. In addition, the individuals coped in different ways, in a manner distinct to their personality, character, strengths and convictions. Each inmate's account is a study, to be scrutinized, to learn from our responses to their reactions under circumstances of extreme duress.

Now, half a century later, we still try to comprehend and analyze not only the perpetrators, but the victims as well, for much can be learned about mankind in dire circumstances trapped without possible escape if we more fully grasp their personal travails.

The author changed a few names to protect the feelings of relatives, who might possibly be pained to know that their dear ones had to use means that in different times would be considered objectionable or even worse to try and survive. Perhaps the reader can honestly ask how he himself would have been in a hopeless situation; what price to pay for a chance at life?

The book recounts the sagas of young individuals who desperately wanted to live and who fought for and lost those they loved. We catch a glimpse into the torment of decent individuals who reached the end of their tether and yet were not willing to give up, hoping to live to see the end of the war, if for no other reason than to be there when retribution came.

I believe we can learn a great deal about man's naked emotions in the final battle against insurmountable odds. The reader will be interested in the differences in reactions and responses to the unprecedented maltreatment of European Jewry.

Vera Schiff, the author of this work, is herself a survivor of the Nazi rule of terror and shared her incarceration with most of the individuals depicted in this book. Only an insider can truly understand and discuss those years with authority; for most others the experience is truly beyond imagination.

Although historians and students have written much of the Holocaust, it is only the survivor who can with full authenticity depict how it really was. All else is speculative and often incorrect. How can an outsider know how each day unfolded, how hunger, the ever-present death threats, physical torments, passions and loves were handled? Nothing could prepare a normal human being for a comparable situation. Who can say how deep a man can and will stoop to ease his suffering?

We can also contemplate, and many an inmate did, not only the qualities of mankind, but indeed religion and God Himself. While European Jewry emerged from the Holocaust decimated, many believe that true faith and worship suffered an even worse fate. Some devoted and pious Jews accused God, and found Him guilty.

It is also obvious that the survivor has no other agenda but to report about the true events that typified the Nazi period. She is motivated by her desire to preserve the memory of her dear ones and to cast an exposing light on misunderstood or incorrectly reported facts.

The survivors, often misunderstood, present a disquieting and uncomfortable reminder of a past many in the world wish forgotten. Many may carry feelings of a vague guilt of less than heroic comport, that perhaps they were remiss in not doing all they could to save the persecuted Jews.

Immediately after the Second World War, most nations did not know what to make of the handful that went through the fires of hell and lived to tell their tale. Some thought that most survivors were damaged and warped by the experience; others believed they were bound for a criminal future. Quite to the contrary, most survivors lived an honorable and productive life, wanting nothing more than to make the world see.

This anthology is such an attempt, perhaps one of the last few, penned by one with the unfortunate, first-hand knowledge. All we can endeavor to do is to learn from these accounts of our not too distant, tragic past and hope for the often repeated "Never again."

Hitler's Inferno

Foreword

To write about the worst phase of our history is not easy; indeed it sparks off momentous difficulties for the survivor who embarks upon such an endeavor. It is painful to reopen the scarred wounds and one more time reflect upon the tragedy that befell us. But there is a compelling force nudging me, reminding me that my debt to those who lost their voices in the Holocaust is not settled. Then, during the dark days of Hitler's rule of unprecedented brutality, the wholesale murder of Jews, aided by twentieth century technology, escalated into genocide of unparalleled proportions—indeed, the catastrophe assumed unmatched dimensions.

Most of us—the best of us indeed—did perish. Europe's soil became soaked with Jewish blood, turning the continent the Jews loved and worked for into an unmarked mass grave. It ended the century's long presence of Jews in the heart of Europe, leaving only a handful surviving the carnage. In some parts of Europe, 90% of Jews were wiped out. In some countries, the statistics were worse; in others, slightly less overwhelming. A new crime entered the tormented history of mankind: Genocide. The annihilation of Jews was a brainchild of the Nazis, conceived in secrecy by Hitler and his cohorts. The apocalypse unfolded exactly as the sinister script projected it. It was orchestrated mainly by the members of the SS elite units and was perpetrated behind the walls of the modern-day torture chambers: the concentration camps.

In the first stages of the mass murder, the world pleaded ignorance, giving a benefit of doubt to the Nazis. In later years, namely from 1942 onwards, the disbelief was only pretended, for the Allies knew well enough what came to pass behind the tall walls and barbed wires. But the world preferred to remain silent, tacitly in cahoots with the mass destruction of the Jews, hoping

that the Nazis would resolve the cumbersome "Jewish question."
What better way to do away with the stiff-necked Jews, who
refused to vanish from the pages of history like a tiny homeless
people should do? And, what's more, the crazed Nazis did the
dirty work for the other "civilized" nations, who could put on an
air of exasperated anger while staying out of the mess and keeping
their hands clean. Yes, the world knew all too well, but they
wanted the Nazis to finish the job undisturbed.

It is the tragic truth that the dying inmates of the camps
believed—to their last labored breath—that the world at large did
not know, that the dark secret was concealed by the master
manipulators: the Nazis.

During the long three years of my incarceration, I saw many
die and all of them, for as long as they had voice and strength,
whispered their fervent wish, "Should you survive the catastrophe,
bear witness, tell the world about the infamies and horrible
tragedies inflicted upon innocent men, women and children." I
cannot recall a single one of them, approaching death, whose lips
did not mouth the words: "Bear witness! Let the world know about
our innocent martyrdom!"

Few of us lived up to the legacy and fulfilled the obligation
towards the millions of our victims. While it is true that the world
did know, still we were charged by our dead to testify about the
modern-day Huns. Our only justification is that it was not easy to
come back and relive the days of terror, which dwarfed the
Spanish Inquisition, the pogroms, the forcible baptismal, killing
and looting of the days gone by.

I was no exception. I, too, wanted to forget the unforgettable,
push back or out of my mind the nightmarish years that followed
me persistently into my fitful sleep, forcing me to meet our
tormentors over and over again. It was an uphill battle, but we
would not concede that we could not win. We refused to admit
that the Holocaust changed everything. Not only the fabric of our
families (mostly non-existent, wiped out during the onslaught), but
all our decisions, plans and ambitions were skewed and distorted
by the experience seared deep into our subconscious.

Only towards the end of my days did I accept the fact (which
I spent most of my life valiantly fighting against), namely that

though we have physically survived, that part of us died there in the horror camps. The remaining part that tried to regenerate into a normal human being was injured, often motivated by the torment we experienced. We were liberated, but never really free. To some extent we remained captives and victims of Hitler's devastation long after he blew his brains out. The effects of human depravity we witnessed were etched into our beings, and we could not erase it, no matter how hard we tried.

In the book: *Theresienstadt: the Town the Nazis Gave to the Jews*, I described my experiences before, during and briefly after the Second World War. My second book is dedicated to the special people who were nearest and dearest to me. Some were my relatives, others friends; and a few were people whose fate was so distinct and riveting that I took the liberty to depict in a shortened form their destinies during the Holocaust. Neither book was easy to write.

TABLE OF CONTENTS

A map on page 6 shows the locations of the concentration (labor) camps and death camps that the Nazis created and administered.

Photographs appear on pages 8, 34, 64, 114, 164, 198, 244, 289, 292, 339 and 343.

Prologue

It was a unique pleasure to collaborate with my mother, the author, in bringing this work to light.

After reading *Hitler's Inferno: Eight Personal Histories from the Holocaust*, I was deeply moved. I was well acquainted with the Holocaust through frequent dinner-table conversations with family and friends, as well as my readings. Even so, I was magically transported into the very lives of wonderful human beings battling for their very existence during those turbulent and intriguing times.

The author with first-hand experience sets the background, historically and individually, placing the reader in the shoes of our heroes caught in the web of destruction. The stories are intimate, colored by rich descriptions of relationships born out of familiarity with the times and subjects.

Each account begins with the individual's pre-war life, family and other central relationships. We share their experience of the coming winds of war, their reactions, futile attempts at escape and their journey to and trials in the various concentration camps. Each report is inimitable, a product of the being and setting.

Their journeys to, and struggles in, the concentration camps are presented in a matter-of-fact manner, aimed at accuracy without embellishment or motive. The reader will see and feel through the author's lens of familiarity, which clarifies and reaches one's core through empathy of the human experience.

The accounts are meant to be historically accurate, a testimony witnessed by the author, close relatives and friends. This anthology describes their desperate decisions; to survive or save loved ones—all in a setting not of their making, sentenced to death because they were Jews. A question echoed in my mind: What would I have done?

I write this one-month after the World Trade Center and Pentagon disasters, as the world spasms in another war of intolerance that threatens to engulf the globe. Some have, more and less gently, questioned the value of "another Holocaust book." Is there relevance and importance here?

The historical documentation, by itself, of eight courageous lives, with the shrill Holocaust deniers' voices and the diminishing numbers of aging survivors, is tragically relevant. The revisionists of history call for vigorous rebuttal. In addition, the author's unique presentation brings fresh access and insights allowing for study of the times and human behavior under extreme duress.

Many a Jew, time and again, on leaving for certain death, would look back at those left behind, often family or friends still with a chance at survival, and say or mouth the words: "Do not let them forget us! Let the world know what happened here to us!" Why was this so important for them? Is it for us? Perhaps there is a lesson they wished we learn so their deaths would not be in vain. For the author perhaps some promise is fulfilled.

Some may associate the title, *Hitler's Inferno* with Dante's literary masterpiece. Dissimilarly, Hitler's was no work of fiction, but a manmade hell. Dante depicted nine circles of torment commensurate to differing infractions; Hitler required only one, but like Dante, established progressive levels of anguish. Hitler's version is the more real, its embers still glowing and threatening to re-ignite.

In these eight stories, the author shows man's dark side with its cohorts while simultaneously bringing light to the potential and grace of life burning within each, even in the cruelest of subjugations. The continuing, age-old battle for tolerance is opposed by dogma, ignorance and violence. Humanity, in its regressed states, has and will stoop to levels unknown in the animal kingdom. Our destructive potential and tendencies, our immaturities, now exponentially amplified by our technological prowess, menace mankind's very survival. Evil deeds and wrongs must be grappled with on all fronts, with all our fortitude, or another Holocaust will fall upon us and our children. Many have stated that this will be no easy task. I believe it will require a true understanding of our "nature" while nurturing wisdom, courage, love, intelligence and maturity.

MDS 10/11/01.

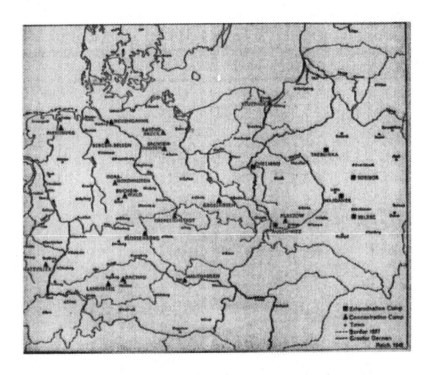

Concentration Camps (triangles) and Death Camps (squares) in the territories occupied by Germany during the Second World War (1939-1945). All the death camps were located outside the German Reich in occupied Poland, the so-called General Government where the Waffen SS exercised total control. The difference between the treatment of prisoners in death camps and their treatment in the concentration camps was one of degree, not kind. For most inmates, being sent to either kind of camp amounted to a death sentence.

Helen: Beautiful Mistress

The "Small Fortress" today in Theresienstadt.
It was in this place of torture and death that Helen's lover,
the Elder of the Jews, Paul Epstein, met his end.
(Photo courtesy of the author.)

All I could do was stare in awe. Never before had I seen such a stunning woman and one with so powerful a presence. Leading the way into the "Hamburg" barracks was the gaunt "Alteste," the elder in charge. Following was a short, colorless woman well beyond her prime, and behind her walked a tall woman of such radiance and beauty that she seemed to illuminate the shabby, gloomy hall.

We were in the concentration camp "Theresienstadt," and it was there I first saw Helen. The all-too-powerful Alteste assigned her an adjacent bunk, and while Helen busied herself with the arrangement of her bundles, I could not help but fix my eyes upon her.

She was a tall, slim, well-shaped girl, whose poise and finesse were a singular mixture of elegance and sensuality. She had thick, almost black hair, somewhat softened by a shiny titian glow. It fell to her shoulders in smooth waves. Her oval face revealed classical loveliness; her complexion resembled translucent alabaster. Her cheeks had a slight shade of pink, and her large, almond-shaped eyes glittered. Her lips were sensuous, and when she smiled she displayed two rows of snow-white teeth. In different times such a woman would have been assured a brilliant future for her exquisite looks.

Later I discovered that in addition to her looks, she had charm and a sharp mind combined with savvy and flair. Probably she felt my gaze, for she lifted her head and on noticing my barely concealed admiration, she smiled, and said: "I am Helen. What is your name, and how long have you been stuck in this place?"

And so began our friendship. Helen was my senior by some seven years. When we first met she was 24 years old, worldly, experienced, sophisticated and married. I was none of the above. At 17 I was inexperienced, naïve, trying to learn the ropes and traverse what seemed to me to be a labyrinth in the complex, alien world of a Nazi concentration camp. I truly loathed and feared my innocence and inability to manipulate events to my advantage. To be a guileless, innocent young girl was the worst single liability in the German detention camps for a Jew.

Although heartbreak and ill luck had marked Helen long before we met, no one would have guessed it by looking at her. The fact that she was a target of much envy was perhaps not deliberate on her part, but it nonetheless met with her full approval.

Moments later while we chatted, another unheard-of violation of the camp's protocol occurred. A young man entered the hall where only women prisoners were held, passed quickly by the speechless Alteste, and handed Helen a small parcel. It was John, Helen's husband, who, at the risk of harsh penalties, violated the taboo that prohibited men from entering the women's barracks.

John either did not know or considered the risk well calculated. There was no other way to smuggle in some food and, as every inmate soon learned, hunger was one of the worst curses of the camp. John didn't look like a fool or a man bent on suicide; rather, he was tall and slim, probably in his late twenties, and his bespectacled face disclosed seriousness and intelligence. He handed the parcel to Helen, gave her a perfunctory kiss, and quickly vanished into thin air. To my teenage imagination this was the gallant knight who was willing to risk all for the lady of his heart.

Perhaps Helen wanted to set me straight, because as soon as John left she began to talk about her marriage. She usually referred to John as her "best friend." Whenever Helen talked about or to John, she used cordial and warm expressions and tones of voice, as one would use while speaking to a dear friend. Even to me, a total novice in the field of love, it was clear that she was not in love with her husband. He, in turn, looked at her with unconcealed admiration and affection.

Helen told me that she chose John because he was a decent, reliable chap, whose courage and intelligence were legendary. His professional standing as a physician was another asset; even in captivity a medical doctor might have a better chance of survival. Another reason was that John loved her in the most devoted and selfless way, grateful just to be around her. She was certain that John would make no demands on her and would tolerate her every whim. Helen liked the scenario of a man slavishly enthralled by her, doing her bidding, asking for nothing in return.

John had been overjoyed by Helen's choice and so were her parents. Not only did they delight in her choice, but they also appreciated the expansion of their small family with a young, competent, decent and smart man, whom they had known and loved since his childhood.

Helen and John married in a quiet ceremony in the local synagogue officiated by the local rabbi. In deference to the ominous times of Nazi occupation, they had no celebration and in attendance were only the two sets of parents; no friends were invited.

While Helen's parents were genuinely happy, John's parents were less than enthusiastic. They could not help but worry, for Helen had a questionable reputation. In the opinion of the small town burghers, she was a seductress, a flirtatious girl who toyed with men's feelings. Some compared her to the biblical paradigm of a female sinner. But John's parents kept their concerns prudently to themselves; their only son was ecstatically happy. Helen was the only girl he had ever loved, and he desperately wanted to marry her.

John believed that his looks were common, and though he had an outstanding intelligence, he was not the type to charm this beauty off her feet. While John's greatest asset was his mind, Helen had only a marginal appreciation for the academic or abstract disciplines, which were hardly of interest to her. He thought it a small miracle that Helen had accepted his proposal of marriage.

Helen, in turn, did not pretend to suddenly fall for him; she conceded a sisterly kind of affection. She didn't conceal her reasons for consent, freely admitting that she was scared of her uncertain future. John was not in the least perturbed by her honest admission. He nursed the naïve hope that, given time, she would learn to love him for all the kindness and care he would shower on her. His conviction is proof that even a very smart man can behave like a king-size fool. It was to be a short-lived bliss, for soon the newlyweds, along with Helen's parents, were called upon to present themselves for deportation.

Unfortunately for Helen, she was born Jewish in an era which would be marked by its attempted annihilation of all Jews. The rich reservoir of Jewish culture and tradition, emanating from Central and Eastern Europe, was to be obliterated.

Helen hailed from a small town in Bohemia's northeast, where her father owned a well-established, prosperous dry-goods store. Her arrival was welcomed as a miracle by her middle-aged parents, who had almost given up hope of being blessed with a child. Perhaps understandably, they doted on little Helen. The little girl born to them was from the get-go exceptional. She was a lovely baby, much indulged by all around her, partially because she had the knack of getting her way by hook or crook. Helen's mother, who never seemed quite convinced that she was so fortunate to have this attractive child as her own, yielded to the every whim and wish of little Helen.

In due course, Helen was enrolled in school, which placed few demands on the intelligent child. Helen's parents spared no expense to expand their daughter's education and early on supplemented her studies with music instruction. Helen was one of the lucky few that were endowed with a wide scope of aptitudes.

When Helen reached her teens, it became obvious that this enchanting girl was also growing into an exceptional beauty. Few failed to notice, and soon young Helen turned into a flirtatious girl. She enjoyed the admiring looks of the local boys, who did not dare to ask her for a date.

But soon two dark shadows entered her young life.

The first danger affected the world at large. The dark clouds of the Nazi movement, which took foothold in Germany, signaled the rapidly approaching storm. As if hypnotized by an evil magician, many European Jews trembled and feared the dim today, to be followed by a portentous tomorrow. The atmosphere in Helen's hometown was quickly poisoned by the gloomy shadows of the impending catastrophe. It appeared that the outrageous destruction that might befall the Jews would dwarf any and all previous calamities that had plagued them during their long and tattered history.

Helen's family had lived for generations in northeast Bohemia and had precious few connections to the world at large.

They lacked the sophisticated contacts or worldly experience which might have helped in those forbidding times. Helen's parents made some half-hearted attempts to purchase the over-priced and almost unattainable certificates which authorized immigration to Palestine. Only a few could be had, and at an exorbitant cost. Helen's parents were well aware that they could not come up with the funds demanded by Great Britain, the mandatory power of Palestine. The British colonial office restricted issuing of these certificates to an absolute minimum in order to pacify the Arabs, who strongly objected to any additional Jewish presence in Palestine.

It was at this time that Helen had her first brush with puppy love, followed by heartbreak and complicated by a seemingly unsolvable impasse.

In 1938, Helen's parents decided to retain a new piano teacher whose musical experience and reputation surpassed the small town instructor. Paul S., a gifted choirmaster and music teacher, took over Helen's piano instructions, furthering her overall knowledge of the world of sounds. He began to commute twice a week from the neighboring city to enhance Helen's proficiency and mastery of the instrument.

Paul was young, handsome and much attracted to his 19-year-old pupil. And Helen, too, liked the more mature Paul. He seemed a man of the world, towering over the awkward local boys. Before long she fell hopelessly in love with him, and the more mature and sophisticated Paul responded in kind. These piano lessons were always given in Helen's home, where the student and her instructor were for most part all alone. Soon the music lessons were laced with passionate kisses and embraces, which led to a fully consummated affair.

Had anyone known of the affair, it would have been considered shocking. No reputable young girl from a respected Jewish family would have considered losing her virginity to an impoverished, married Gentile. Helen was passionate, impulsive and eager to explore her sexuality with the man she believed she loved. She had complete trust in him and never queried him about precautionary measures.

Helen had limited knowledge of sexual matters, although her mother had offered a much-embarrassed heart-to-heart talk, almost skirting the issues of the facts of life. Only later, when Helen reached puberty, did a more explicit chat with the maid cast some light into the world of love. But that was as far as Helen's knowledge reached. In the schools of those days, the topic of sex was never covered; even matters like pregnancy and physical hygiene were not included in the curriculum. Folks then believed that if they handled sex in hushed silence, it would somehow preserve a girl's virtue.

It was therefore only a matter of time before this illicit affair became a scandal or carried even more serious consequences. Unfortunately for Helen, both happened.

She became pregnant. Initially she ascribed her symptoms to her guilty conscience, but eventually she knew that she was in trouble. Paul fell apart when she shared with him her concerns; he quit his job immediately and vanished. It was his firm belief that Helen's parents would handle the situation with utmost discretion and concern for Helen's reputation, all of which assured him of his chance to escape unscathed. Paul did not think for a moment that Helen would not rely on her parents, who in turn had the means and wisdom to deal judiciously with the problem.

As matters stood, Helen confronted the consequences of her infatuation painfully alone. Initially, even the bold and courageous Helen was fearful, and the first person she asked for advice was the maid. She recommended some folksy, old-fashioned remedies, in the form of some herbal teas and high jumps from a ladder, which well-nigh killed Helen without achieving the desired result.

Next, the maid suggested hot baths and then some pills, which she supplied and which only succeeded in making Helen sick to her stomach.

Several weeks passed and Helen was becoming frantic .In those days to have a child out of wedlock would ruin any young girl. Helen realized she had to, regrettably, involve her parents. The news shocked her mother, who never made room for sexual intimacy outside marriage. But she knew that there was little time to waste. The family physician was drawn into confidence, confirmed Helen's condition and placed her somewhere in the third month. He refused to perform an abortion or even recommend a colleague. Helen's despondent parents frantically searched for a quick and quiet solution to their dilemma. They became privy to an address of a woman in Prague, who was a back alley abortionist, supposedly much experienced and reliable.

Apprehensively, mother and daughter took the first train to Prague, rented a room in a quiet hotel, and set out for the only person who they thought could still help. They found her in an old, decrepit high-rise, where she had a small flat. The building was filled with the smell of cooked cabbage and onions, and though mother and daughter were dismayed and discouraged, they knew that they could not be choosey.

Helen's mother, clutching her purse containing a letter of introduction to this woman and her exorbitant fee, caught her breath as she pressed the doorbell of the apartment. A not very friendly and less then clean elderly matron opened the door to them. They gnashed their teeth, but followed her into the dark hall, which opened into a kitchen where soup bubbled on a stove.

The abortionist knew all too well what brought the two well-dressed women to her doorstep. She scanned rather perfunctorily the letter handed to her and without further ado she agreed to perform the illegal abortion. But she added a few words of caution. Helen's pregnancy was quite advanced and the interruption could lead to complications.

The abortionist seemed pleased with the fact that both women planned to remain in Prague for at least a week. They would stay in proximity to good hospitals, to which Helen should be transferred in case of any bleeding or serious discomfort.

In a grumbling, gruff voice, the abortionist insisted on a promise that under no circumstances were they ever to mention her name. If complications in the form of fever or hemorrhage were to arise, they had to deny any criminal intervention and just ask for medical assistance. Helen's mother, much frightened at having heard of this possible outcome, wanted to leave, but Helen was adamant; she was determined on terminating her pregnancy, no matter the risk. Only after they had promised never to breath her name and had handed over the envelope with money, did the abortionist agree to proceed.

She wiped her hands on her dirty apron and beckoned Helen
to the kitchen, instructing her mother to stay behind. Both women
were ordered to be quiet, not to utter a sound, for any irregularity
could attract the attention of jealous neighbors, who might
summon the police. Abortion at the time was not only illegal but
considered a major felony and would potentially net the
abortionist as well as the woman many years in the penitentiary.

Events unfolded very quickly. The woman ordered Helen to
lie on the kitchen table; she placed a ball of wool in Helen's mouth
and told her to bite hard, should the pain become unbearable. The
gag smelled of onions, and Helen nearly vomited even before the
woman proceeded with the horrid butchery.

First she took out of a drawer some crude instruments with
which she set about to dilate Helen's cervix. Helen thought that
she would die right then and there, sprawled on the grimy kitchen
table. But she knew better than to cry out. She bit hard, hoping to
get the torture over with as fast as possible. She was unaware that
big tears rolled down her face.

It did not dawn on Helen that the next step would be even
worse. The woman forcefully injected some soapy, caustic
substance into Helen's uterus. Helen felt as if her womb would
rupture, tear wide open any second, and her death was a foregone
conclusion. When she thought she could no longer keep from
screaming, the woman declared the intervention complete, ordered
Helen off the kitchen table, removed the gag, and asked her to
leave and remember all her instructions.

Mother and daughter left holding on to one another and
returned to their rented room. According to the abortionist, Helen
should lose her baby within 24 to 48 hours after the surgery.
Helen's mother sat next to her bed the entire night, watching over
her daughter's fitful and troubled sleep.

All seemed well during the early morning hours. Helen,
though obviously sad, was in no discomfort. Then, around midday,
Helen developed severe abdominal cramps and, before she could
reach the bathroom, blood began to gush as if some internal faucet
had flown wide open. The stream strengthened, and Helen looked
in shock as her living blood poured onto the shabby carpet.

Luckily, her mother kept her cool, recalling the instructions issued by the abortionist. She had as a precautionary measure retained a taxi for the entire day, and now she hurriedly summoned the driver to help transfer Helen to the nearest hospital.

By the time they reached the emergency room, Helen was unconscious. She was immediately placed on a gurney and hurried into surgery. She was anesthetized and her womb packed with sponges to stop the hemorrhage. Another surgery followed to remove any residual tissue from her scalded uterus. The physicians worked feverishly, as Helen's life hung in balance.

Her mother held a constant vigil praying passionately for her daughter's life. She couldn't blame Helen for the unfolding drama. Self- recrimination was the order of the day. She as a mother had failed her daughter, and now poor Helen was in the throes of death.

It was hours before they wheeled Helen, stabilized, out of the operating room and into the intensive care unit, where she remained overnight. Helen's mother phoned her husband and told him that all had gone according to plan. She saw little purpose to have him panic and come running to Prague.

Over the following days and weeks, Helen was gravely ill and literally battled for her life. For though there was no more bleeding, a serious infection took hold. The treatment of such a deep pelvic infection in the pre-antibiotic era required a monumental effort and usually was doomed to failure. Helen tossed in her bed, delirious with high fevers and pain.

It was two months before her youth and determination prevailed and Helen recovered sufficiently to be discharged. The attending physician informed the two women that Helen's health was restored, but her likelihood of ever bearing another child was minimal, although not entirely impossible.

Helen and her mother spent another two months convalescing in a spa. There Helen regained most of her strength, beauty and, eventually, some of her spirit, although she lost some of her sparkle and self-confidence.

Upon return both women were awaited and enthusiastically greeted by Helen's father, whose tears of joy at seeing Helen in relatively good shape were mixed with sadness for the pains she had been forced to surmount. Helen would hardly ever speak of this event, and when her mother alluded to it, Helen would immediately try to switch the topic of conversation.

The comely young Helen, by that time already 19 years old, grew into such a beauty that she became the desire of every man's dream. She was swarmed and courted by the town's young men, but to Helen it was now only a play; she no longer wanted to love another man.

Conditions deteriorated rapidly for the Jews trapped in the two western provinces of the torn Czechoslovak republic: Bohemia and Moravia. The family was stripped of all their possessions, the thriving family business was expropriated, and a German manager was appointed and eventually declared the legal owner. They lost access to their bank accounts, and any other assets they had once possessed.

The Nazis issued many ordinances and prohibitions transforming the life of Jews into a virtual house arrest. Their mobility was curtailed by an official decree. To be instantly recognizable, they were commanded to wear on all outer clothing a yellow patch in the shape of a Star of David, inscribed with the word "Jude" (Jew), at all times.

Helen surprised all and rose to the challenge. She developed a practical approach and independence in the face of so much adversity. In the rare case that a solution remained obscure, she turned to one of her many admirers, who unfailingly rushed to her rescue. Her suitors came from all walks of life, and she gratefully accepted their advice, suggestions and help, but remained aloof and uncommitted to any of them.

The dark times worsened daily, and it was only a matter of time before the Jews were to be torn from their homes and sent to the far distant camps in the East. It did not take long for Helen to recognize that the challenges ahead, including her responsibilities to her elderly parents, might lie beyond her abilities. The elderly couple did not do well; they coped rather poorly even before the more dramatic change of deportation to the concentration camp. Helen decided that the most prudent step would be to marry, and so secure a partner and companion for this hazardous time. Helen combed through her many options and finally settled on the boy next door, the serious, quiet young man, who already had concluded his studies; his chosen calling was medicine. John S. would be the ideal partner for the hard, arduous days to come.

As I observed Helen, I thought that if I could be anything like her, I'd be able to improve our lot in this godforsaken place. I was certain that a woman like Helen could persuade the cook to ladle her serving of soup from the bottom of the cauldron, where all the turnips, pieces of potatoes and peels settled. I thought that perhaps by watching her closely, I could learn some of her know-how and self- assured manner.

Helen craved approval and wished to be treated with high regard, all of which I quite candidly felt for my mentor. Flattered, she continued to chat with me, asking about the rules and regulations of life in the camp.

Helen's unique beauty did not go unnoticed by the handful of men responsible for the administration of the camp. All the members of the Council of Elders were well aware that they were living on borrowed time. For that short span they had special privileges, which they used prudently and well. These men had no freedom of movement outside the camp, but within Theresienstadt they wielded enormous power. They never went hungry. They had any amount of the camp's usual grub and slop and often enjoyed "normal" food, smuggled in or bartered for favors or services rendered.

The Council of Elders was responsible for the camp, and they reported directly to the Nazi commandant. At the helm of the Council stood a man who was in charge of the entire administration of the camp. The members of the Council of Elders and, in lesser degree, the men who handled the food distribution were the most privileged. The cooks and bakers were the uncontested upper class. Then there were the craftsmen who maintained the camp's infrastructure, but more importantly worked for the SS commander (e.g., cobblers, tailors, plumbers and electricians).

They all worked within the camp, but after hours slugged it out for food and other commodities. With these desirable commodities they could engage in the brisk black market of the camp. All edibles had a price, usually converted into the camp's currency, namely cigarettes. Smuggled-in jewelry was exchanged for food or medicine. The suffering inmates lacked all the basic necessities of day-to-day life in a camp.

This clandestine trading could bring the inmate into grave jeopardy, for if caught he might be shot immediately. The prisoner could also be transferred to the jail also known as the "Small Fortress," where torture and death reigned supreme. Actually many a jailed man in the Small Fortress prayed for death, for the torment there was so outlandish that release by any means was the much wished-for outcome.

Another form of punishment was deportation to Auschwitz. The offender (black marketer or other transgressor) would be designated as "S.B." (*Sonder Behandlung*, which meant "special treatment," i.e., gas immediately upon arrival without selection).

The SS men and some Czech policemen did not miss the opportunity to enrich themselves, either. They professed to hate us, but they did not mind feasting on our Jewish carrion. The Jews were nearing total annihilation; this might be the once-in-a-lifetime chance to fill their coffers with valuable loot.

The rank and file of inmates suffered with hunger and ailments resulting from the subhuman conditions that prevailed in the camp. The inmates who fleetingly wielded enormous powers used and, at times, abused their special privileges. They did not go hungry, and they were housed in a separate section of the barracks, in small garrets, which offered the luxury of a modicum of privacy. Clearly they lived incomparably better than the average inmate, but they also knew that because of their special positions the sword of Damocles hung over their heads by a very thin thread. They would be sent to their deaths at the whim and pleasure of the commandant, at the moment he deemed suitable. There were few pleasures available which would distract the nagging fear of one's impending end. Perhaps the only way to obtain a moment of oblivion was to share love with someone or, failing that, to engage in casual sex. The members of the Council had the enviable advantage of privacy in their small attics, a luxury beyond the reach of the ordinary inmate.

Helen could choose among the many, and she took full advantage of her physical attributes, securing for herself a nearly pain free incarceration. In Theresienstadt, she pushed her other concerns aside, concentrating exclusively on improving her slim chances for survival. She was convinced that later might come the time to sort out her feelings, should she be among those who would last to see the day of liberation.

Meanwhile John, her much tried husband, was patently unhappy about her flagrant infidelities, although he was accustomed to sharing her time and favors with other men. John knew that Helen would never bear children, and he ascribed her conduct, at least partially, to her traumatic abortion, which left her barren.

Helen tried to turn me into a proficient manipulator and was often frustrated by my lack of talent in following her example. Helen was not only beautiful, she possessed a keen intellect and although she was deported to Theresienstadt much later than I was, she was a quicker study.

A woman of her ingenuity, to me, was a revelation. Helen had no other female friends, perhaps understandably, and it was my dubious distinction to be her only friend. In reality, though, I was more of a disciple, a follower and admirer. Helen in turn needed someone to confide in, a person she could open up to, someone who would know all, yet would not be judgmental, envious or jealous.

Other than me, Helen trusted her mother, who accepted all her escapades and loved Helen unconditionally, but was deeply embarrassed by her daughter's flirtatious and suggestive conduct.

Helen did not stay long in the jammed, uncomfortable lodgings of the "Hamburg" barracks. One of her admirers arranged an allocation of a small alcove in one of the dilapidated old houses vacated by the forcibly relocated Gentiles. Helen encouraged me to visit and chat about the camp's latest gossip. Like most other inmates, I was perpetually famished, and Helen would frequently offer me her day's ration, for she usually had better fare, supplied by one of her many suitors. Actually, she referred to the daily rations as revolting, but most of us fought tooth and nail for every potato peel or sliver of rotten turnip.

Helen's mother remained in "Hamburg" barracks, but was transferred from the loft in which I lived to a smaller hall with fewer women and received a lower bunk. Helen's father was taken care of in a similar manner. Although Helen shielded them from many of the camp's harsh realities and they were spared much suffering, both passed away several months apart, having lived in Theresienstadt for a relatively short period of time.

Helen considered herself to be alone, for although John dropped by frequently, she no longer regarded him as her spouse. With the passing of time, John became a vexing nuisance and Helen, never known for her tact or finesse, told him so in no uncertain terms. She would recount all this, notice my disapproval, and then laugh heartily about my touchy feelings.

Then, one day I came for a visit and noticed a significant change. Usually she was upbeat and extroverted, rather boisterous, with an infectious and cynical sense of humor well related to our unattractive realities. It was a surprise to find her somewhat subdued and pensive, yet not particularly worried or anxious. She talked very little, which was completely out of character. I knew better than to pry.

It was a much gentler and more tractable Helen who, a few days later, began to tell me about the powerful transformation of her life. She had met a man who, for once, deeply impressed her. Although Helen was loved by many and had numerous affairs, she had never truly loved anyone. Admittedly, she cared more for some than others and bestowed her favors rather liberally. More often than not she used men to satisfy her insatiable sexual appetite and to help with her needs for safety in the camp.

It appeared that Helen had met someone who impressed and electrified her. I did not ask who he was, for the less known, the better. But Helen in her excited state volunteered his name, violating the unofficial, unspoken rule calling for anonymity.

I knew the man, every single inmate in the camp knew him. He was none other than the Elder of the Jews, Professor Paul Epstein. The Elder of the Jews for the short duration of his reign was an enormously powerful man. He would take orders only from the SS and within the camp proper he was the uncontested authority.

Paul quite recently had replaced his predecessor, Jacob Edelstein, in this high profile, dangerous and time-limited position of prominence. It was the iron-clad rule of the Nazis to appoint the head of the Council, the "Elder of the Jews," to a short period. Those Jews in whom the Nazis vested power soon knew too much, and it was this knowledge which disquieted the Germans.

The Elder of the Jews was also well aware that his, and the Council's life, hung by a thread which could be cut by the German commandant at any time. The Elder's realm encompassed the life and death of all inmates. He was aware of the number and destinations of the dispatched transports. His assistants compiled the lists of those who had to leave the camp; they controlled vital food supplies and important work assignments. The decisions of the Elder were never challenged. The Nazis only issued orders as to how many inmates are to be deported and to what direction and purpose they would be destined. The rest was up to the Elder and his Council.

Edelstein, the first Elder, was well-known to most of us from his work in Prague, where he was a prominent official of the Zionist organization. He was a kind, decent man who knew the likely outcome of the inmates' upcoming annihilation and had no doubts about his own short-lived assignment. Still, he would find it within himself to talk to people, encourage them or offer a smile or a kind word. He made himself accessible, attempting to support morally and emotionally the many distraught inmates. His successor, Professor Epstein, was a totally different individual. They contrasted like day and night. Epstein was a more reserved, serious and reticent man. Through no fault of Epstein's, Edelstein was sent to his death, accused by the camp's commander of sloppy administration and creative bookkeeping, ostensibly resulting in inconsistencies in the census of inmates.

These charges were trumped up and few understood why the commandant bothered to indict Edelstein in the first place. Hundreds of transports were arriving with thousands of individuals, in each a mixture of living and dead. Other transports were, in turn, leaving at a rapid clip, and people were dying in droves. A mathematical wizard could not have kept an accurate count for the SS. If it had not been a tragedy, it would have been a farce.

Paul Epstein was reputedly a brilliant and cool intellectual, a one-time philosophy professor at the prestigious University of Berlin. His arrival was preceded by rumors that he had the inclination to be more like a German than a Jew and that he was a cold, unapproachable, self-centered, almost arrogant man. He proved to be all that and much more. He was a handsome man in his late thirties, well-groomed, and his was a striking appearance when passing through the squalor of the camp. He was supposedly appointed by Berlin headquarters where, as a representative of the Jewish community, he had routine dealings with the SS head office. Theresienstadt's SS commander at that time, Anton Burger, was pleased with the choice of Epstein, because his German, unlike Edelstein's, was accent free, and his mannerism and posture were "German."

Helen and Epstein became lovers. Helen was totally enthralled with her new lover; she had never met anyone quite like him. He became her first and last great love. It had to be love at first sight, for Helen changed into someone completely different from the moment she first laid her eyes on him. Suddenly gone was her flirtatious and vivacious self. Helen became transformed into a near-teenager who had experienced the first brush with love. She could not think, concentrate or talk about anything except the miracle of their shared love. She was convinced that they were destined for each other; two people ideally suited for each other.

Helen and Paul were brilliant, passionate and ambitious, and both had few scruples that would hinder or prevent them from taking what they craved. They differed in their conduct, however; while Helen was passionate and physical, with unbridled desires that she needed to still, Paul was disciplined, well-controlled, at times appearing cold and heartless. Most of Helen's pleasures were derived from the emotional and physical aspects of life, whereas Paul's main interests lay in intellectual pursuits. They were bound together, however, by an all-consuming passion for one another, which knew no boundaries or restrictions.

They craved each other's company as much as their physical love. I hinted only once that an association with the Elder of the Jews was extremely risky and that, while his eventual death was assured, she might be sentenced to die with him as well. In other times Helen did not tolerate admonitions or unsolicited advice, but, being in love, she took my concern in stride.

The thought of living without him made her shudder and her preoccupation with survival seemed to fade. In her past Helen was never faithful to any of her men; now she became fastidiously monogamous. She was like a teenager in love living for the moments they could be together, and she resented any interference. In all fairness they had little time for each other because Paul lived and functioned under unimaginable pressures. Daily he faced the Nazi overlords, managed the day-to-day life of the camp, and warded off the many threats promising to engulf the camp and his own existence.

Moreover, he had to come to terms with his own impending death in as brave a manner as he could muster. Somehow he accepted his own demise in a cool, rational and resigned fashion, at least outwardly. While most of the men and women in Theresienstadt frantically searched for extended survival no matter how brief, Paul radiated serenity.

Helen, who never knew the meaning of physical faithfulness, was devoted to Paul with monastic, unwavering resolve. She often said that she could not even imagine kissing another man, let alone having sex with anyone but Paul. Helen was smothered by the gamut of emotions often affecting women in love. Paul responded to their involvement in a different manner. Unlike Helen, she was not his most significant affair of the heart. However, he was impressed by her, relishing her beauty and responsiveness to their sexual union.

Helen, as the mistress of the most powerful man in the camp, became a powerful person, wielding influence beyond some members of the Council itself, yet she barely used it. In her transformed state she was light years from manipulations; all her thoughts and energies were focused on Paul. She was so absorbed that she seemed to barely notice her parents' fading health. On their death, Helen's grief was brief.

While Helen's affair with Paul became a target of sordid jokes and salacious remarks, John, Helen's much-tried husband, began to unravel at the seams. He hoped the day would come when he would be the recipient of the deep love and faithful devotion which she so lavishly bestowed on her seemingly undeserving lover. Moreover, there were no doubts in John's mind that this very public affair endangered Helen's life. Perhaps it was his attempts to separate her from Paul that led Helen to ask John not to come anymore; he was not welcome. Even as a friend he had become objectionable.

Almost overnight, John willed himself to be free and to overcome his anguish. To this end he would need a woman in his life. In the children's ward, his assigned station, worked Lilly, a pretty nurse who never hid her admiration and affection for the serious and caring physician. John, with cool deliberation, started an affair with the adoring Lilly, and soon enough John surprised himself; he could stay away from Helen without the excruciating torment that had afflicted him previously. He was immensely grateful to Lilly, whose love helped him regain his freedom and self esteem, and though he could not reciprocate her passion, his affection for her grew.

Helen did not have to work, but her anxiety was mounting with every passing day. She knew that time was running out for her as well as Paul. The time of reckoning came shortly after the inspection visit by the International Red Cross. All went well; the inspection team was thoroughly fooled. Some said they allowed themselves to be. Still, the camp's grapevine had it that Epstein would be disposed of. We knew that this type of gossip was often based on fact and would be followed by specific action. I saw Helen only briefly during those frantic days, and she seemed deeply distraught. She hardly spoke with me and was filled with panic for Paul's life.

A few days later, some of her worst premonitions became tragic realities. The SS commandant sent Epstein on an errand outside the walls of the camp. Epstein, as Helen later told me, suspected a trap but had no recourse; he had to obey. Initially he thought, or rather hoped, that they would shoot him in the back for attempted escape. But SS Rahm, the then commandant, wished for more than the life of Epstein. He wished to dispose of the entire Council. He singled out Epstein, however, for the harshest, most violent execution. He decided to jail him in the notorious "Small Fortress," a one-time maximum-security prison adjacent to Theresienstadt, where conditions were unimaginably inhuman.

Clearly, the trumped-up charges of Epstein's attempted escape were preposterous. Not only was the accusation an inconceivable fabrication, but it made no sense at all.

Helen never saw Paul again; he was shot in the back of his head, executed gangland style by the guards in his cell. Theresienstadt was awash with rumors that before he was murdered, he was brutalized, hit with violent blows, stomped on, his bones broken. His tormentors inflicted gashing wounds, tore out his nails, and knocked out many of his teeth. Then they shot him, letting him finally expire in a pool of his own blood. We did not know if the circulating rumors were true or not, but those familiar with the methods of the Nazis believed every word of it.

Back in the camp all the members of the Council who served with Epstein were rounded up along with their families and ordered to the barracks where those destined for deportation were ingathered. Not one of them or their families was to be spared. The commander was adamant; all the former mighty and influential Jews had to die, and Helen was included, right on top of the list.

I was reluctant to seek her out. To say that I was apprehensive is an understatement. I held my breath as I knocked on the wooden planks that divided her from her neighbor's cubicle. Inside I found Helen, pale, upset, filled with fear and anger. She paced restlessly. She would mumble words I could not make out, then her muttering would stop, and she would march in silence back and forth.

Finally she regained some composure and began to make some sense. She complained bitterly about Paul's sudden disappearance. She had heard of his "attempt to escape," and she was raging that they concocted such a bizarre lie to end his once glorious life.

Helen was consumed with panic and impotence, imagining the torture inflicted upon Paul. She reproached herself for the failure of her attempts to convince him to commit joint suicide. Helen even showed me the sleeping pills she had bartered on the black market. There were more than enough for the both of them.

Now her only hope was that perhaps the commandant might spare him and simply enroll him in a deportation order, right along with the rest of the Council. To this end she petitioned the SS

commandant for an interview, in which she would implore him to
allow that they be deported together. She waited for the return of
the sentry, who for a hefty bribe carried the message of her heart-
rending supplication to the commander. She told me to leave and
to return that evening. By then she might know if she achieved her
objective or if her petition fell on deaf ears. Little did Helen know
that even had Rahm wanted to grant her this favor, it was no
longer a possibility. Paul was already dead by then, lying on the
floor in a cell of the Small Fortress, his body disfigured beyond
recognition.

Nevertheless Rahm granted her an audience, but was not
ready to tell her the news about her lover and watch her react in
despondency. Might not a woman like Helen when distraught
become violent, attack him, or faint in his presence? Who knew
how she might respond? Rahm was not taking chances to find out.
If she were to turn violent, he would have to shoot her point blank
and that, too, was an unpalatable option for him. The SS
Obersturmbannfuehrer Rahm had known her for quite some time
and felt a strange affection for this one-of-a-kind beauty.

To comfort her and get her off his back, he reassured her that,
yes, he would allow Paul to join her on the platform of the loading
ramp, and they would even travel in the same freight car. The
entire Council and their families would be kept isolated from the
rest of the deportees in a restricted railcar. Helen thanked him, full
of gratitude for the chance to see the love of her life one more
time.

As she was about to leave, she was surprised by Rahm's
remark that according to the rules governing deportation of
inmates he was obliged to include her estranged husband, because
officially John and Helen were not divorced. Helen paused, turned
around, and asked the commandant to reconsider, for he knew that
their marriage was over; John and she had separated long ago.

Rahm, who did not have the courage to tell her the truth about
Paul, now relished inflicting a blow, this time consistent with the
truth. He repeated with a malicious glee, that he could not exempt
John. It would also cause administrative complications, for John's
current companion, Lilly, had volunteered to join him in the
deportation order.

When I returned on that very last day, I found an entirely different Helen. She was glad and grateful for the chance to see one more time the love of her life, to be reunited with Paul, even though it would be only for a few hours. She mentioned that instead of walking with Paul to the "Chuppah" (the traditional canopy under which Jewish couples wed) to offer her marriage vows, she would be joined with him in their last moments on this earth.

Her mood quickly shifted; one moment she was sad and resigned to her fate, grateful for her share of the blessings they enjoyed in the brief span allotted to them. The next moment she was infuriated, fuming with rage. She then engaged in a tirade about the cynical and malicious commandant who refused to take John and Lilly off the transport list. Some moments she sounded crazed, no longer of sound judgment. The combination of suppressed fear and fury against their undeserved fate made her rave and curse, cry and smile, all within a few short moments.

I felt downhearted. I liked Helen, and through her tales I learned to admire Paul. Helen was a good friend, her character blemishes notwithstanding. I was keenly aware of the impending loss of a friend of remarkable caliber. As we embraced for the last time, my heart pounded. She kissed me, thanked me for my friendship and pressed into my hand a bundle of clothes she would not need anymore. I could not thank her or even talk for that matter. I held in my arms a living, warm Helen, and I was aware that tomorrow or the day after she would be a small pile of ashes.

The following day, under heavy guard, the Council members and their families were led to the loading ramp and quickly shoved into a separate boxcar. From some distance, I clearly spotted Helen, as she walked, tall and proud, to the train, her eyes feverishly scanning the ramp for Paul's presence. She still was gorgeous; her beauty could not be suppressed even in this hour of her supreme torment. I followed her with my eyes for as long as I could recognize where she was, recoiling with pain thinking that tomorrow by this time she probably would be dead, having lived a sum total of 25 years.

The loading was quickly completed, and the train jerked off into the northeast, destined for Auschwitz. I never saw Helen again. I only know that upon arrival the entire Council was separated from the rest of the transport members. They were denied selection, placed on a waiting lorry and driven off to the gas chambers. Among them had to be my beautiful friend Helen. All were gassed the same day they arrived at Auschwitz.

Later I managed to gather some information about John and Lilly. They arrived in Auschwitz with the rank and file, the fatal connotation "S.B." (*Sonder Behandlung*) was not attached to their names. They were subjected to a selection process, sorting out the healthy and strong ones for the forced labor camps and sending the weak and old, the "useless," to their deaths in the gas chambers.

John was deemed strong and of use and therefore was sent out from Auschwitz to a work camp near Buchenwald. Tragically the inmates assigned to the camp had to toil in the quarries, under brutal and subhuman conditions. John did not last long; he was unaccustomed to hard physical labor. Already weakened by malnutrition from his stint in Theresienstadt, he was forced to work at backbreaking speed. The prisoners received little food and were poorly sheltered. He died only a few months before the final victory of the Allied forces.

The only survivor of the foursome was Lilly. I met her in Prague, shortly after the Russian army liberated the city. She looked drawn and haggard, was skinny and had oozing sores, but it was obvious that she would recover. We handful of survivors would gather in a small coffeehouse, which became our unofficial meeting place. There we exchanged information and news, and hoped to meet someone who just came back. We all waited anxiously for some relative or friend to show up, only most of us did so in vain.

Lilly would, without fail, show up every single day. She would wait for John with stubborn tenacity, hoping with every passing day against fading hope that he might come back. She questioned every returnee about John. Perhaps someone saw him or knew something of his fate? For most, the wait was futile; our expectations were shattered daily. But we would return again the next day and the day after that. None of us could stay away or admit that all was lost.

I met Lilly in that coffeehouse every single day. By the end of August we could no longer deceive ourselves. Though we thought we would not be able to face it, we now had to admit and accept that not one of those we were waiting for was still among the living. Most of the late returnees were back; the sick who languished for months in hospitals in foreign countries were also repatriated. The initial stream, later reduced to a trickle, by August had dried up.

Late one afternoon, after yet another futile wait, Lilly got up, embraced me and said, "John will not return. He must have perished, and I have to stop coming here every single day. This is tearing me apart; I cannot sit here and have my hopes shattered day after day. I must give up. I have to try to begin a new chapter in my life." As she spoke her eyes filled with tears, and then she whispered softly, "I loved him so very much."

George: Musselman

Starving Death Camp inmate (Musselman). These prisoners,
as a result of prolonged starvation, lost their will to live.

George was not really our first cousin. His mother was my father's cousin, which made George my second cousin, a trivial detail of no importance to us. The family felt close, generally interacted lovingly, and could care less exactly how akin we were to each other. When George was a teenager and my sister and I were only small schoolgirls, we saw in him the embodiment of sophistication and charm. Our little girl's eyes saw the prototype of the accomplished young man. George, often and readily, accompanied his thrilled cousins to the theater or concert, providing the adult escort to many of our social outings. These were the good years.

He had flocks of friends, a few brief love affairs, numerous flirtatious peccadilloes, but his most serious commitment was to his studies. He viewed his chosen profession more as a privileged calling than as a skill to assure a livelihood. Though he excelled at many sports and enjoyed an easy rapport with people, he was monomaniacally devoted to his field of science, the healing of the sick.

My sister and I not only loved and admired George, we were frankly proud of him, basking in his achievements. He was several years our senior, having in 1938 completed his penultimate year at the prestigious Charles University Medical School in Prague. He was handsome, athletic and had a marvelously winning personality. Most found him charming, and he was popular with young and old alike. He did not share much of a resemblance with our side of the family. We had olive complexions and dark, wavy hair. George was nearly our opposite. He had light blue eyes and his thick hair was light brown in winter and sun-bleached, almost blond in summer. He was a tall and handsome fellow with an exceptional intelligence. All predicted a brilliant future for my cousin George.

Then fate struck. Czechoslovakia fell, to be ruled by the expanding power of the Third Reich. Like any other Jew, George was expelled from school. In short order, all centers of higher learning were closed permanently with the pretext of student dissidence and disobedience to German decrees. Nazi indignation flared in the wake of an attempted demonstration, staged by students, to mark the liberation of the republic on October the 28th. Fortunately, George didn't live in the dormitories, which the Germans ransacked that night with dragnets, arresting many university students. He would have been apprehended and sent without trial to a concentration camp with the rest. Most of those promising young men never returned. In the ensuing months, most of their families were summoned to police stations where they were handed their children's few worldly goods and a small simple box containing their ashes. That was all that remained of the select elite, the academic hope and pride of so many families and a nation.

George and his more providential peers could find no work and were left penniless when the Nazis seized all Jewish assets. George searched for work; any would have been good enough, but there were just no opportunities. Many offered their services for minimal pay as the jobless soon grew desperately poor and hunger chased them into the streets. George worked for a while with the sanitation crew, then hauled coal for some weeks, and later became employed by the Jewish hospital of Prague as a jack-of-all-trades.

In the course of those tough times, George remained somewhat optimistic, but maintained a realistic attitude. He concluded that he needed to educate himself politically; the crisis demanded an understanding of the swiftly unfolding events. He hoped to join one of the many resistance cells rumored to have sprung up in the Czech heartland.

However, fate prepared a different scheme for him. Before he could pursue any of these plans seriously, the Nazi occupiers began the deportation of Jews from Prague. George and his parents were summoned to join a transport leaving the city on September 4, 1942. The 1,000 people were delivered to Theresienstadt, where families were torn apart; parents and spouses separated. George's father joined the many men cooped up in the one-time military barracks, while his mother was dispatched to another designated for women. George was subject to the usual screening process for a new inmate, and then ordered to a commando unit, that was compulsory.

This assignment, lasting 100 days, called for hard manual labor. They were ordered to build wooden bunks and clear the grounds destined for the construction of additional barracks and huts. These were preparations readying the small town to accommodate the upcoming expulsion of Jews from many European countries.

When the 100 days (*Hundertschaft*) were over, George was given a new work order. Most hoped to work under a roof, for the weather in Central Europe is capricious, and winters can be wickedly cold. Since most inmates wore inadequate clothing, their only chance of living longer was to find some protection from the elements. George's saving grace was his having nearly completed his medical studies, which included training to perform autopsies and report in a more or less scientific manner the findings. He was commandeered to the mortuary, an assignment that might have prevented his deportation to the East. George hoped fervently that his protection might stretch out to include his parents.

He immediately reported to the commando, which was responsible for many assorted tasks. First and foremost, they had to collect the many bodies, the daily harvest of death in Theresienstadt. The group would trudge behind and alongside a hearse, pulling it like beasts of burden, piling high the cadavers on their way to the crematories. If the heap was too high, the entire macabre mass toppled and, like a scene from hell, the many stiff bodies fell and scattered in grotesque postures, inflicting additional indignity on the pitiable, soiled corpses.

In the fall of 1942, hastily constructed crematories had replaced the mass graves, which no longer could absorb Theresienstadt's daily harvest of death. Before the men threw the bodies into the large ovens, it was their ghastly duty to pry open the mouths of every deceased and wrestle out all the gold teeth. The next step was a thorough inspection of all body cavities for valuables and, lastly, the procedure was to cut off the hair of the dead and only then, when the Germans fully satisfied their thriftiness, could the dead be cremated. Indeed the Germans did not tolerate any possible waste. Rumors claimed the hair was used as a sealant in the production of submarines. It was hard to believe; perhaps it was just one of the unsavory rumors circulating in the camp.

The promise given to George that his parents were immune from future deportation was broken soon enough. A few months into their stay in Theresienstadt, they were included with a group of inmates heading East. George's valiant efforts to reverse the order came to naught and his attempts put him in jeopardy of being sent with them.

In the late fall of 1942 the camp commandant, *Obersturmbanfuehrer* Siegfried Seidl, had a brainstorm. For some time he had wanted to bestow a certain degree of respectability to his camp and to reverse the ugly hearsay relating to activities in the mortuary. He searched for some gloss which would cover the various operations of the camp with a patina of honor. The ultimate indignities perpetrated on these lifeless bodies could be shrouded in a scientific, medical aura.

Finally, a rather brilliant thought flashed in his mind. The crematories would continue to serve as the collection place as before, but they would also be assigned a scientific task, to research and obtain data from these unique cadavers. The study was to accumulate information about the type of ravages caused by prolonged starvation on young and otherwise healthy individuals. Seidl wanted all this data summarized and written up into a scientific report, as if compiled by a reputable medical center. It was not to differ from regular postmortem summaries and have the appearance of research aimed at expanding medical knowledge.

The man in charge of the mortuary, which included the autopsy suite, knew of George; his nearly completed studies, and reliable and accurate working habits. He therefore recommended George for this new, almost farcical assignment. Not only did George know how to properly perform autopsies, but even more importantly, he was familiar with proper documentation, which seemed of great importance to SS Seidl. The latter sought recognition for himself and the camp he commanded and hoped to ingratiate himself with Gestapo headquarters in Berlin. It was his unflinching ambition to be considered a serious, scientifically minded commandant, who would make a great contribution to modern medicine. The large number of bodies available would make the study that much more credible, meeting all the criteria of a serious research project. The repository would still be the station for stripping the corpses of their useful contributions to the Reich, but would also gain respectability as a place of scientific research.

The only truly beneficial side effect of this pseudoscientific charlatanism was the added stability to George's life. He was unofficially responsible for the pedantic and precise autopsies, which he alone documented and furnished with the authenticity of a real and systematic investigation. He was able to distance himself from his work. For him the bodies he dissected ceased to be someone's loved ones. They became objects to study the effects wrought by long-term deprivation. For that reason, he was able to report to me the autopsy findings of my sister and parents. To him, then, it was professional discourse; to me, listening, it was tantamount to emotional hemorrhage.

I sat silently through those sessions, because I understood that he meant well, and he felt it to be important that more people should know the findings of his work. The SS categorized this project as confidential; the only ones who surveyed and filed his data were the Germans.

The effects of long days spent among mounds of corpses exacted a heavy toll. Even the newly built crematories could not cope with the rising death rate, and they were always behind schedule. George was well aware that he owed his remaining in Theresienstadt to this particular "project," but he could not help but feel more and more depressed by his work. Even a hardened "researcher," on occasion needed to pause and think of all the talent and living and dreams destroyed in the name of the Nazi master plan for "racial purification." Slowly his cheerful disposition faded, withered by the tragedy unfolding before his eyes.

At some point during those many months, he determined that all of us were doomed. There was no sense in contesting such overpowering might or attempting to fight wickedness of such gargantuan proportions. The world as we knew it had come to an end, and George came to believe that the only meaningful protest

was to somehow sabotage German orders, regardless of the
consequences. However, life in Theresienstadt did not lend itself
to any effective action. Little could be organized in the fickle
situation of a camp in a continuous state of flux. The surge was
rising and ebbing, as Jews were shifted from one end of Europe to
the other and then to their deaths.

Almost two years had passed since George began his
pseudoscientific work, diligently documenting all the atrophies
and ravages caused by starvation and subhuman-like conditions.
The camp's commandant was delighted with the reports, written in
meticulous and punctilious handwriting. The records were
compiled and organized in the same manner that such a project
would have been handled in a reputable research center.

All this impressed the commander, a layman with a deep
admiration for research compiled with such exactitude. The
commander nursed the hope of earning appreciation from his
Berlin superiors, who could not fail to notice the contribution
presented by such an under-funded project, placed in front of them
in neat calligraphy. The abject crimes they perpetrated did not
bother the members of the "master race."

However, George reeled under the weight of his perceived
share of guilt in the project. He blamed himself for not joining his
elderly parents at the time of their deportation East. They, like
many others, were never heard from again. George began to relive
the final parting, the last good-bye shared in front of the gates of
the "Schleuse," the barracks earmarked for deportation. Often
during his sleepless nights he would conjure up their image
somewhere far away in Poland, worrying how they might cope
with the rigors of the bitterly cold winter months. At times, he
wondered if they could possibly still be alive, both being in their
fifties. He fought these thoughts and didn't want to sleep because
in his restless slumber he suffered nightmares. He saw his parents,
two old and emaciated people, barely holding on. They came to
resemble the withered bodies on which he daily performed postmortem dissections. In different times, few would call people in
their early fifties old, but in the camps, a new yardstick measured
all.

In Theresienstadt, the commandant issued orders forbidding autopsies on those over forty. Their deaths were of no interest; their demise was taken for granted. On other tormented nights, George would ponder the persisting hearsay informing of mass gassings of Jews somewhere in the East. The frightening uncertainty offered fertile ground to believe the unbelievable. Was it possible that mass murder was actually going on in the East? Could mobile vans adapted with their exhaust rerouted into the cabin, flooding it with carbon monoxide, be the way rumors indicated? Was there a trace of truth to the gossip of large installations in the East busily snuffing out the last breaths of the Jews by choking them with the gas "Cyclon B," an insecticide? Was this his parents' reward for lives filled with honest work and upright citizenship? George became more jittery and distraught, sleeping an hour or two, then waking up haunted with some nightmare.

Perhaps all this emotional torment compelled him to leave, just to get away from his ghastly work and find out what really was in store for the Jews deported to the East. George was in a class by himself, for he felt relief when the grapevine had it that the camp, Theresienstadt, was about to be liquidated. The rumors had the camp outliving its multipurpose existence and about to be dissolved. Large-scale deportations were therefore imminent to remove the inmates, leaving behind only those needed to dismantle the last traces of Theresienstadt and return it to its original small town appearance, thus concealing the camp's wartime existence.

Although he was privileged, protected by the strong arm of the commandant, George failed to appreciate his good fortune. Even the extra rations, an additional portion of soup and bread, meant to keep him working, did not elicit George's gratitude. He wanted to leave, never to return to this work. He was near emotional collapse and deportation would save him from insanity. And as is nearly always the case, the rumored action materialized. Perhaps the SS encouraged these leaks as trial balloons to prepare the inmates for the upcoming events?

Beginning in September 1944 waves of transports began to move out to an undisclosed destination. Theresienstadt was always intended to be a transit camp and saw many transports leave, but this was always an action dispatching only several thousand people. The fall of 1944 seemed different. It appeared that one and all would leave, abandoning the garrison town to its last surviving inhabitants: the copious fleas, mice, rats, lice and bedbugs.

George could care less if a few inmates were left to strip the barracks. He was filled with the desire to leave, never to dissect another young, emaciated body and then write a neat, impersonal report. He felt an overpowering need to flee the many lifeless faces that haunted him. The persistent qualms he felt about his work had grown to self-reproach.

His wish was fulfilled in October of 1944, when he was ordered to join a transport leaving in forty-eight hours. A new identity was conferred upon him. This time the substitute for his name was "EM 328." Like the others, he inscribed it on a piece of cardboard and suspended it around his neck. He packed the few things he still possessed, placed them in his torn knapsack and joined the rest of the people in the barracks. Empty boxcars awaited their reluctant cargo on the railway tracks. Few bothered to take leave of those left behind. All believed they were witnessing the well-synchronized liquidation of the one-time "model camp."

George sought me out to bid me good-bye. He was not one to just drop out of sight, no matter how heart-rending our parting might be. He was, after all, my last living relative in Theresienstadt, and he wished to reaffirm our family ties and memories of better days, when our hopes ran high, when the sky seemed the limit, before all our expectations were smashed to smithereens by the Nazi persecution.

We did not prolong our good-byes. We kissed, wished one another survival or, if that was not in the cards, then an easy death—the more likely case for any concentration camp inmate. In the unlikely event that we should live to see Germany's defeat, we agreed to look for each other in Prague. In addition, we would be on the look out for each other in any camp we would be moved to, just in case we could help each other. George smiled sadly when I spoke of Prague; he had little faith that we would see our hometown or each other again. Nevertheless, I insisted that the Germans were losing their quest for world dominance. They were suffering losses in assorted battles and fate had turned the tables on the seemingly invincible Axis. Perhaps we stood a chance, if we could endure a little longer and the war's end came in time for us.

Then George hugged me and whispered in my ear: "Vera, be brave, and just in the case you do return, live a happy life, but never forget what came to pass to so many during these apocalyptic times." We looked at each other for the last time, dry-eyed. You can hardly cry at your own funeral, and it was this sensation that filled us. I looked at him for the last time; he was still his handsome self, though infinitely sad, thin and aged beyond his years.

The cardboard sign dangled around his neck, appearing disproportionately large and looming menacingly on his chest. An ugly image hit me; the rope around his neck was an ever-tightening noose, which we, in spite of all our fretting, circling and manipulating, could never escape. The thought had barely flashed through my mind when I rebuked myself; one could not afford the luxury of such defeatist sentiments.

During our hurried parting, I tried to encourage George. I kept insisting that we would make it; we were young, and we would return safely to Prague, to freedom and a new life. We kissed for the last time, and he quickly marched off. I followed his shrinking silhouette, as his tall figure mingled among other inmates, eventually vanishing in the crowd. For a heart wrenching moment, I could not move, but then I reminded myself that George was young, still quite strong, and he might stand a chance. With luck, we might see each other again. If only the war would come to a quick end, with a complete defeat of the Nazis!

I never saw George again. He was correct when he considered his chances, or perhaps he had a premonition when he doubted his return. In the course of my relentless efforts to piece together his fate after Theresienstadt, I happened to meet a chap who was deported at the same time as my cousin. They left together, spent the entire stretch of time at the same place, and he was there during George's last painful moments of life. We met after the war and, as we sat together at the foot of the stairs leading up to the castle of the Czech kings, he recounted to me my favorite cousin's fate. The radiant sun darkened, turning dim and receding into a total eclipse as the news I heard blotted out all the glory of the near perfect day in freedom. Soon all in me was cloaked in sorrow and deep pain.

Frank was George's good friend. Their comradeship was formed years back, during their studies at the medical faculty. They remained close through the years of persecution and in Theresienstadt, where Frank worked as an orderly, assigned to the surgical ward. By sheer coincidence, they found each other in the courtyard shortly before the loading of the trains began. They remained together when pushed into the packed freight car, where already people were fighting for breathing space. The car was overcrowded; everyone standing and soon many, especially the very young and old, fainted, and some died even before the train left the station. They were propped against the wall, because there was no room to lay them down. The car was equipped with only one pail for human waste and during the entire journey, which lasted over two days and nights, no food or water was provided.

The time spent in the boxcar was a nightmare, even for the seasoned inmates who had spent a long time in a grim place like Theresienstadt. Inside the boxcar bedlam reigned. The crowded prisoners died in growing numbers. Many lost their sanity— shouting, crying, praying and begging some invisible being for redemption. The overpowering stench nearly suffocated them and slowly most lost heart, sinking into despondency. Their time in the sealed boxcar was an infernal experience. George and Frank were convinced that nothing worse could come their way. Unfortunately, they were wrong. Soon they were exposed to an even more horrid encounter, which seemed scripted from the worst possible hells.

The train came to an abrupt halt. The car was kept throughout the journey in near darkness, and most were disoriented; nobody knew where they were or the time of day. The entire journey was spent in twilight, which broke in through tiny cracks in the walls of the car. On top a little window, barred with meshed wire net, let in a few rays of light. The murky shadows plunged most into deep pessimism, but as the train came to a halt, George and Frank became hopeful again. They could hear orders shouted outside the car, and somebody flung the door of the boxcar wide open, briefly blinding the people inside.

They peered outside, slowly discerning a platform lit by floodlights. They were not given the time to adjust, but were commanded to step out of the car as swiftly as they could. It soon became obvious that the SS men in charge of the unloading were furious and accompanied their orders with blows at those appearing too slow for their liking. George caught a thump on his back, so ferocious that he stumbled and would have become the victim of an enraged SS man had Frank not pulled him some distance away. He whispered urgently to George, "Let's get out of the train, later we will see what happens." He prodded George, who, still half stunned, reeled to his feet on the brightly lit platform where the railway tracks ended.

Their first impression was one of shock. The men supervising the unloading for the Nazis had to be prisoners, too, for they wore identical striped uniforms and caps. They mercilessly brutalized the newly arrived, striking the staggering, half-dead people trying to comply. George also noticed that the men had color-coded triangles attached to their tunics, but he could not fathom their meaning. One of the zebra-like men dealt George a blow with his truncheon, and the sharp thwack to his neck brought him back to reality. He would have finished him off, had Frank not came to his rescue again, pulling George out of harm's way.

It was an unwritten law that an inmate who fell while beaten would be flogged to death and the SS supervising the beating might provide the coup de grace and shoot the man on the ground. It all depended on the mood of the SS officer. At times, it might please him to watch the slow death of a victim and, on other occasions, he would lose patience and finish the job. More often than not, the SS would leave the dirty work to their vassals, the commando unit charged with the duty of receiving new transports. Rarely was an SS man willing to dirty his shiny boots or his immaculate uniform, unless it became obvious that the men of the commando unit were having difficulty coping. The prevailing chaos was controlled and quelled at the first sign of undue turmoil. The SS men on duty would intervene immediately by shooting into the crowd, killing as many as they wanted, on occasion even including the inmates of the commando unit responsible for moving the masses of newly arrived from the cars to the end of the ramp.

At the end of the ramp stood an officer whose perfectly pressed, clean uniform, shiny buttons, and boots polished to high gloss, stood in sharp contrast to the grimy, bedraggled Jews. The keen contrast was so striking that even the lined up, dead tired inmates noticed that their dirty, unwashed bodies, wrinkled and soiled clothes placed them into a different category, far below the spotless officers of the SS unit.

Frank and George knew from Theresienstadt that in any selection they must appear healthy and fit for work, and artisans or craftsmen stood the best chance. Now as they approached their final moment of selection, they glanced at the officer whose handsome, bored face was distorted with the haughty grimace of a man required to dispose of an unpleasant task. As he separated the newly arrived into two groups, he showed all the signs of a man weary of his assignment, and perhaps to lessen the monotony he whistled a tune from the opera "Aida." Without a word, he signaled those in front of him to one side or the other. By far the larger group was shown to the right, where a large cluster of frightened people huddled together. The left side consisted of a few men and women, all young, strong and obviously in better shape. All drawing near the powerful officer prayed for a signal to the left, but few had their prayers answered.

At some point, it became obvious that most would not survive that dark night. The air was saturated with the pungent stench of burning flesh and hair. Not far off one could see the outline of tall chimneys, billowing curls of black smoke into the silent night sky. For the first few moments, George thought it not unlike the crematories in Theresienstadt, the fires consuming the day's harvest from illnesses, starvation and violence. A sinister, fearsome suspicion began to gnaw in his mind. Like most veterans of Theresienstadt, he had heard the rumors of mass gassing and wholesale murder of Jews in the East, but he, like most others, dismissed them as too unbelievable. Even the Germans could not perpetrate such an absurdity. He could not whisper his fear to Frank who stood right next to him; the prohibition of talk was strictly enforced. Nevertheless, by the expression on his friend's face, he could deduce that he, too, was filled with dark fears and daunting premonitions.

Soon they stood face to face with the dapper officer, who enthusiastically, even if out of tune, continued to whistle. George was fascinated by the spotlessly white, shimmering gloves of the officer. Everything on the man seemed unblemished as if just taken out of a display window. The SS man scanned George with cursory interest while asking if he had any skill. George, well prepared, replied in a rehearsed tone that he was a carpenter by trade. This answer appeared to please Dr. Mengele, the "Angel of Death" responsible for separating those to die this very night from the others still capable of delivering their pound of flesh to the German war machine. The thrifty Germans wished to squeeze those still useful for hard labor until they dropped off, no longer worthy to live.

George and Frank passed selection that night, beckoned to the left side, where they along with a few others waited for further instructions. The majority went to the right and was ordered to climb onto waiting lorries, which drove off when filled to capacity. Not far away the human cargo was unloaded and ordered into contrived showers, which instead of water discharged fumes emanating from pellets containing Cyclon B. The insecticide snuffed out their breath, albeit after lengthy suffering. Their remains were incinerated in adjacent crematories, the visible buildings with the tall chimneys.

Meanwhile the group destined for forced labor was ordered to march to real showers. Their heads were shaved clean and a number tattooed on their forearms. This all-important number represented their new identity. Right after the steamy shower, they were run into the dark, cold night and, while still in motion, someone threw some clothing, which they caught in midair. Most of their garments were scraps of dirty, torn rags, some bloodied, but they put them on nonetheless for they were freezing and scared of the striped old-timers who supervised the activity. Then they were issued wooden clogs, which were randomly paired and hardly suitable for walking. Considering that the SS wanted everything done on the double, these shoes were the least appropriate. Dressed, they were ordered to turn into a nearby barracks, lie on the bare floor and remain there for the rest of the night.

This was the first day George and Frank spent in the bizarre world called Auschwitz. This was a different place; totally dissimilar to any other entity man, in his checkered history, had ever created. In all Nazi camps, people were famished, became ill and died in droves. In every such camp Jews were overcrowded and as a matter of routine, beaten, tortured and starved. Yet, all that seemed to be a man-made horror. It was in the extermination, the death camps where men's faith in God was completely shattered. Here, all day and night, for years, thousands of men, women and children were murdered, poisoned or choked to death by lethal gas, systematically, methodically, their murders encouraged, sanctioned and authorized by a government.

Here even the devout and pious began to question, and at times curse, the Almighty. Ultimately this led to the total collapse of all religious precepts and concepts. To the myriad of Nazi crimes was added the shattered faith of the reverent ones, many who went to death robbed of all that once had offered them sustenance. They exhaled their last breath, cursing and condemning the One they had lived for and whose laws they obediently followed for much of their lives.

In Auschwitz, anger blotted out the whisper of the prayer for dead, the "Kaddish," the traditional glorification of God, which Jews recite in the hour of the loss of a loved one. Instead of the traditional praise for all God's deeds, the pious turned their angry eyes at Him, confronting Him with the worst possible accusation: God was charged and found guilty of the murder of an entire people. Their last breaths, snuffed out by Cyclon B, were expended on a blasphemous malediction. The pain of untimely death and the premature extinction of the physical, temporal existence was made worse and magnified many times over by the loss of faith in the justice of the One God. While the Jewish past was arduous, never before had any suffering moved the observant to condemn and forsake their faith.

George was lucky. His stay in Auschwitz was relatively short. In just a month, he was selected, along with Frank, for duty in a forced labor camp. Even this short period marked George with indelible scars. His good-natured disposition had vanished, replaced with bitter sadness. Both men left Auschwitz in another cattle car destined for an unspecified location. This time the conditions prevailing in the car were different. Though they were tightly crammed, the mood never sank as low as on their previous journey. The group was comprised of young men, all in relatively good health. Moreover, the journey was shorter and within a few hours the train stopped. They were ordered out into the open.

They arrived in another camp, called "Dachau." By then George was already a seasoned inmate, one who graduated with flying colors from Theresienstadt and Auschwitz, having learned the basics of survival and quick adaptation. He learned swiftly and mastered the skill of spotting new dangers and dodging perils, some of which differed from camp to camp.

Dachau seemed to offer George a new lease on life. He rallied quickly, adjusted to life in the somewhat improved conditions; the food was better, the barracks were of superior quality and the main advantage was the absence of the menacing gas chambers. The permanently billowing chimneys of Auschwitz affected every thought and moment of his life there. Here he felt free of the heavy burden of the relentless reminder of the incessant murder in progress. The living quarters, even those assigned to Jews, were much less crowded in Dachau, and in a better state of repair. Not only were the barracks roomier, but the inmates also received better clothing and warmer blankets. The general mood and interrelationship of the inmates was incomparably better. One could say that at times it was almost civil.

There was still a lack of food, but the inmates were not nearly as famished as in Auschwitz or Theresienstadt. In addition, physical hygiene was attainable. The facilities in Dachau were inside the barracks so that the inmates could reach them without traversing long distances, with long delays and many accidents. The lavatories were adequate in number and kept clean, not always flooded, forcing the inmates to soil their clothes while wading through to use it. Additionally, the abysmal filth in most other camps was a hotbed for the spread of infectious illnesses. In Dachau, the need to attend to one's physical necessities was no longer a nightmare.

The age group of the inmates attributed to the improved
situation. Most were young, healthy men, excellent material for an
efficient and much-needed work force. These superior conditions
explained the resistance to contagious diseases, which aside for
gassing was the main cause of death of the older, debilitated
inmates under the subhuman conditions in Theresienstadt and
Auschwitz.

Within the fenced walls of Dachau existed different
subsections. Some housed political prisoners, another those
charged with economic sabotage, dissident clergy, etc. Within the
compound, there were sections for several diverse groups of
prisoners. Dachau held a relatively large contingent of political
prisoners; another consisted of religious offenders and a third the
omnipresent habitual criminals. Intermingled within the
hodgepodge were homosexuals, Jehovah's Witnesses and gypsies,
all human categories deemed undesirable. As always, when
Gentile inmates were involved, even in separate, secluded
quarters, the prevailing conditions were immeasurably better.
These were the noteworthy dissimilarities, but Dachau also shared
common features with the rest of the camps; for example, the
grapevine, the vital information supply, without which most
inmates could not have coped.

In less than a fortnight, our twosome heard of a powerful
Kapo who happened to be Czech. The man, a Gentile, was an old-
timer and the trusted friend and confidant of many within the
inmates' power circle, a man who could pull many strings. George
and Frank could hardly afford to be shy or rely on their own
greenhorn status. A contact with someone of one's own nationality
in a position of authority was a godsend. Actually, they perceived
it to be a near-miraculous boon. Using the camp's grapevine, they
quickly sent a message to the one man who could come to their
rescue and perhaps be the difference between life and death. The
reply was quick in coming. The Kapo let them know that he would
come to see them and look to their needs. That certainly was the
best piece of news they could have hoped for and was followed by
much-improved moods and spirits.

The Kapo was one of the few political prisoners promoted to
that rank. Kapos were usually picked out of the many habitual
felons the Nazis trusted to do their dirty work with the same

attitude. Through the grapevine, George learned that this powerful co-national was imprisoned for being an active member of the Communist party and had already spent the last two years in Dachau. This information was extremely pertinent, for nobody, even a Gentile, could last for such a long time in a concentration camp, unless he was a wizard of sorts. Men of such caliber had a sixth sense for eluding danger and had to be in a circle of powerful comrades, who compiled an invisible armor of contacts to shield them from every impending peril. Another skill of equal importance for any long-term prisoner was to know how to pretend zealous efficiency at work (particularly within sight of supervising SS guards) while conserving his energies. The Czech Kapo had to know all that and would be imminently qualified to teach them the ropes of Dachau.

Dachau was unlike the two camps with which George and Frank were familiar. Theresienstadt, for example was in a state of perpetual flux. People were arriving and leaving; even those belonging to the inner circle saw little as permanent in the infrastructure of the camp. The transient character of Theresienstadt did not lend itself to the organization of any meaningful resistance. Few bothered to use their imagination even for simple tasks such as the improvement of their immediate vicinity. Dachau, in contradiction to Theresienstadt, was not engrossed with the all-encompassing panic of impending transports to an undisclosed dangerous destination. It goes without saying that Dachau differed from Auschwitz, where the continuous wholesale murder did not allow the inmates, not even those wielding power and temporarily exempt, to foster thoughts or hopes of potential survival.

In Dachau, some of the inmates died of natural causes, if you could call starvation and its complications natural death. Many more lost their lives while preparing or carrying out acts of sabotage or falling prey to German snooping or infiltration by a mole in individual resistance cells. Then there was the German practice of executing many hostages as collective punishment of a group suspected of disloyal activity or in retaliation for an unauthorized deed. When a group was apprehended and earmarked for retribution, they were either hung or shot. Escape from this complicated web of threats demanded intelligence, shrewdness, courage and other talents, all of which the Czech Kapo possessed.

When he finally visited his two newly arrived countrymen, he surprised them. Somehow, they did not associate his good and neat appearance with his post in Dachau. He was a tall, handsome man in his early forties, with a wholesome exterior, well groomed and for all intents and purposes none the worse for his lengthy incarceration. The long detention did not leave a visible mark, so much so that, if clad in different garb, not prisoner's stripes, he could have passed anywhere as an ordinary citizen. Here they met the master of the art of day-to-day survival in a lethal place like Dachau.

George and Frank were keen to learn, and he was willing to guide. He not only taught them all about who and what mattered, he also pulled some strings and arranged a work assignment they would have never even heard of, let alone become a part of. The Kapo knew of the best work places, where the inmates received augmented rations and sheltered from the elements. Within Dachau an entire munitions factory, dug underground, was engaged in the production of a super-secret weapon, the V1 rocket. The Germans pinned high hopes on this new weapons program and made it their most important secret project. The German Air Force would become the sole master of the skies once this new missile became operational. If the two friends were assigned to the subterranean munitions factory, they would be unavailable for medical experiments, a Nazi research project for which only young Jews were handpicked.

Dachau was one of the camps, which boasted of an extensive research program, partially underwritten by drug companies and using vast populations of available human guinea pigs willingly provided by the camp's administration. The German Air Force made use of this windfall of free human test subjects for their research, exploring the effects of high altitudes on humans. The unfortunate men involved in this experiment were placed in a special chamber, built exclusively for this purpose, where the pressure was altered, simulating conditions at high altitudes. Most of the victimized men died during the tests, and the few who did survive their torment in the "sky ride machine" were killed immediately upon conclusion of the experiment. The purpose of this research was to enable German doctors to examine the effects of high altitude on the human lung, which as a rule burst. In addition, other organs, some of which suffered fissures and other damage were inspected and thoroughly documented by the physicians for their pseudoscientific research.

Another lethal danger loomed for those selected for the "freezing tests." In this "experiment," the prisoner was forced to stand outdoors, in below-zero temperatures. When he eventually fainted, they revived him by warming him up. The test was then continued for several hours. All the victims of this obscene "research" were killed immediately when the experiment was called off, if they had not succumbed beforehand. There were other tests with X-rays, trying to determine the right dose required for sterilization. The Nazi blueprint for the world of tomorrow required the extinction of lower nationals like the Slavs, and X-rays were the planned mechanism for mass deprivation of reproductive powers.

Eventually the gods of war had a change of heart. In 1943, Allied forces landed in North Africa and in the East the Soviet Union began a major counter offensive. The winds of war began to blow better tidings for the much-tried Allies. The Germans pinned their hopes on the new weapon, hailed a miracle: the Fau One or V1, which would not only return dominance to German hands, but also bring the war to a rapid end, forcing the Allies once and for all to their knees. All these changes proceeded at a snail's pace, coming nearly too late for the almost extinguished Jews, most of whom could no longer muster whatever it took to live a short time longer. The Western Allies' solemn and sanctimonious promise to avenge Jewish martyrdom, stated for the record that the spillage of Jewish blood would not go unpunished, offered little comfort to the nearly annihilated remnant of Jews. The last few survivors teetered on the brink of collapse, and few nursed hopes of living to see the day of victory, of truth, over the Nazi hordes.

While the Nazis pinned their hopes on the new "miracle" missile, which would destroy England, some were reluctant to believe that they could claim the final victory. Even those who doubted they could win were unwilling to relinquish their primary goal of killing every Jew under their rule while they still could. The murderous frenzy increased. Eventually their hallucinatory hatred placed the goal of Jewish extinction ahead of their military needs, of even self-defense. In their crazed agitation, trains urgently needed for logistic military reasons were diverted to transport Jews to their deaths. Little else seemed to matter, except the wholesale murder, the successful conclusion to the "Final Solution of the Jewish Question."

June 1944 marked two events of immense importance. The long-awaited and much wished for Allied invasion in the West opened the second front. June 6 marked the day the Allies crossed the Channel and landed in Normandy. Within a few days, the Soviets staged a new offensive, and the once mighty Wehrmacht began a free fall into quicksand. It was at this point that they based their faith on the new weapon, which would restore their military superiority and usher in their final victory.

With an almost childish trust, they expected and took for granted that their beloved "Fuehrer" would produce the wondrous missile, capable of destroying all their enemies. As a child believes that the tricks performed by a magician are real, the Germans blindly believed that Hitler would produce a final act of magic, restoring their victory. Hitler encouraged these delusions, dropping trial balloons of gossip about the nearly completed miracle weapon. The reality finally sunk in only by the end of the war, when the Germans conceded that nothing, absolutely nothing, could have saved them from their well-deserved defeat and condemnation.

When George arrived at Dachau, faith in the effectiveness of the V1 was faltering though far from being written off, and the inmates assigned to this commando unit enjoyed privileges as few others did. The extra rations and exemption from medical experiments were much coveted and valued as a lease on life. Our twosome was much relieved when they were informed of their enrollment. They knew that their powerful protector, the Czech Kapo, had to pull quite a few strings and grease a few palms, but they landed amongst the best jobs in Dachau. For a few weeks, all went well, and just when they had almost relaxed, lulled into believing that they might remain unscathed till the end of the war, fate intervened again. As before, the first hint of trouble began with a whispered gossip, insisting that trouble was brewing in the V1 plant.

Supposedly, the upper echelon of the engineering department was unhappy about the slow progress of the work and had information pointing to sabotage at the production site. The immediate reaction was one of panic, for the German practice was to punish the entire work force with mass reprisals. As anticipated, the German retribution was swift and massive. Scores of men and women were summarily shot. The SS did not bother to investigate or differentiate between those who might have been guilty, and those who were just bystanders, uninformed of the attempts to slow down the final stages of the project.

George and Frank knew their last hour was near. They didn't think that they had the slightest chance of reprieve and since they were not religious, they spent their time reminiscing about their past. However, they forgot or underestimated the powers of the Czech Kapo. Although they felt they were done for, *he* did not concede defeat.

Using his versatile channels to the German commanders, he bribed a man rumored to have the ear of the SS officer ordering the punitive measures. For a fortune the man was willing to try and plant a thought in the Nazi's rather rigid and obtuse mind to exempt those who were recently assigned to the commando, for they could not be culpable of this subversion. He stressed the need of upholding German justice if for no other reason than the historical record. There was an additional reason for some circumspection; many members of this particular commando were Gentiles and if some were conceivably innocent, they should be given the benefit of the doubt. In the end those believed innocent, the late joiners, were punished rather leniently, merely expelled from this desired assignment.

George and Frank could hardly believe their lucky stars! They were ordered to join another work unit, one toiling outdoors, clearing stones and preparing the frozen ground for future construction. On hearing the news they were euphoric, but before long they began to feel the pinch. They were bitterly cold when the mercury dipped deep below the freezing point. They had no warm clothing to protect themselves during the long hours of work outdoors. In addition, their extra provisions were taken away, making them dependant on the usual starvation rations. Moreover, their acceptance into their new commando was rather cool and reluctant. As men previously of the V1 group, they were ostracized for fear of being identified with those close to the many men executed for treason. They understood that for a while they were "untouchables," pariahs, too hot for the rest to approach.

In spite of all the new hardships, they were grateful just to be alive. In their new work unit, they were treated more like beasts of burden than laborers. They toiled for long, hard hours, so as not to arouse the ire of their supervisor, a brutal and sadistic Kapo, who drove them mercilessly. With all their strength they lifted, carried and pulled, exactly as ordered, only to avoid the blows dealt by the brutal Kapo. He enforced inhuman speed, which none could maintain, and in response, he beat them on their backs, necks or heads, wherever his club landed.

During this winter, George and Frank starved and froze bitterly, but the lunatic Kapo who took pleasure in spilling the blood of those he ruled with an iron fist aroused their main dread. His foul mood brightened only after he satiated his urges. As a rule, he randomly picked an inmate and beat him mercilessly till he bloodied him and, more often than not, killed him. Only this pacified him for the day. The fact that in the pre-war, normal days he was a serial killer, partially explained his perverted tendencies.

Exposure to these conditions proved hard for both men, but George weakened at a faster pace. George fell victim to many illnesses, but never dared report to sickbay, fearing that the enraged Kapo, who checked the list of ill inmates, would offer as he stated "his own treatment." This consisted of beating the man to death, and George wanted to lie low and live to see the end of the war.

Frank was more resilient; although unwell himself, he was not as badly off as George, whose worst affliction was a bowel infection. His loose bowels put him through hell, with sudden attacks of fevers and cramps, which left him weak and spent. George was lucky; if not for Frank, he would have likely died quite soon after the transfer to the outdoor commando. However, Frank nursed, washed and fed him to bridge the remaining days to liberation.

The miraculous day arrived in mid-April 1945, when the longed-for and prayed-for moment finally arrived. From daybreak, the inmates could hear the distant rumblings of motorized units. With bated breath, they listened, the sound growing steadily stronger. The tension in the camp was nearly unbearable. Silent anxieties and expectations thickened the air, until it was almost palpable. Soon the dull rumbling reverberated with the roar of tanks and motorized units. To the inmates this mechanized clanging sounded like heavenly music, the most wondrous clamor they could hear, for it signaled the unbelievable: the hour of liberation.

Then came the magic moment, when the soft shouts rose to a tumultuous roar: "Freedom! Freedom! The Americans are here!" All the men who could walk or even crawl tried to reach the fence to see with their own eyes their liberators embodied in the American GI's. Only yesterday, few would have dared to approach the perimeter strictly forbidden to the inmates. Any man approaching the fence was shot from the watchtowers, which were manned day and night by guards armed with machine guns. Now most felt the need to see the liberators with their own eyes. Some still doubted; perhaps the Nazis had staged this provocation as a pretext for more bloodletting. However, this time they were wrong; the unbelievable was truly a reality.

On the day of liberation, George was lying in his bunk, his consciousness blurred by spiking fevers. Frank rushed to the barracks to share the wonderful news with his best friend. He had to shake the feverish man to full awareness and then he almost shouted into his ear, "George, buddy, we made it, the Americans are here and we are free. As soon as you feel better we will go home, back to Prague to freedom and a new life."

He was yelling at the top of his voice, but half way through his words his voice broke and he began to cry. He hugged the gaunt body of George, and they both wept, overcome by the powerful moment they were experiencing. He kissed George and whispered in a cracking voice: "Listen, stay put. I am going to look for a doctor and some medicine, now you will recover in no time flat." Then he helped George back to his bunk and ran out.

The news Frank brought spelled life to George and though weak, emaciated and ill, he became fully alert and aware of the uniqueness of the unfolding events. Left alone in the empty

barracks, George was overcome by the burning desire to see
for himself his liberators, to partake in this long-awaited, almost
spiritual scene. He, too, wished to be part of the final act of the
savage war, be a witness to the poetic justice of the Nazi defeat.
He was not going to be robbed of the greatest moment in history.

Slowly he crawled out of the bunk, nearly keeling over in his
attempt to stand up. He realized that he could not walk or stand,
but he would not give up on his powerful urge to join the rest in
their first free moments after endless suffering. George reasoned
that he might try to crawl to reach the fence to see an American
soldier; to him it would be proof of the end of the Nazis. A living
GI had to be an emissary of God, who had belatedly decided to
restore sanity to the world. Slowly George crawled out of the
barracks, excited and ready to welcome his saviors. He wanted to
join the feeble skeletons who stared in disbelief at the uniformed
American soldiers, who came to represent angels from heaven.

At first many an inmate thought he was experiencing a
mirage, but finally, when realization came that these were men of
flesh and blood, few remained dry-eyed. The few with energy left
screamed for joy; others shouted greetings, but most just stood by
or lay on the ground, overcome with happiness and gratitude. The
hope of seeing this day had sustained them through unimaginable
sufferings, indignities and beatings. It was this moment which they
envisaged while gnashing their teeth as lashings tore their skin,
mixing their blood with exasperated tears. It was the shimmering
mirage of this moment, which carried these true survivors to this
glorious day.

Tragically, most had not lived long enough to see this evil
toppled and erased from the face of the earth. Nevertheless, for
those who did, it was their first genuinely happy moment.
Unfortunately, for some, it was also the last one. Dachau was not
the first camp liberated by the American army, but still the sight
confronting them did not fail to shock the soldiers. The many
dead, lying among the living, the emaciated Musselmen, the torn
and ragged inmates with their hollow eyes and spidery bodies
startled the American boys who had a passing and marginal
experience with Nazi camps.

Some of the liberators, moved by the enormity of the misery spread before them, tried to help in their own way. On impulse, they offered food to the starving men, who almost drooled upon hearing words like "cookies" or "chocolate." Though they meant well and their intent was noble, they might just as well have shot the inmates dead on sight. This normal fare was lethal to many who had starved for a long time and whose digestive systems were atrophied and racked with infectious diseases. Most long-term prisoners lost on average over 50% of their body weight. At the time of liberation, most tipped the scale at sixty-five pounds or less.

Though George was in desperate shape, the news Frank provided was the needed shot of adrenaline. Suddenly he found the energy to slowly crawl to the fence. With hindsight, I wish he had not, for had he remained in his bunk, Frank would have arranged for his transfer to the hospital and, with a little luck, he might have been saved. Many of the "living dead" were restored to life in the various hospitals the Allies quickly assembled.

On that April day, George dragged his spent body towards the fence. He had to rest after every exertion, but he persisted, finally reaching a vantage point where he could see the American boys. He noticed their pained expressions as their gaze fixed on one sight after another in the yard of Dachau, to them an unprecedented display of human misery.

For George, though, this was a moment of happiness. The sight of the liberators moved him so much so that he began to cry. He sobbed like a child, tears flowing down his hollow cheeks, forming rivulets in the grime, distorting his once handsome face. Nearby, watching, stood a young boyish soldier, who was deeply touched by the plight of the man collapsed in front of him. They had no language in common and even if they had, George was much too weak to engage in meaningful conversation. The tenderhearted young American, touched to the core of his soul, thought of a way to show his compassion and offered George some food. He rummaged in his pockets and found some K-rations, which he passed to my dear cousin. He handed him some cookies and a chocolate bar.

George had not tasted such heavenly fare for years. He had to be convinced that he had died and woken up in heaven. George always had a sweet tooth, which in normal times he kept under careful control, but I doubt that on that April day, in his condition, the word "self-control" crossed his mind. In different conditions George, who had nearly completed his medical education, would have recognized the perils of ingesting food while reeling with high fever and months of famine. The young American had to see the ravenous hunger reflected in the eyes of the man on the ground. He understood that the feeble wretch could neither stand nor even sit to reach out for the offered tidbits. The kind-hearted man unwrapped the chocolate, then passed on to him the cookies, one by one, and when he saw that the man still searched for more, he found a tin of ham and opened it for George.

Something must have snapped in George's mind. He devoured all that the soldier handed him, without restraint or regard for his condition. He never paused; he only ate and then ate some more, not unlike an animal famished for a long time. He could not let go of the food, which he'd missed for such a long time. He would finally still all the gnawing hunger pains, which had tormented him and ravaged his innards for so long. The kind American soldier meanwhile began to help another inmate, who lay prostrate near George. He assumed that George had fallen asleep, not realizing that his act of mercy had caused George to faint.

Meanwhile Frank, who went to find medical help for George, had a hard time finding the staff of the camp's infirmary and his attempts to solicit the help of the Americans were hampered by lack of a common language. The entire compound was a madhouse, the turmoil reached hysterical proportions, and Frank soon gave up on his search for a physician. He slowly threaded his way back, hindered by the many who walked, crawled or sat outside, witnessing the miracle. He navigated through such a thick throng that it took him some time before he reached the barracks. Once inside he rushed to the bunk and discovered to his shock that George was gone.

Frank was well aware of George's very poor health, and he almost panicked when he saw the empty bunk. He frantically asked around, and some men who noticed George crawling out pointed Frank in the general direction. Frank knew that George could not be far, that he had to be within steps of the barracks. He soon noticed George in his torn, striped uniform, lying crumbled on the ground. Nearby a young soldier smiled kindly and mimed that George ate a lot and now was sound asleep.

Frank bent down and within seconds recognized the terrible reality. George was not sound asleep; he was unconscious and near death. He was lying flat on his back, his face was dark blue, and he was having difficulty breathing. Immediately Frank tried to resuscitate him.

He worked long, all to no avail. This man, his companion during their studies in Prague, with whom he shared the hells of Theresienstadt, then Auschwitz and Dachau, was slipping away. Frank worked like a man possessed. He continued resuscitation long after George was no longer among the living. He could not stop, until finally some people, watching his efforts, tore him away from the body of my cousin and his best friend. Frank did not even notice that as he worked, trying to breathe air into George's lungs, tears streamed down his face. Somebody wiped them off, but nobody could abate nor sooth his heart-rending pain. What a heartbreaking tragedy to die on the day of liberation!

It is a matter of speculation whether George aspirated his vomit or if he died due to a shock to his fragile system, which was suddenly heavily overloaded. Perhaps it is immaterial to consider what caused his death. It's the finality of the loss which is so tragic. The young solider was disconsolate, blaming himself for the death, and Frank tried to console him. There was no way the American could have known how to handle something so jarring as a starved Musselman. It was no more the fault of the American, than of the hunger-crazed George, who lost all control, bringing about his own demise.

A strange, humbling pain wrings my heart whenever I ponder George's last hours. For years, he eluded the wickedness of the Nazis, just to find his death in the hands of misplaced but avoidable kindness. I mourn him, along with the many others I loved and lost. They could fill much ground in a cemetery, but I do not have a single grave of any of my family members who lost their lives during the Holocaust. Their ashes are scattered over much of Central and Eastern Europe. If you could translate sorrow into tears, I could fill an ocean, but this relief remains denied to me.

With the passing years, I realized that I am grateful for the brief moment of George's happiness. He lived to see the defeat of our archenemy and, unlike the rest of my relatives, rejoiced even if only for a few moments in the victory of right over wrong.

For a long time I raged against the young soldier who unwittingly brought about my cousin's demise. In my pain, I blamed him and though even today I wish he had been either less compassionate or more knowledgeable, I know that his actions were prompted by kindness. Having known George, I am convinced that he was gratified to meet another human being who wanted to help a much-abused, anonymous Jew in a German concentration camp. Indeed, on that day he was happy, if only for a few brief moments!

Rita: Love Triangle

A transport of Jews awaiting selection on the Jewish ramp
beside the railroad tracks at the entrance to Auschwitz.
Most of those pictured did not live to see another day, but were
sent immediately to the gas chambers. A small minority, usually
young men and women, were selected to work as slave laborers
until they, too, were too exhausted to be of further use to the
German war machine and were then also sent to the gas chambers.

I first met Rita in Theresienstadt's sickbay where she was assigned to the non-medical auxiliary team. She soon became a casual friend, someone with whom I enjoyed chatting without growing overly close. Her fate is intriguing.

Rita was both young and beautiful. She had the appearance of an exquisitely dainty but precisely chiseled china doll, the kind we used to admire behind the glass enclosures of display cabinets. Rita could have served as the model for the delicate "Sevres" dolls in figure, face and grace.

It is not simple to breathe life into words that would do justice to Rita's pulchritude. She was of medium height, slim and well proportioned. She moved effortlessly, with elegance and without undue hurry. She stood on two perfectly shaped legs, very slim with narrow ankles. Rita seemed refined and fragile. I often thought that she should have carried a sign reading: "Fragile, handle with care!" But her appearance was quite deceptive; Rita was tough as nails. Few women, even those over six feet tall with the muscles of a professional athlete, could measure up to Rita. It was not only her physical resilience (which she rarely had to prove), it was her will to live and do the utmost for herself, which were the hallmarks of her persona.

Rita's face was framed by pitch-black wavy hair, which shone with a distinct luster. Her complexion was flawless, snow white, and her gray-green eyes were bright and sparkling. There was something cat-like about Rita, especially her eyes, screened by long eyelashes, giving her an air of impenetrable mystery. She had a long, slim neck, held at a slight angle, somewhat coquettish and provocative. Despite the camp's shabbiness, she seemed mysterious, fragile and elegant. She had enormous appeal to men who styled themselves as the strong protector of the dainty belle.

Rita enjoyed a sheltered childhood in her native Vienna, the capital of Austria. Her wealthy parents lavished not only affection on their only pampered child, but also their free time and largesse.

They were not particularly perturbed that their darling Rita showed little academic aptitude and even less willingness to apply herself, thus falling short of expectations. Her parents were content to notice the promise of loveliness and elegance and were convinced these would provide a comfortable future for the child they adored.

Since creation men have been attracted to beautiful women, and it was therefore a given that Rita attracted swarms of suitors who scampered for her favors. Had she lived in ordinary times, she would have followed the well-charted course for girls from affluent homes. Typically she would have her debut into society, then a period of dating, well chaperoned of course, during which her parents would pick out the most promising young man Rita would have consented to marry. From then on it was to be: forever after, Vienna style; a child or two; a household run by servants; and a husband who would take great pride in her elegant appearance, style and skills to entertain and charm his friends and business associates. They both might fill their customary roles and perhaps even be happy together.

On the other hand, they might become bored and follow a different course where they might be unfaithful to each other with discreet dalliances that conformed to the norms of contemporary Viennese circles. Rita would not have rocked the boat, for one of her most driving characteristics was self-indulgence; she loved luxuries and desired an easy and relaxed lifestyle.

However, Rita did not have the luck to live in a time suited for a young socialite. The thirties in Europe were cataclysmic times, a devastating epoch for the Jews of Europe. Particularly hard hit were those who lived in the central and eastern parts of Europe, which possibly were the worst localities for the "chosen people."

Rita was born some six years after Austria's defeat and surrender following the First World War. The vanquished and diminished Austria could not come to terms with the new reality of being a humbled, small country. The sudden loss of the glamour and grandeur of the imperial era hit the Austrians with devastating force. The elegant and eminent capital city, Vienna, presided over a shrunken nation.

Austria became a hydrocephalic midget, whose bizarre and abnormal shape and structure may have contributed to her aberrant and insane behavior. Austrians prided themselves on their *"Gemuetlichkeit"* (easy going attitude) and the Habsburg dynasty, which ruled Austria, and the mighty Austria-Hungarian empire for centuries. They believed in the motto: *"Bella gerund alii, tu felix Austria nube,"* which loosely translated means: "Others should expand in wars; you, lucky Austria, do so by marriages."

The defeat of 1918 was followed by the overthrow of Austria's monarchy. The new republic was troubled by a weakened economy, aggravating labor issues, and the extremes of the political spectrum, which clashed violently. In 1934, the rightist government lead by Chancellor Engelbert Dolfuss was overthrown in a coup during which the diminutive Chancellor, dubbed "Duodecimo" for his small size, was murdered. The gang of Nazi criminals who murdered Dolfuss perpetrated a particularly revolting and atrocious transgression. Mortally wounded, he was left to bleed to death, all medical help denied by his assassins.

The man who followed him into the office of the Chancellor, Kurt Schuschnigg, could neither command the respect nor gain the affection of the disgruntled Austrians. They lived in denial of their new reality and longed for the good old days of glory for their once great and mighty empire. This tumultuous unrest was effectively exploited and utilized by the rapidly growing Austrian Nazi party, led by Seyss-Inquart, a man without scruples or conscience.

For a long time the Jews of Austria ignored the gravity of the situation. They refused to acknowledge the threats, which were written all over the Austrian national scenery. Most cultivated the irrational hope of riding out the waves of hostile, bitter anti-Semitism endemic, inherent and ever-present in all layers of Austrian society. The Nazi ideology greatly exacerbated the traditionally latent form of Jew baiting, bringing tidal waves of hatred to new, hitherto unknown heights.

Despite all, most Jews, including Rita's parents, trusted that conditions would improve, once the depression of the downtrodden economy lifted and signs of improvement appeared on the horizon. Regrettably, just the opposite happened. Following several provoked incidents, Hitler occupied his prior homeland, Austria, in the spring of 1938. He received a hero's welcome; the Austrians were jubilant, for once more they had become a great power. Following the "Anschluss" (annexation), Austria became an integral part of Germany, considered and treated as an equal partner, and with great pride the Austrians claimed the "Fuehrer," Adolf Hitler, as well as many members of the top Nazi brass as native sons of Austria. The motto of the Nazi party was: *"Ein Volk, ein Land, ein Fuehrer"*: "One people, one country, one leader."

The Jews of Austria were engulfed in tidal waves of loathing and ensnared in mortal danger. Most began the last ditch scramble for an escape hatch, but times were tough; no country offered refuge to the endangered Jews. There were a few exceptions; some found a country willing to take them, but those were the very rich or famous Jews, and the rank and file remained stranded and unwanted. Even the world-renowned Dr. Sigmund Freud left at the last minute in 1938 for London; otherwise he, too, might well have joined the procession of the doomed.

Rita's parents, like most, failed to secure a visa and were trapped. The dark clouds gathered over the heads of Austria's Jews as their Gentile compatriots joined with gusto the wild orgies of anti-Semitic belligerence. The Austrians were more than just grateful for their new "Fuehrer;" by and large, they shared his beliefs in Aryan mastery based on the crude dogma of racial and blood superiority. The Jews in turn were defined as inferior, subhuman, vermin-like humanoids.

Hitler, a son of Austria who rose to the pinnacle of power, handed the Austrians the veritable *"Panem et circenses,"* meaning: bread and fun times, galore. Jobs became abundant as Hitler re-armed the military, in violation of the Treaty of Versailles. Moreover, the Nazis appropriated all Jewish assets and in the process began the torment. The Austrians excelled in this thievery and outdid themselves in heaping pain and humiliation on the defenseless Jews.

So proud were they of their "heroism" that they took snapshots of their playful trifling with Jews. Many of these photos were kept for posterity, showing Austrians pulling and cutting hair from the heads or beards of men, ridiculing them; forcing them to scrub sidewalks (often with their fingernails or toothbrushes), and attaching degrading posters to their prey. To put it bluntly, the Austrian anti-Semite reached its pinnacle, all courtesy of the "Fuehrer," Adolf Hitler.

Then came the night which seared an indelible mark on Jews then, and forever after: "Crystal Night," the night of broken glass. The Nazis of Germany initiated this well-orchestrated, destructive attack, which spread to Austria, where it assumed even more extreme proportions. The outburst of frenzy and the criminal acts perpetrated exceeded even those of their German allies in savagery. Jewish lives were in jeopardy, many synagogues set ablaze, countless Jewish shops broken into and looted. Glass shards covered the streets of many Austrian and German cities. Thus the name: "The Night of Broken Glass." Bloodied and impoverished by harsh laws and penalties, the Jews got the message; they could not ride out this new wave of hatred. They faced annihilation on an unprecedented scale.

Panic seized the Jews of Austria. The air was filled with the dark premonition of an impending disaster. Jews were robbed of all they owned, stripped of all civil and human rights, becoming targets free for all to abuse. They were removed from all walks of life that regular citizens took for granted: forbidden the use of all public institutions like schools, hospitals, libraries, parks, public transit, etc. Jews scraped along the margins of a society to which not so long ago they not only belonged, but also in no small measure contributed by devoted work in many professions. A few measly years ago Jews were an integral part of the Viennese art scene, represented a significant segment of the scientific community, and were heavily involved in cultural, social and humanitarian endeavors. They provided more then their proportionate share to Vienna's golden era, when the city was known as the cultural capital of Europe.

In utter disbelief, stunned by the terror, the Jews helplessly watched their rapidly approaching doom. No longer being allowed access to public institutions, many of which they once founded and helped to maintain, the representatives of the Jewish community of Vienna set about to pick up the pieces. They followed the example of their German brethren who, only a few years before, had to go down the very same path.

Under the Nazi rule all public facilities, schools or hospitals were forbidden to teach, admit or treat a Jewish student or patient. The only available facility was the Jewish hospital in Vienna that was reserved for Jews only. In bygone days, Vienna had an extremely illustrious reputation as far as medical care was concerned, and in better times, many famous physicians were Jews who had flourishing practices in Vienna.

According to Nazi orders, all medical doctors of Jewish origin were barred from practicing their profession. The Viennese Jewish community had more physicians than needed; however, there was a dire shortage of nursing staff, and all Jewish women, irrespective of age, were encouraged to join the "voluntary" units of nurses' aids. While the number of properly trained professional nurses was minuscule, the Jewish "volunteers" kept the hospital operational in spite of the substandard supplies, crowded conditions and absent municipal support.

The next step in the process of Jewish persecution began with the much-feared deportations to unknown destinations somewhere to the East. The resettlement and even worse, the concentration camps, began to shape up as an unavoidable reality. Most Jews were initially only vaguely aware of this looming menace, which all too soon turned from mere gossip into a nightmare and then to stark reality.

Rita did not cope too well with the many restrictions curtailing her freedom, the rigidly enforced curfew, the shortages of all commodities and the fear of an unknown, forbidding future. Rita resented these joyless times; the material deprivation came as a revelation, and she, like most, still did not quite grasp the extent of the peril ahead. She responded reluctantly to the request of the Jewish community officials to join the other able-bodied women in caring for the ill in the overcrowded hospital and the adjacent, substandard old folks home.

Rita loathed the drudgery of hospital work. Frankly, she was disgusted with the care of the sick, often becoming nauseated by the stench that blanketed the ward, overflowing with human misery. She nearly fainted when asked to empty bedpans, plugging her nose, sickened. She scoffed at hospital work; girls like her were not meant to soil their hands with such unappealing drudgery. She looked regretfully at her lovely, fine, long manicured nails that were unaccustomed to manual work, unaccustomed to cleaning the receptacles for human excreta.

In all fairness, it was an unfortunate place; while it was called a hospital, it was such in name only. The absence of sufficient medical, hygienic and logistic supplies for the overcrowded facility would have prompted any health official to order the immediate closure of the institution, but in the eyes of the Nazis, the facility was just right for the Jews of Vienna. Rita worked without enthusiasm and lacked empathy for the unfortunate charges in her care.

The head nurse soon gave up on her, tired of listening to the repetitious complaints about and from Rita. To free herself of this lackadaisical deadweight, she transferred Rita to the adjacent old folks home, to minister to the old and chronically ill.

The head nurse was pleasantly surprised with the unexpected success of the transfer, noting an improvement in Rita's attitude and performance. This metamorphosis was not achieved by the sudden awakening of compassion in Rita's self-centered heart, but rather by the presence of the young physician in charge of the old folks home. Rita thrived in the presence of men; she loved to flirt and tease and exercise her charm over them.

Heinz was a dedicated practitioner who genuinely cared for his patients and spared no effort to ease the suffering of the aged under his care. But times were tough and even the young had a hard time coping with the shortages and the ever-mounting challenges of day to day existence.

Heinz could not help but notice and be deeply impressed by the new addition to his staff. Her beauty and grace, amidst the decrepit and shabby environment, stuck out like a long stemmed red rose in the midst of a field of nettles. His obvious admiration and delight in her presence were not lost on Rita who, after all, was an expert on men and their esteem and approbation for her.

The young man's awe had an astonishingly stimulating and beneficial effect on Rita; it spiced her working day, and the flirting and toying with her smitten admirer was right up her alley. She came to work on time, in high spirits, for if Rita loved anything, it was the cat and mouse game in which she remained the uncontested winner.

Heinz was struck with Cupid's arrow almost instantly and fatally. Rita enjoyed watching and manipulating his growing intoxication and passion. Her work ceased to be boring and gained meaning in her eyes, now that she had a reason to hurry to the hospital; she loved to watch Heinz' admiration and ensnarement in her web of flirtatiousness. Later she confided in me that it was not love that she felt, not then or ever, but he became her handyman, arranging, providing and removing as many obstacles as possible from her cumbersome life.

Heinz took pains to become indispensable to Rita and ingratiate himself with her parents. He had used his connections with non-Jews to the benefit of his patients, but now as he took charge of Rita's life and comfort, she required more of his attention. He knew a number of black market racketeers who sold food, the kind consumed in normal times.

Moreover, his contacts within the Jewish community kept him posted on the dates, specifications and destinations of the frequent transports. The removal of Jews from Vienna proceeded at an alarming rate, and Heinz navigated skillfully the murky world of surreptitious information gathering, vital, but out of reach to most of the Jews of Vienna.

Rita depended on Heinz's help, his caring presence and willingness to shoulder some of her problems. Before long, Rita could not manage life without him and that was exactly Heinz's wish; he hoped to become indispensable. Heinz was no fool; he did not delude himself with the illusion that Rita truly loved him. He acquiesced to the fact that she needed, and in her way, perhaps liked him. Heinz surmised early on, that Rita was a spoiled, pampered girl who hated any exertion related to work. From that he deduced how to conquer this belle. If he were to continue removing most difficulties and chores from her, she would stay with him. He was proven right.

On one rendezvous, between kisses, he proposed marriage. Her response was evasive, but she continued to ensure that his ardor did not diminish over the next several months.

Time was running out, a fact not lost on the lovelorn Heinz. He decided to drive the point home with forceful bluntness, to save her, in spite of herself. He used their next tête-à-tête for what he considered a drastic intercession. He told her in no uncertain terms that he could save her only if she would marry him. She could benefit enormously, for he could arrange for himself and his family resettlement to a better and safer camp: Theresienstadt. That camp, by his information, was not an extermination camp, but a detention camp, for the prominent and well-known Jews of Europe.

This piece of news did catch Rita's attention; as it was, she was petrified by the thought of deportation from Vienna. Moreover, she knew she would not qualify for Theresienstadt, the concentration camp for the privileged, on her own. Suddenly a glimmer of hope began to shimmer; perhaps she could save her life by attaching herself to this young man, who loved her dearly and, better yet, knew the ropes in this wicked new world. She did not dismiss his proposal offhand and asked for time to think matters over, to which Heinz enthusiastically agreed. He was pleased; he understood that he had hit the raw nerve of terror and that she would consent to marry him. A few days later, Rita somewhat halfheartedly accepted Heinz's proposal. Her obvious lack of enthusiasm did not dampen his zeal. He was on top of the world.

Amidst the frequent and jarring deportations of Viennese Jews to localities in far-away Poland, no one heard of and cared even less to learn about the promise of resettlement to Theresienstadt, referred to as "the best of the worst." According to the hearsay, this camp was located in nearby Bohemia, a relatively short distance from Vienna, and that alone provided some comfort and sounded significantly more attractive. Only a few Jews with an international recognition or those well connected to the Jewish community stood a chance of qualifying for resettlement to Theresienstadt. The remaining vast majority, the rank and file, was quickly dispatched to several extermination camps in Poland, Belarus or the Ukraine. The Jews of Austria teetered on the brink of extinction in this prevailing mood of ruin and perdition. It was in that atmosphere that Rita was preparing her wedding to Heinz.

She was a beautiful bride. Leave it to Rita; no disaster was portentous enough to discourage her zeal to be a one-of-a-kind bride. She bartered some valuables for an elegant wedding dress, made of white silk, luxuriously stylish and exorbitantly expensive for the times and circumstances in Vienna of 1941. However, her parents and, even more so, her captivated groom spared no effort or expense to accommodate Rita's whims.

In spite of all, she remained emotionally detached, as if an outsider, uninvolved in the event. For her it was a union of convenience, an insurance policy for better prospects at survival. Rita filled her emotional void by focusing on one matter: the paramount importance of outlasting the onslaught, to keep death at bay. In her heart of hearts, even as she recited her wedding vows, she resolved to re-evaluate her marriage, should there be a later time for her to do so. It all sounds as if Heinz were some kind of a loser. Far from it. He was a dark-colored, sober, serious man, whose intelligent, bespectacled face radiated kindness and warm-hearted friendliness. Only Rita had no use for his outstanding qualities. His dogged and pathetic dependency on her made him – in her eyes – ridiculous and contemptuous.

When she later reminisced about this phase of her life, she admitted contemplating divorce from the moment she accepted Heinz's proposal, but she emphasized that she kept all these thoughts to herself. The brief wedding ceremony was limited to attendance by both sets of parents due to prevailing conditions. A modest celebration followed, after which Heinz moved with his bride to his in-laws for the short term left before deportation. They enjoyed an abridged honeymoon, the highlight of Heinz's life and a monotonous episode for Rita. All his ardor and passion did not make a dent in Rita's heart. Not even the tiniest ripple of emotion stirred the indifference she reserved for the man she married.

Several months later the deportation to Theresienstadt became a stark reality. Heinz succeeded in having them enrolled in the preferred camp due to the gratitude of his many friends and patients and their families for his indefatigable work in the service of the old and ill of Vienna. Rita accepted the call with a relatively calm frame of mind. She persuaded herself that they had a chance of avoiding the death camps in Poland, though Heinz did not withhold any information about the nature of Theresienstadt, which was labeled a transit and holding camp. Even a small increase in one's lease on life counted, and they considered their destination to have such promise.

Heinz, you may have guessed, took it upon himself to arrange for all that was needed. He packed the 120 pounds of items permitted, tied the knapsacks, rolled the blankets and fastened them securely on top. Then he prepared the square cardboard signs, which every deportee was required to suspend with a rope around the neck. On these signs were painted large, legible numbers, the new identity given to each new inmate. Once on the road to the "Final Solution," Jews were to be demoted and depersonalized, known only as a number, bound for liquidation. In Theresienstadt, the antechamber to hell, or perhaps the first circle, inmates were still known by their names, but further along the road, they were to be known only by their number issued at deportation or the one tattooed on the forearm.

Heinz applied himself assiduously to lighten some of the pain and burden of the strenuous journey. It was his task to function as the transport physician and this duty allowed some personal freedom and access to information. He was a shrewd man, who knew how to use his privileges to the utmost without drawing unwanted attention, and still supply Rita with as much comfort as the constrained situation allowed. Heinz could secure space only to four people's removal to Theresienstadt. He used the two remaining for Rita's parents, forsaking his own mother and father, who remained temporarily in Vienna.

The four arrived in the camp in relatively good shape, the trip being a comparatively short one. The men and women were billeted to separate barracks. Rita and her mother were assigned to the "Hamburg" barracks and allotted the lower of the three-tiered bunks.

Rita's father was mindlessly shunted aside into a small room in a barrack reserved for men, where he joined some 20 men already crowded in there. It would not even have qualified for a pigsty. It was chock-full with elderly men, the air saturated with an overpowering stench. Half the men were on the verge of death, victims of the omnipresent bowel infection, the notorious "Terezinka." Rita's dad lasted only a few days, as he developed a

violent case of diarrhea and quickly passed away. He left this
world almost unnoticed. Rita took the sad news in stride. Like
most younger inmates, she understood that the older folk did not
stand a chance. Life was much too harsh, stripped of all comfort
and disregarding the needs of the aged.

Heinz received his assignment and reported to work in the old
folk's barracks, where death ruled supreme. Only patients dying
and near death were sent there. Most physicians dreaded this
work; they could not stave off the flood of misery without
adequate medical equipment or drugs. Neither was available in
Theresienstadt's old folks home. They could not allay the woes or
ease the pain of the dying. All they could do was look on while the
death toll rose ever higher and higher. The ward was blanketed in
a pungent odor emanating from the dead and dying, many lying in
their own waste, covered with numerous lice and rats feasting on
the hapless corpses.

Heinz had no recourse but to report for work in the old folk's
barracks; the better-connected Czech physicians invariably
managed to avoid working there. Heinz remained confident that
with time he, too, would establish contacts and improve his and
Rita's lot. The Jews of Vienna did not carry great clout in this gray
and somber garrison town. There were only a handful of them,
mostly celebrities or their relatives, serving as window dressing,
their illustrious names sheltering them from deportation to the
East. Therefore, members of Dr. Sigmund Freud and Theodore
Herzl's families were permitted to die in the garrison town of
Theresienstadt; they were allowed to linger there for a while, just
in the outside case the world inquired about them.

Heinz needed time to find out where the real power rested,
how the dynamics and undercurrents operated and what
inducements mattered to those who wielded power. He was well
aware that this closed microcosm had its own hierarchy that he
needed to learn to manipulate to his advantage.

At the time of their arrival, power rested in the hands of a
small coterie comprised of the leaders of the Czech Zionist
movement. They were a close-knit unit, who earlier had organized
the illegal smuggling of young Jews to Palestine. They continued
to work together, their friendship cemented by common dreams

and many perilous missions planned and executed. From the inception of Theresienstadt, they assumed the positions of power, which they guarded closely and jealously, rarely permitting an outsider into the inner circle of real authority.

Within the perimeter of the camp, they wielded great power; they decided who would be sent to the eastern extermination camps. The German headquarters issued broad directives: how many young or old, healthy or sick, children or adults were to be enrolled. The rest was up to the Council to work out. This favored group lived, ate and was clothed incomparably better than the ordinary inmates. They appropriated some garrets or tiny cubicles and adapted them for their quarters, thus creating a modicum of privacy. All this resulted in a much higher standard of living than the rank and file inmate could ever hope for.

However, there was a momentous drawback to these privileges. While they had the best the camp could offer, they had a short life expectancy. Periodically the entire council would be earmarked for removal and death; deported to Auschwitz, their names annotated with two letters: S.B. (*Sonder Behandlung*, meaning: "special treatment," in Nazi parlance death by gas, no possibility for selection to forced labor camps). In due course, a new Council would be installed and so it went on and on in a tragic roundabout.

The duration of any Council was never the same or known. They lived and died at the pleasure of the Nazi commandant. The Nazis sought to rid themselves of any witnesses to their crimes, the men who saw and knew much too much. Every appointed member of the Council was well aware that his stint would probably be of short duration, to be terminated at the pleasure of the SS commandant.

Though this was common knowledge, man hardly gives up all hope. Most prayed fervently for the miracle of an early defeat of Germany on the battlefields, which at the time appeared rather remote. Still, many kept their faith that the Almighty would come through for his beleaguered "chosen people." Man is a strange creature, many already jammed into the gas chambers, awaiting the noxious fumes of Cyclon B to rob them of their breath, still

prayed invoking the powers of God, beseeching Him for a last
minute miracle. None ever came.

In Theresienstadt, every inmate had to work, and Rita was no
exception. She was appointed to the camp's untrained work force
and therefore retrained to help and assist the overburdened nurses,
trying to cope with numerous patients in an ambulatory clinic. The
treatment room was filled with narrow cots largely used for minor
surgical procedures. Many inmates, debilitated by malnutrition
and poor sanitation, suffered from infections like boils, carbuncles,
and a host of excruciatingly painful, festering lesions. Only a
precise surgical incision to drain the suppurating pustules brought
relief and the potential of healing. Most of these surgeries,
although brief, were very painful and without analgesics; most
patients had to be restrained, for the agony on incising these
suppurating sores, without anesthesia, was beyond imagination.

The bulk of Rita's duties consisted of cleaning the used
instruments and keeping the clinic reasonably tidy. This was a tall
order and very hard labor. The physicians and nurses had no
dressings, cotton wool, gauze, ointments or clean towels to wipe
the purulence. Once the lesion was opened it drained a great deal
of pus, which was sopped up with whatever was available. Then it
was another patient's turn.

Not a soul worked there of her own volition; not only was the
day one continuous flow of patients, it was an exacting duty,
which took its toll on both the body and soul of those ministering
to the ill. The uninterrupted piercing and agonizing screams grated
the nerves of the medical workers. The ward looked and sounded
like a medieval torture chamber. Indeed the agonies, even if
unintentional and therapeutic in intent, were on occasion worse
then torture from the dark ages. The steady stream of human
misery, the putrid odors, the confined overcrowded space,
accounted for the many arguments triggered by frayed nerves.

In Theresienstadt inmates were neither gassed nor received
lethal injections. The station caring for ambulatory patients was
not called the *Revier*. Medical help was hampered by the lack of
material (syringes, cotton, gauze, drugs or analgesics), but patients
were not killed.

Few would choose such drudgery, but in the camp, an inmate had no choice. He or she had to comply with orders and report to the station assigned. The 12-hour shift felt truly like an eternity as the parade of human torment broke and shattered even the strongest among us.

When Rita began her stint in the infectious ward, she was awash in disgust and self-pity until the day a new physician was ordered to the "ambulatory station," as it was euphemistically named. Viktor was a fully qualified surgeon who was charged and entrusted with the task of reorganizing the work in the notorious ward. He was a friendly, cheerful man who surprisingly managed to retain his positive attitude. He, too, was a newcomer, whose physical and emotional resources were yet to be depleted.

Viktor began his work, supported and liked by the tough, veteran crew. He was one of those rare individuals who spread good cheer and was popular with people. Although he could not offer any incentives, he had the gift of charm that stimulated his coworkers to follow suit. When Rita first set her eyes on him, she was electrified. He had personal appeal and though his demeanor was domineering, he was softened by his appeal, which few were immune to.

Certainly, Rita could not resist, for this man struck her as never anyone before. She loved his looks; he was indeed very handsome, tall, slim, his wavy hair was light, chestnut colored. Even in the dismal station, he retained both class and elegance. Viktor was Heinz's true opposite. While Viktor was easy going, projecting optimism, Heinz was a worrywart, assessing all in the cold light of stark reality rather then nursing any hopes that might soon to be dashed. While Viktor was tall, slim and fair, Heinz was swarthy and of a very average appearance.

There was more to Viktor than his handsome, winning looks; he commanded the respect of men and had a magnetic effect on most women. His decisive and cheerful disposition was enhanced by his wit and jocular style. Even the wretched surroundings could not erase his personal flair; to the contrary, it seemed that his ebullience lifted some of the omnipresent desolation. He seemed to bring some hope to a place of utter despair and, even more importantly, his kindness with the abject patients was soothing, invariably the main succor he or anyone could offer.

Viktor alone somehow held on, showing compassion without disgust. Rita, too, was quite different from most of the other women assigned to the infectious station. Unlike the majority of the nurses and auxiliary staff, who were by and large rough, tough and unkempt, having given up on their femininity, Rita tried to be well-groomed. Her beauty – at least in the early stages of her incarceration – was almost unaffected by the squalor of the camp. Clean and well tended, as only a recently arrived inmate could be, she was strikingly beautiful. The longer interned prisoners' faces had hardship deeply etched into their features. Rita's gestures and expressions, especially when Viktor was near, were those of an unburdened, kind and flirtatious woman, who knew her sway over men.

On occasion I would stop at the infection station, delivering some recycled material no longer usable in the operating room, like hand washed bandages or dull instruments. I was prepared for Rita's surly face, her lovely features distorted with disgust and disdain, letting everyone know, without uttering a word, of her hate for the work there. Then, on one of my visits, I ran into a different Rita; she was animated, lively, radiating good cheer. She was no longer surrounded by an air of abomination and boredom oozing from every pore of her body. She was no longer dragging about, tired and sickened by all around her. The new Rita was alive, energetic and an involved worker.

I soon discovered the cause of this meteoric shift. One did not need keen sight to notice the warm glances and smiles exchanged between Viktor and Rita. Soon all heard the gossip reporting the new, burning passion of this unique affair between the two straying lovers. Both were married, but their entanglement flared up quickly and with a fiery intensity. Both were locked in marriages of convenience, which some time ago seemed opportune, but here in this transit station heading to death called Theresienstadt they found a shared rapture. Somehow everything else took a backseat to their newly found ecstasy and if they ever thought of their spouses, they dismissed them as ghosts of their past lives.

Rita did not surprise me; it was Viktor whose unflinching, almost demonstrative show of affection was startling. He was worldly, had his share of indiscretions, yet in the past he never embarrassed his wife, perhaps because of their ten-year-old son, Eric, who was the spitting image of his father. Viktor had been devoted to him.

All this changed abruptly; it appeared that the two lovers had eyes only for one another. Illicit affairs were not particularly rare or even considered outrageous in a camp, where people tried to seize a few last moments of joy during their earthly existence before Cyclon B snuffed out their last breaths. Even in those circumstances, this romance was one-of-a-kind, totally out of proportion. They spent every moment of their time together to the exclusion of anyone else. They ignored all their previous commitments, to Rita's dying mother and Viktor's wife and son. The ugly world of Theresienstadt became Rita and Viktor's oyster shell.

If Viktor's wife was perturbed, she did not show it. She took it all in stride as rumors circulated that she was used to Viktor's straying, philandering ways. Viktor was supposedly never faithful to her, but mainly for the sake of Eric, and appearances, they kept his affairs under wraps, presenting themselves as a happy couple. Eric never found out, but when his father fell in love and behaved like an intoxicated teenager, he felt abandoned and neglected by the father he adored. Here Viktor's wife rose to the occasion, explaining that the father's rare visits were not that Viktor loved him less or that he was remiss in his duties, but rather due to the great demands made on the life of a surgeon in this place where his skills were so needed to relieve pain and save lives.

It was much worse for Heinz. Rita's still very much infatuated, hapless husband all but fell apart when he admitted to himself that his wife had fallen head over heels for another man. He was wise enough to know that nothing he could say or do would affect Rita. However, he could not let go, he loved her much too much. Steeped in his wretchedness, he hit upon a plan so perilous that it led to his undoing.

Heinz must have been insanely desperate when he embarked upon the only way left for him to acquire some bartering chips for the Theresienstadt black market. In the camp's unwritten price list, every desirable item had its worth. The generally accepted and universally valued items were cigarettes, followed by hard currency, jewelry, and food all the way down the ladder of the camp's desiderata. Heinz had none of those luxuries for in the camp, physicians were paupers, and had no access to the other highly preferred commodities.

However, Heinz did not overlook the one option before him: morphine. Many suffering intolerable pain bartered all they possessed for the painkiller to diminish their torment. Heinz hit upon this risky and immoral scheme, though he had to override his own revulsion for this vile plan, but eventually he decided that yes, he would use morphine as the vehicle to lure Rita back.

In the shabby, pitiful barracks where Heinz tended to the sick and dying, morphine was in short supply. On occasion, in irregular spurts, some would become available and allotted to those in the direst need for analgesia. Heinz used to be a man with self-respect and high professional and personal ethics; once a dedicated physician who truly cared for his patients, who loved and respected his calling, he now lost all discretion. He was a man obsessed, enslaved by his compulsion and addiction to Rita and his longing for her.

Once he embarked on that slippery slope, he could not backtrack. He stole the morphine like a common thief and exchanged the drug for food and camp luxuries, like a bar of soap and toothpaste, items that in the life of an inmate were unattainable extravaganzas. Rita accepted his gifts, never asking how he acquired the spectacular items that he gave her. It is telling of Rita's character that she never questioned the source of his sudden "affluence." Heinz was grateful that he could see the love of his life, even if only as the delivery boy for his presents. On occasion, if he had a more stunning gift, she would kiss him and on a rare occasion allow him to make love to her. These were moments of sublime bliss for the pathetic burglar, Heinz. Rita deliberately rewarded him for special extravaganzas with sexual favors, to spur him on, whilst ordinary gifts barely elicited a kiss or perhaps a smile. The pitiful slave tried for more and more special gifts, just to share Rita's favors. Heinz had lost his dignity, self-respect and bearing.

Rita passed some of the delicacies along to Viktor, which they might consume together during their clandestine dates, while exchanging snippets of jokes about Heinz's dogged attachment and total disregard for his personal safety. Was it not hilarious that the man they cuckolded supplied his unfaithful wife and indirectly fed her lover as well? Both agreed that Viktor was in more than one way indebted to Heinz. Rita and her lover found the situation uproariously amusing.

For a while, Rita basked in her happiness. She thought she had the better of Heinz. Not only did she ride the high wave of reciprocated love and passion with Viktor, she still could take advantage of a man, her husband, if only by name, to supply her many needs and so avert much suffering and deprivation. She exploited Heinz's slavish love shamelessly, slowly driving him over the edge, into a deep abyss into which he would drag her unwittingly along.

In the beginning, Heinz pilfered small quantities of the narcotics, but gradually he stole more and more, eventually brazenly taking it all. It would seem that he had a death wish or no longer cared if his continuous embezzlement was detected.

Meanwhile in the old folk's home many a nurse saw the much-changed Heinz and silently wondered. Another puzzle to most was the total lack of narcotics. While in the past the supply was erratic and totally inadequate, now it ceased entirely. The narcotics were locked in a small box to which only Heinz and the head nurse had access. Heinz became an instant suspect; in his dazed state, he seemed to be an addict who took the drugs for his own personal use.

Once the head nurse became suspicious, she began to monitor the locked box more closely as well as the only other person with its access. Slowly the unbelievable became indubitable. All the evidence pointed to the physician-in-chief; he was the unscrupulous thief. The first conjectures were met with misgivings, but the longer she shadowed Heinz, the more she became convinced that she was not mistaken; Heinz was guilty of misappropriating the opiates.

The head nurse consulted with the handful of other nurses whom she confided in and involved in the spying. All recoiled with horror. Life in the camp abounded with all sorts of infamy, but the debasement of a physician by stealing medicines from his patients, whatever his reasons, was a new low. The nurses deliberated and pondered for some time about the correct manner to handle this loathsome deed.

In the end, they decided to report Heinz to the director of the camp's health care system, who was also a member of the Council of Elders responsible for the entire camp's management. The nurses' decision was not taken lightly; they were well aware of the consequences of their report. Heinz, if found guilty, would be deported, along with his family to another camp, where conditions were most likely far, far worse.

Heinz was rather surprised when he received the summons to present himself immediately before the Council of Elders. Although some anxious thoughts crossed his mind, he dismissed them, for no one else had control of the drugs but he and the old head nurse. Not a soul would suspect him of any wrongdoing; was he not a well-liked and respected physician?

Who would doubt his integrity? All knew him to be a devoted doctor. Heinz was genuinely convinced that his impeccable reputation put him beyond suspicion. Heinz was so engrossed in his wheeling and dealing and his obsession with Rita that he never considered his behavior. However, when sent for by his superiors, he began to wonder and with mounting fears contemplated whether the time of reckoning was at hand; perhaps the hour of his undoing was approaching?

His dread of discovery was accurate. At his hearing, the physician in charge addressed him curtly, informing him that they knew he was the one who stole from the anguished patients and was therefore immediately dismissed from any further work with the ill. For the time being, he would work in a labor detachment at a construction site. He then invited Heinz to defend himself, elaborate on the charges, or at least add something in the way of an explanation. Heinz broke down, began to sob, unable to articulate any defense.

The senior man glared with nauseated contempt at the crying man. What a pathetic weakling of a man, thought Dr. Munk, the director of the camp's health care system. At the time of the greatest tragedy to befall Jews, this young man behaved like an obsessed teenager, an immature, irresponsible, sniveling scoundrel. Dr. Munk was not a heartless man. It was one thing to be a victim of unrequited love, but it was an entirely different matter to rob patients of their needed relief. As it was, everybody knew about his private tragedy and while most felt pity for Heinz, all judged him no longer fit to function in the capacity of a medical doctor. Heinz not only violated his Hippocratic Oath, a pledge sworn by every physician, but he also behaved as a corrupt, despicable scoundrel.

Finally, Heinz was informed that he, along with his family, would be included in the next transport leaving Theresienstadt eastbound, probably within a month. Heinz still in tears begged the man, with his voice breaking, not to include Rita in the deportation order. The disdain in the eye of the elderly physician softened to a near compassionate glance. "What a spineless wimp you are, so totally enslaved by this obsession for your wife. And what a manipulative courtesan she is, to exploit your pathological dependency." He stared at Heinz with boundless derision, reminding all that these were not times to indulge the immature infatuations of a lovelorn cuckold.

He rejected all pleas, and Heinz was informed that not only Rita but also her lover and his family would be deported. The Council did not pass judgment on the adulterous affair; rather, they condemned Viktor's moral failings. It was concluded that he showed abysmal indifference and stooped just as low to benefit from theft of the ill-begotten narcotics destined to ease the suffering of the very ill, old folk. His moral fiber was judged deficient; he should have stopped Rita's exploitation and domination over her lovesick husband. Moreover, it was the consensus of the Council that Viktor, also a physician, should have suspected Heinz to be the nefarious source of his sudden windfall. The Elders stopped short of marking Heinz with a "*Weisung*," the designation for those to be denied selection, condemned to death by gas right upon arrival.

I happened to run into Rita within a day of Heinz' downfall. She still did not know the extent of her own misfortune, but realized that Heinz was caught, dismissed and demoted to work at a construction site. Much of her radiance was toned down. She still believed that the storm would blow over and with Viktor she would learn to make do without the extras and still prevail. They would learn to live with the gnawing incessant hunger and adjust to it like most other inmates.

As it happened, this was but a pipe dream. The sentence was much harsher. Rita and Viktor could not ride out the storm. A few weeks after Heinz's conviction, one thousand Jews were ordered from Theresienstadt. As sentenced, all the members of the sordid triangle were enrolled. Tragically, that included Viktor's much-tried wife and his young son. It was the unalterable order of the SS commander that families were to be deported together.

Fate was not merciful to Viktor. He had to be a part of and witness, upon arrival in Auschwitz, his family's selection. Right then and there all mothers with children under sixteen years of age, were sent to the right, for they were deemed useless, unfit for work and therefore undeserving of life. Inasmuch as Eric and his mother were deported because of Viktor's culpability, they both lost their lives because of his philandering with Rita.

Viktor, who never suspected that his reckless behavior would exact this horrendous price, fell apart, when he realized that his innocent, most-loved son had to expiate his father's sins. Those who met Viktor in and after Auschwitz agreed that he was a broken, changed man, unable to recover from the shock, blaming himself for Eric's and his wife's deaths. He was disconsolate, burdened with guilt; he sank into deep depression, unwilling to fight any longer for his own survival. Recoiling with guilt and the consequences of his offence, he no longer cared to live.

All three protagonists: Rita, Heinz and Viktor passed selection by Dr. Mengele, who assessed them to be good prospects for hard work, and each was dispatched to a different forced labor camp. Rita's luck had not run out yet; she was ordered with the rest of the inmates into the barracks, where as was the routine, her hair was to be shaven off. A young SS officer in Auschwitz for a day's orientation visit was startled by her luxuriant appearance. Although he could not prevent her hair being shaved, he took notice of the number tattooed on her forearm. He pulled a few strings and arranged for Rita's transfer to the camp he commanded.

The young officer was the notorious von Biebow, the commander-in-chief of a large concentration camp in Poland. Following his wishes, Rita was transferred; he sought her out and ordered her removal from the barracks allotted to the rank and file. He arranged a small cubicle, all her own, for living space and instructed the senior Kapo to leave Rita alone.

Though officially a regular inmate, she instantly became inviolable. Rita was exempt from the backbreaking toil, to which the rest of the women were subject. Most of the women slaved from dawn to dusk in a munitions factory. Rita became a privileged person. She had enough food, was nicely and warmly dressed, had medicines when the need arose, and nobody bothered the concubine of the powerful commander. She was there for von Biebow's pleasure alone and remained his mistress for the remainder of the war. Although she was spared all the privations, she lived an insular existence, ostracized by the other inmates as well as the underlings of her mighty lover. Few cared to lock horns with the notorious, much-dreaded von Biebow.

Rita's and von Biebow's affair was unique, in that von Biebow was an SS officer. The other liaisons were between inmates who were in a position of power and their mistresses. A relationship of an SS officer and a Jewess was almost unheard-of. The risk of being caught or reported would be ominous. No Nazi officer would survive *"Rassenschande,"* sexual connection with a Jewess. He would be put to death at once, for in the Nazi jurisprudence this was the vilest crime of them all. Rita would follow suit, only the execution of a Jew was routine in any camp; the shock would be only the transgression of the highly positioned SS man.

Meanwhile Rita lived in her solitude worried sick, anguished over Viktor's survival. She knew that the odds were stacked heavily against him. He had a slim chance of escaping unscathed; he lacked physical strength, never having been the athletic type. Moreover, he was unaccustomed to physical exertion or the backbreaking drudgery of the forced labor camps.

Nor did Rita underestimate the depth of sorrow and guilt that weighed heavily on Viktor, further diminishing his resolve. He never made a secret of his devotion to Eric, for whose death he now had to feel responsible. Rita, on the other hand, was a hard nut to crack; she readily ignored the hateful glances of the other inmates. She understood that they envied her for her soft captivity and simultaneously held her in deep disdain. They loathed her for her selfishness, never sharing her extras with her famished, less fortunate sisters.

Von Biebow treated Rita well, she was never lacking in the basics, and he even brought her some luxuries, like toiletries, silk stockings, scarves and trinkets. Then, in the fall of 1944, von Biebow began to change. He showed definite signs of nervous tension, at times seeming distraught and drinking much too much hard liquor. He began to bring her some real valuables, precious jewelry and some hard cash in Swiss currency.

Although in the past he never discussed with Rita Germany's war effort and destiny, now he began to confide his most distressing concerns. The vagaries of war had stopped favoring the "master race." Germany suffered repeated set backs on the battlefield and the prospect of a final victory for the Third Reich was quickly fading. Von Biebow advised Rita to try and socialize with the other inmates, just in case of Germany's defeat. Should that happen, he would try to flee, but Rita's best chance would be to join and blend among the rest of the inmates. Only in that way could she count on escaping attention and punishment for having been the commandant's concubine for quite some time.

Von Biebow, in his function as a camp commandant, accumulated a small fortune. He appropriated much of the valuables that inmates smuggled into the camp. Most deportees tried to bring a small nest egg in the form of gold nuggets, diamonds and hard currency, which they stashed in secretly sown pockets or hid in body cavities. The thorough fleecing of those alive and dead yielded the contraband. Concerned about Rita's future, he decided to provide her with some gold and jewelry that she could use to buy or bribe her way to freedom. Indeed Rita had a magical way with men; even an SS officer, a camp commandant, worried about her safety. Her porcelain, classic beauty awoke chivalry in the men who loved her, bringing out the best in them.

That is not to say that Rita cared for her Nazi protector; he represented a mere conduit for her survival. The only man she really loved and cared for was Viktor. She lived in the memories of their past happiness and spent hours imagining their reunion and lives after the war.

Rita began slowly to mingle with the other inmates, especially after roll call. To her astonishment, she encountered a brick wall; the women despised her, loathed her presence, and old envy turned into vicious malice. Rita thought they would be flattered to socialize with the mistress of the commandant; she did not expect such abhorrence. While Rita intuitively always understood, manipulated and bewitched men, she was out of sync in dealing with women. She could, almost by reflex, satisfy the desires of men and have them love her, but women were another kettle of fish. She could never establish rapport with any of them, never having had a sister or a close female friend.

The sordid affair of the mighty SS commandant and his lowly mistress Rita, was supposed to be a closely guarded secret, concealed from prying eyes and ears. In the camps little remained hidden from the watchful Kapos, who in turn had within the lower ranks their informants and favorites. Therefore, it traveled through the intricate web of this interdependent hierarchy, where all relished in sharing juicy, salacious gossip.

An affair between an SS man and a Jewess was a rare occurrence, and it was von Biebow who stood to lose the most. If caught or denounced and convicted of "*Rassenschande*," he would face the death penalty, his eminent post notwithstanding. His liaison with a Jewess violated the Nuremberg racial laws, which decreed the death penalty for sexual relations between a "pure" German and a Jew. Even lesser fry could not escape the ultimate penalty for disobeying these racial regulations. The blood purity was so sacred to the Nazis that they knew no leniency if they caught a sinner in violation of their laws. They took their absurd racial theories with deadly seriousness.

Von Biebow was also nobody's fool. He knew what was important in the hierarchy of the Nazi party. He cultivated those who mattered; those he deemed important to have well predisposed towards him, just in case some charges were leveled against him. Many were indebted to the generous commandant and would probably be skeptical of any accusation of wrongdoing.

They would quash any charges, dismissing them as malicious gossip. Rita, if accused, would be killed, no questions asked, but then she was doomed anyway, and every inmate stood at the edge of the precipice, having only a brief while before tumbling down.

Towards the end of 1944, the German armies were in full retreat on all fronts. It was evident that Germany was about to lose the war that ushered in what was to be the thousand-year Reich and world domination by the "master race." Even the most dyed-in-the-wool SS man began to falter in his zeal, no longer giving much thought to the Jews. On the horizon was the foreboding cloud spelling doom, and it overshadowed all other considerations.

Von Biebow and his ilk realized that the hour of the Allies' victory was at hand. Their minds were preoccupied with preparations for flight, fake aliases, hiding places and surgical removal of their tattoos. It was compulsory for members of the SS elite units to have a tattoo in their left armpit indicating their blood type. In their frantic search for a viable defense, their guilty past had to be obliterated and a new, false identity invented. Suddenly even a Jewish mistress, in the heyday of Nazi rule a mortal sin of racial debasement, could be spun to be an alibi.

Von Biebow was rather realistic about his upcoming fate. He knew that he had to avoid, at all costs, capture by the Russians advancing quickly from the East. The Soviet high command made it perfectly clear that every SS man taken prisoner would be executed without a trial. The indescribable bestialities perpetrated by Hitler's elite units explained such raw frontier justice, and the members of the SS elite units were easily identified by their tattoo. Once seized, an SS man was summarily shot. Now yesterday's masters of life and death panicked when faced with their own impending execution. Their only hope was to escape to the West, where American divisions were marching into the German heartland. There was not a German serviceman, from the high command to the last foot soldier, who did not attempt to reach the American lines.

The news spread like wild fire and was convincing enough: The Americans were taking into captivity members of the SS along with ordinary soldiers. More importantly, the Americans were treating their captives leniently and well, perhaps too well.

The Americans never experienced German atrocities on their very own soil. They lacked understanding of the ruthlessness and inhuman cruelty the SS units were culpable of and had inflicted on Russia's population.

It was no secret that during the final stages of the Reich's fall and with the ensuing confusion, the German ranks broke into a panicky, bewildered retreat. Many an SS man took advantage of the disarray and escaped. Lackadaisical guards, or worse, often guarded the already captured German POWs, many interned in makeshift camps, enabling many a Nazi criminal to flee justice.

In addition, the deposed but immensely wealthy SS members and their families hastily scrambled to assemble an underground organization to facilitate the escape of one-time SS members to countries that were safe and sympathetic to them. Most of South America opened its doors wide, especially Argentina, which deserves special mention. It was this country, then governed by the dictator Juan Peron, a kindred soul to Nazi ideology and himself a devoted fascist, which sheltered some of the most odious and notorious Nazi war criminals.

The "ratline" whisked the Nazis from Germany to the Vatican, where they found temporary shelter. Many well-appointed diplomats and highly placed clergy supplied the fleeing Nazis with false documents, new identities and, on occasion, when deemed necessary, even plastic surgery, to alter familiar features of the Nazi chieftains. It goes without saying that most former SS members had the incriminating tattoo surgically removed from their left armpit. The hastily established organization was named and achieved notoriety under the codename "Odessa," an acronym for *"Organization der ehemaligen SS Angehoerigen"* (Organization of former SS members).

The world, still unwilling to take in the handful of wounded Jews who survived the Nazi genocide and languished in displaced persons camps throughout Europe, now opened their arms wide to the victimizers, the Nazis. I think it is worth mentioning that the Nazis after the war had vast fortunes, much of which they stole from their victims, while the surviving Jews were dispossessed, totally impoverished and reeling from devastating personal losses.

During and in the aftermath of the Second World War the ethics and morals of mankind hit a new rock bottom.

Von Biebow joined his terrified, scurrying cronies trying to reach the American front lines. When he took his leave from Rita, he gave her more gold and money, to improve her chances of buying her way out of her predicament.

The inmates felt that Rita, in her heyday, never gave a damn about them and made no attempts to help them, though she had the means. Now at the war's end the other women inmates began to devise their own escape plans, and their odds were improving, for the presence of the SS guards was thinning, dwindling quickly as many took to flight far from the scene of their crimes. None of the SS wished to be caught red-handed by the Russians with their *"corpus delicti."* For the Germans, the spring of 1945 was a time for anonymity, dissociation from past affiliations with the Nazi organization. It was also a time when victims and victimizers suddenly and surprisingly shared a common purpose. Everyone plotted and planned his or her escape, but no one wanted to have anything to do with Rita.

When Rita passed by, all hushed whispering stopped. She was completely ignored, glared at with open hatred and ostracized by one and all. At times, she would hear a hissed threat that presaged her death at the hands of the irate women. Rita knew she was in danger and in her panic lost the little practicality and common sense she possessed. Rita was not used to fending for herself. She had moved from her parents into the pampering hands of Heinz and, when his hour passed, von Biebow's. Men were always eager, enthusiastic, and even hell-bent to take care of Rita. That is, up until the spring of 1945.

With every passing day, Rita's anxiety reached new heights. Rita was convinced that the other inmates, who just a short time ago envied her, now waited for the opportune moment to attack and make her pay for her perceived lowly role of the pampered concubine. Even more inciting was the general opinion of her being a traitor, a quisling who betrayed them for the soft, cushy life in the arms of an SS man, the same man who tormented them.

Now Rita regretted her lack of foresight; if only she had befriended some of them, given some bread, explained herself and professed some sense of loyalty and identification with them, irrespective of their pathetic, repulsive and dirty appearance. Even von Biebow had encouraged her to mingle with the inmates and find haven among them. By then, it was too late; the women saw through her phony attempts. Now the gray throng of emaciated women loomed as a major threat and she waited, not like a lone wolf but more rather a scared mouse, for the attack by those whom only a while ago she considered a useless, dying heap of walking corpses.

Before long, her trepidation reached a peak, and she made clumsy efforts at bribing some women who appeared susceptible, with absolutely no luck. Rita was a master at wrapping men around her little finger, but she had no experience, and even less talent at establishing rapport with members of her own sex. She was incapable of devising her own escape, and she slowly resigned herself to the fate that willed her death at the hands of her fellow Jewesses. Perplexed and completely at a loss of how to proceed, she passively awaited her fate.

Then, to her great surprise and joy, an older woman approached and offered to help if Rita paid generously with jewelry and money. Rita eagerly consented and offered a small fortune to her if she would help her get out safe and sound from the clutches of the angry swarm of women. They devised a plan predicated on Rita's total compliance with the instructions of her more experienced, self-appointed guide.

The escape was scheduled for the very next night. Tense with bated breath, Rita awaited the two knocks on her bunk, which was to come in the dead of night. This was the signal for Rita to get up and join the other woman in a run for the fence.

It was a dark, moonless night in April when Rita followed her in the direction of the wire fence encircling the compound. The older woman had previously cut an opening in the mesh of the fence and camouflaged it well, making it undetectable to the inexperienced but prying eye. Now as they crawled towards the opening, the woman motioned to Rita to hand over the arranged payment. Rita passed the wrapped bundle which in normal times amounted to considerable wealth; she kept a small amount of money for herself, which she stuffed into her underclothes. The tough, seasoned woman worked quickly; taking possession of the bundle and on reaching the fence moved some twigs from the no longer electrified wires, and Rita slipped into freedom.

Rita breathed a sigh of relief and began to run. She was instructed to run into the nearby forest and keep moving as long as the darkness of night protected her. Then, as day approached she was to hide and carry on again after sunset. Eventually, some distance from the camp, she was to come out and seek help from local farmers to whom she was to say that she was a Gentile worker drafted into forced labor by the Germans in Austria.

The Polish peasants were in general quite anti-Semitic, and therefore Rita had to deny having anything to do with Jews. Her appearance confirmed her words. She appeared well fed and dressed. No Jewish escapee from a concentration camp could look comparably well. Her story was very believable. Rita committed all this to memory and was now about to begin her run for freedom. The night was dark and she could not see a thing, but she began to sprint in the direction the woman suggested.

Her dash was short lived. Within minutes of her start, someone pounced on her. She felt several pairs of hands grabbing and pulling her down to the wet ground. The first thought entering her mind was that the few SS guards still on alert had caught her and, with von Biebow gone, there was nobody left to intercede on her behalf! Then she heard hushed Yiddish words hissed around her.

A dark thought flashed like lightning through her mind. She was about to die, by beating, in this craggy, wild forest at the hands of the beastly women who designated themselves her prosecutors, judges and executioners, all rolled into one. They believed that they were delivering earthly justice to the sinner. What an ignominious death for a beautiful woman!

As often in moments before death, a flurry of reflections rushed through her anguished mind. At first, she cursed her gullibility that any of the inmates would come to her help, even out of greed. How naive of Rita to trust that the woman wanted only gold and money! She could have taken it all away by the sheer force of her fists; nobody would have come to her aid. Rita was convinced that all the inmates conspired against her, bringing about her final moment.

Soon blows rained on her body, and all Rita could do was scream and beg for mercy. She promised them money, a lot of it. She had a small fortune hidden in Vienna, and she promised to give it all, but soon she no longer could talk. She tried to protect her face, pressing it into the wet moss, but her voice failed as her consciousness flickered. The women lost all control and struck her indiscriminately, ferociously and violently.

The last thing Rita felt was her head ablaze from the many blows. Her arms and legs felt like burning torches of agony. The women targeted their worst pummeling to her abdomen and pelvis. They directed their punishment, guided by their primitive verdict, to that part of her body, the most offensive, by which she procured the many favors from her lover, the commandant.

Rita did not know how long this beating continued; the last thing she remembered was the taste of sticky, metallic-sweet blood on her lips. Several of her snow white, pearly teeth were knocked loose in her mouth, and she felt a burning sensation on her cheeks where she sustained deep bruises. As she mercifully sunk into unconsciousness her last thought was of Viktor, "What a pity not to see him again." In leaving this world, her last flashback belonged to the glory of her grand love.

However, Rita was not to die, not on this night anyway. The women did not intend to make it easy for her; she was not be let off the hook, not as yet anyway, for they wanted to torment her, make her pay for her betrayal and total past disregard for her hungry, suffering sisters.

When Rita came to, she was lying on the floor back in a barracks, bound with ropes, gagged, dirtied, covered in caked blood and hurting all over. Soon her rousing mind flashed a warning signal; she quickly remembered what happened and quickly shut her swollen eyes. She decided to lead them down the garden path; they were to believe that she was in her last death throes, lest they start tormenting her all over again. The women left her more or less alone, convinced that she could no longer feel their blows and satisfying their abhorrence with an occasional kick, while others spat on her, passing by her motionless body.

She could not even approximate how long she lay there. Her consciousness was shifting from high alert to mindless oblivion. Her only recollection was beseeching God to grant her a quick death and release from her excruciating pains. She was convinced that she had many broken bones; she could not move an inch without pain.

Whenever she came around, she pricked up her ears to listen to the plans the women had in store for her. What she overheard did not fill her with hope or confidence. From their terse remarks, she extrapolated that they intended to slowly and deliberately torment her, till she succumbed to her wounds and injuries.

Fate once again intervened; Rita's life was not to be extinguished in the marshes of the inhospitable Polish countryside or in the drab barracks of the camp where the women dragged her after her capture.

The women who punished Rita so cruelly, deliberated her fate. Some suggested killing her forthwith and leaving the corpse behind. Others objected, considering it too merciful for the "SS whore," as they referred to her. According to the consensus, Rita was not suitably punished yet. Finally they decided to drag her along and continue their protracted punishment if opportunity arose while on the march. Rita listened, cold with fear at their words, while concentrating on maintaining her role of a deeply unconscious person.

Moments before the march began the women poured a bucket of water over Rita, forcing her to open her eyes. They ordered her roughly to get up and not pretend infirmity caused by injuries. If any of her bones were broken and she could not march, they promised to finish her on the spot; otherwise she had better try to join them on their last odyssey. To Rita's and their surprise, she got up; clearly none of her bones were fractured. She had massive soft tissue injuries; she was black and blue over her entire body, her eyes swollen shut, her lips and cheeks had deep gashes and bruises; nobody would have guessed that this was the lovely Rita.

Before they all set out, the women decided to shave her head, ripping and pulling most of it in clumps with sadistic and malicious pleasure. The remainder of Rita's thick and rich curls was shaved off, as time was running out on their malicious amusement. Once they completed their handiwork, they inspected the mutilated and disfigured Rita, altered beyond recognition. The bare skin on her skull bled, her face was black and puffed, her body bruised as she staggered, trying to keep herself upright. Her tears, mixed with blood, ran down her cheeks in reddish rivulets, giving her an absurdly pathetic appearance. The women were pleased; they had chastised their sinful sister well.

Lastly, they smeared tar over her baldhead and sprinkled chicken feathers, which then remained firmly stuck to her skull. This was the traditional stigma directed at women who had intimate relations with the enemy. They continued her torment by continuously beating, spitting and swearing at her. They called her outrageous names, "whore" and "slut" being some of the gentler ones. Rita sobbed quietly, the last thing she wanted was to anger them; as it was, she had many doubts she could overcome her ordeal. She kept stumbling along, aware that this was her one and only chance of seeing better days.

Although her face and body were a solid layer of bruises, her general condition much surpassed the rest of the women. This was the best card in her hand; the rest of the marchers were exhausted, run down and malnourished, most of them at the end of their strength and generally gravely ill. Rita's normal diet throughout her incarceration spared her the devastating effects of chronic malnutrition. In little over a day the moving columns began to fall into disarray as the women began to stumble and drop by the wayside, dead or dying. The SS guards accompanying the marchers simply shot them or just abandoned them where they keeled over, leaving them to die.

While every hour of the death march wrought more havoc among the women, near the end of their tether anyway, Rita began to recover from her many injuries. Her otherwise intact health was helping her mend. Rita continued to march at a steady pace as the ranks thinned.

In the early spring of 1945, Europe's diseased body was comparable to a hugely distended abdomen filled with pus and decay, taut and ready to burst and spill all the putrefaction generated by 12 years of the Nazi's rule of horror. Whatever remained of the Third Reich reached the end of its military power, punctured by Allied shells; beaten to the ground, it began to ooze from its sides and release its deathly contents. The highways and roads of Europe were littered and disfigured by unbelievable sights of death and human misery. The Nazi high command still hoped to obliterate any telltale signs of their crimes by killing off the last surviving inmates. It was their plan to rush the ragged remains of Jews from the concentration camps of Europe to the last operational gas chambers at their disposal, hastily completed in Theresienstadt. Most of the other camps were in the path of the advancing Allied forces, leaving Theresienstadt as the last and only option for their plan.

The thousands of marching Musselmen, prodded by guns and whips, staggered towards Theresienstadt. Their bodies covered with lice and scabs, hungry and worn, they created incredible chaos. Harsh rains and strong winds aggravated their plight. Some attempted to flee, others just walked or stumbled their way inland, moving away from their potential liberators.

They could not stop, lest the Germans shoot them, but their spindly legs could not carry them fast enough on this macabre journey. So more and more fell, finally finding rest from their ordeal. The only beneficiaries of all these deaths were the countless lice, the last legacy of the doomed. In death, all the pathetic Musselmen looked alike. Nobody was quite certain why they were called by that name; perhaps because they staggered wrapped in blankets or rags remotely resembling the loose robes worn in some Islamic countries. Wasted muscles erased their features, their cheeks were hollow and their eyes sunk deeply in the sockets.

With shaven heads, they all seemed apparitions from another planet. In a way, they were; they came out of a different world, one hitherto unknown to mankind. Some were clad in the remnants of their striped, prisoners' uniforms, while others covered their broken bodies with torn blankets or rags. All human dignity and abashment had been taken from them long ago. They were unaware and could care less about their appearance, which reflected the hell in which they spent the last months or years of their lives.

If God created man in his semblance, He must have ached at His debasement. Their appearance reflected their mind and soul. They no longer had any depth or range of emotion or thought; all interests were erased by the one overwhelming, deep-seated obsessive instinct, to still the torment of hunger with food, any food. All else was immaterial; the only thing which mattered was the search for something edible. They searched in the frozen snow along the road as they marched. They would kill for it, for a potato peel or a piece of bread, at times even for a blade of grass –that is, if they had any strength or energy left for a scuffle.

What once were distinguishing human qualities – inhibitions, morality and civility – were washed away by the torrents of abuse, misery and starvation. They moved like shadows of death, like mementos of hell, marked by the Angel of Death. Their physical end was preceded by the eradication of all that differentiated man from the "lower" forms of life. This sad procession of deathly shadows was visible everywhere leaving assorted camps from the periphery of the Nazi empire, on a march that was to end in Theresienstadt.

For months, the death marches, part of the operation euphemistically dubbed "evacuation of prisoners," continued. Both sides were obsessed; the prisoners with food and the Germans by fear of the punishment to be meted out following the imminent Allied victory. Some SS men panicked; exchanging their uniforms for the dirty rags of some inmate, lice and all, hoping that by impersonating an inmate they might escape. Others used their last moments of power for their last hurrah: a killing spree, shooting and beating their helpless captives.

The death marches marked Europe's deepest shame and infamy; at worst condoned, at best unchallenged and silently tolerated. However, our protagonist, Rita, owed her life to one such death march. Back in the camp, the women would have murdered her, after they had satisfied their need to punish her. The hardships of the march sapped their remaining stamina, thus preventing the completion of their vindictive plan. They died one by one, dropping off like flies.

Rita managed to convince one of the marchers to untie her wrists. Her situation improved daily, few in the motley group now having sufficient strength left to strike her. Aside for the strange headgear, her feathery skull, marking her a woman who consorted with the enemy, she completed the march without additional harm. Only a small fraction of those setting out reached the gates of Theresienstadt.

I was standing near the gate when this absurd procession reached its final destination. From some distance, I saw the conspicuous woman whose skull was crowned by whitish feathers. How strange and unusual, I thought; there had to be an SS man with a powerful death wish to engage in an affair with an inmate.

The grotesque bunch passed near me, and suddenly I heard my name called out, loudly and repeatedly. I scanned the group closely, but I could not find any familiar faces. That alone was not remarkable; most returnees were emaciated and distorted beyond recognition.

Again and again, someone cried out my name, and it took me another few moments before I was sure that it was the feather-headed inmate calling. I focused again on her and saw a relatively healthy girl, whose badly bruised face I could not place among my acquaintances. Her cheeks were discolored in all the hues from black to greenish-yellow, and her eyes were swollen, nearly shut. She had dried, caked blood on her face and arms and one ear hung partially ripped off. All that met my eyes was a bruised, recently battered person.

Who was she? She was beaten to within an inch of her life; they had thrashed the daylights out of this concubine of a Nazi. The voice had a familiar ring, and then it hit me, I had heard that voice before, the heavy Austrian accent with the rather high-pitched tone and a specific cadence. When she called out my name again, I suddenly recognized her to be Rita, the aide from the infectious station, whose torrid love affair with Viktor became a legend, even in Theresienstadt.

It did not require special effort to extricate Rita from the circle of women surrounding her; they could not muster the strength to hold onto her. With the exception of Rita, they were all on the verge of collapse. It was evident that she was a privileged inmate; her well-fed body was an indisputable indictment, living proof of her favored status in the camp.

I extracted her from the group of menacing women and to my surprise, once at a safe distance, she barely acknowledged me. Instead, she turned to yell in an angry, high-pitched staccato, "In spite of all your hate, I was von Biebow's mistress." Her entire body quivered, she seemed consumed with hate and spite. She yelled this nonsensical sentence over again till her voice grew hoarse and only then she noticed me watching her in utter disbelief. Rita, being a brazen woman, made even more shameless by her incarceration, did not bat an eye as she recounted the strange story of her affair with an SS commandant who cared for her and by all accounts was in love with her.

In all honesty, I did not have the time, nor cared to listen. I wanted to help her survive, but I was not keen on the details of her love life's subplots. Strangely enough, she seemed proud of von Biebow's affection and did not try to maintain a low profile or keep the story under wraps. These were strange times; most values and the veneer of propriety were erased or turned topsy-turvy. The ugly war and the perverted times turned much of human behavior upside down.

Rita recovered quickly. Her bruises healed, and her hair began to return. Soon she had a cute crew cut hairdo and began to look like her stunning self. Within a few weeks of the end of the war, she was nearly restored to her original condition. Her ear reattached itself at a slightly crooked angle but apart from that, there were no visible traces of her past ordeal. Once she recovered her beauty and was assured of her past radiance, all she wanted was to be reunited with Viktor.

She waited and waited, in what seemed an endless vigil for the one man she really and truly loved. However, her patience did not produce the result. None of the skeletons stumbling back to Theresienstadt, and there were many still marching in after liberation, could remember having seen or heard of Viktor after selection in Auschwitz where he was deemed fit for hard labor and marched to the barracks for further processing.

Two men who stood next to him during selection made it back and recalled his heart-rending anguish while witnessing helplessly his son and wife being ordered to join those sentenced to die. According to their recollection, he stood there stark naked, paralyzed with pain, clenching his fists and gnashing his teeth as his 11-year-old was dispatched to the gas chamber. Viktor supposedly attempted an encouraging wave with tears streaming down his face. Did he blame himself for his son's death? Did he, at that moment, hate Rita? He could not help but remember that if not for Heinz' thievery, neither he nor his wife and child would be standing, at that time, on the platform of Auschwitz, adding yet another drop into the ocean of spilled Jewish blood. Would he have felt less miserable if their deportation had no connection to his affair? Was this his moment of truth? Did his conscience catch up with him when he watched his child, and wife, go to their deaths?

For Rita, who had relatively cushy years of incarceration, now, right after liberation, began the worst period of her life. She suffered much more anguish than the avengers of her promiscuity could ever have imposed on her.

Theresienstadt, liberated by the Russian army, swarmed with many ghost-like inmates who had returned in the wake of Germany's defeat. Rita got into the habit of roaming the camp, approaching returning men to inquire about Viktor. Any scrap of news would make her deliriously happy. Fate seemed to have it in for her. Nobody knew or saw him after Auschwitz. It seemed as if he turned into another grain of sand, drowned in the sea of victims. Rita was a tenacious fighter and refused to give up or accept that he might have died in the quarries of some camp. Most men, who were selected for "life" in Auschwitz at that time, were sent to back-breaking toil with brutal beatings and merciless starvation.

Slowly the numbers of returnees began to dwindle. Fewer and fewer men and women came back into now epidemic-ridden Theresienstadt. Most of the gathered survivors came down with typhus. The Russian medical corps imposed a strict quarantine, shutting down the camp tightly, allowing in only the obvious survivors of death marches, who kept showing up in an ever-thinning trickle.

One afternoon a small group of men staggered in; they were evaluated and recognized as genuine inmates and allowed entry by the weary Russian guards. Quickly, via the camp's grapevine, the news spread that amongst this bunch was a young doctor. To

Rita's misfortune, it was not the man she hoped to see. It was Heinz, though a shadow of himself, more a ghost than a young man. Though he was so weak that he could barely whisper, his first enquiry was Rita's whereabouts. Few practiced social tact in the course of those hard days, and someone informed him in minute detail about her ignominious return. The "friend" was so eager, he not only recited every minute detail, including her decorated feathery head, and explained its significance; he even added Rita's proud admission of having bedded with the notorious von Biebow. For poor Heinz, his love for Rita did not bring him too many proud moments. He paid a high price for his obsession with this unique belle.

Rita, understandably, was in no particular hurry to seek out her husband. But a few days later she plucked up her courage and appeared at his bedside, not so much to inquire about his recovery, but to inform him that she had decided to wait in Theresienstadt for Viktor's return. She advised him of her wish to dissolve their marriage and asked him to initiate the proceedings once he recovered and returned to their native Vienna. None of this came as a surprise to Heinz.

I spoke briefly with Heinz, when he was already well on his way to recovery. He was quite changed; his ordeal in the forced labor camp brought his life into proper perspective. He was no longer the crazed young man who would do anything and everything to please Rita. That is not to say that he was free of his dependency on her, far from it. However, he had regained his balance, could distinguish right from wrong, and no longer seemed the weak man who lost all his self-respect.

He was deeply sorry for the wrongs he committed in his days of compulsion and was determined to make amends to his profession and the patients he would take care of in the future. As for the private aspect of his life, he agreed that he should leave Rita and try to rebuild his own life.

Heinz did not strike me as a man honestly ready to concede to the finite conclusion of his ill-fated marriage. He remarked, as if in passing, that just in case Viktor did not return, perhaps then Rita might have a change of heart and consider giving their marriage another chance. He caught my look of disbelief and hastened to add that he was aware of how absurd and ridiculous his words sounded, but where Rita was involved, he still was far from being indifferent, dispassionate or logical. He still considered her the most desirable female he had ever met and, by comparison with her, all other women paled, seemed drab and uninteresting to him. Only Rita's presence illuminated his days with radiance, embodying the zenith of attraction and loveliness.

When I, less than charitably, commented that he lacked emotional maturity, he, to my surprise, agreed wholeheartedly. He assured me that he was ready to start a new chapter in his life, devoting himself to his patients, to try to make amends for his abominable crimes in Theresienstadt's old folk's home. Before long, Heinz came to take leave of me; the Red Cross offered him repatriation to Vienna. He was well on his way to recovery. He wrote on occasion, but later I moved away, and we lost contact.

Eventually I learned that upon his return to Vienna he was admitted to a local hospital and treated for malnutrition and exhaustion. He recovered quickly and was discharged to civilian life. His medical license was promptly reinstated, and he was offered the position of physician-in-chief in one of the better chronic and geriatric care hospitals. Heinz made rapid progress re-entering the society that expelled him some seven years ago. His well-salaried position was prestigious, and Heinz picked up another source of income when he accepted a position with an elderly general practitioner, who was about to retire. That was just what Heinz was in the market for, and both agreed for the time being to share office hours.

Professionally all went better than he could have hoped for, but there was a fly in his ointment; Heinz found it a complex issue when he attempted to resume contact with his old friends. They no longer shared an easy rapport. There was a deep chasm between him and the Gentile Austrians, who some seven years previously welcomed "their Hitler" with open arms and enthusiastic jubilation. Although most of his friends returned the possessions he hid with them, there was this uneasy suspicion in Heinz's heart, "What did they do during those years while their Jewish fellow-citizens were subject to wholesale murder? Were they opposed or did they silently agree?"

Heinz was well aware of Austria's notorious anti-Semitism and abominable treatment of its Jews. In fact, the Austrians justifiably earned the notorious reputation for being even more violent and vile Jew-baiters and brutes than the Germans themselves. He felt a high brick wall separating him from the Gentile world, one neither side could yet scale. Torn and tormented with many unanswered questions, uneasy in his self-imposed loneliness, Heinz often wondered if he should leave Europe and begin a new life elsewhere, far away, continents away from the stench of the gas chambers which still lingered in his nose and brain.

He decided to postpone any major decision to a time when he might be more levelheaded. Perhaps with time and some distance from the horrid trauma he had just survived, he might gain clarity, if there was a chance for him to re-integrate into post-war Viennese society.

Heinz rented an elegant apartment in the heart of Vienna and busied himself furnishing it with the best and most elegant pieces he could put his hands on. He hardly had any leisure time; during tranquil moments, though, his mind began to drift back to Rita's image. His longing for her did not seem to diminish. He had to regularly fight an urge to take time off, rent a car, drive to Theresienstadt, and see how she was. Every time he came close to caving in, he managed to pull back, conquering his weakness. Rita, for all he knew, was already reunited with her great love, Viktor, and Heinz was determined not to resume the role of the perennial cuckold, if Viktor would not marry Rita. Besides, his cool reason admonished him not to squander his fortuitous opportunity, denied to so many others, to built a new life and a better future. Surely not with Rita!

All went well until a friend dropped in on Heinz. The man had just arrived in Vienna, having recovered sufficiently in Theresienstadt's provisional hospital. They spent a pleasant evening together, sharing a modest dinner and a bottle of wine.

About to take his leave, the visitor asked the wrong question, "Heinz, how are you doing? Do you still miss Rita?" Heinz, who had already downed a few glasses and, unaccustomed to alcohol, had become tipsy, confided to his friend that yes, he missed her terribly, was hurting and longing for her.

The next few sentences from his friend puzzled Heinz. His friend met Rita in Theresienstadt, where she remained alone, refusing to leave, grasping at the thinnest straw supporting her belief that Viktor might still turn up. However, she would not be able to continue doing so for much longer, for soon she would be forced to leave. The Russian medical corps would depart, having successfully contained the typhus epidemic, and the Red Cross would officially return the town to the local municipal officials. They in turn planned to fumigate the ruins, clean and rebuild the town, and eventually transfer ownership to the rightful original citizens.

Heinz was deeply shaken. Somewhere in the depths of his heart he began to spin a web of secret hopes, again. If Viktor did not return, perhaps Rita might reconsider. After all, he understood her; she would not have to pretend to love him. Furthermore, he knew only too well Rita's foibles; she could not support herself or take care of even the most mundane of affairs. Perhaps they could one more time jump-start their marriage, both the wiser, not expecting the unattainable. She would have to come to terms with the fact that the man she loved was no longer among the living and adjust to the thought of being married to Heinz. He, in turn, would give up hope for passion or love from her and be satisfied with her liking him and agreeing to share his life.

However, before he could initiate any proposals to Rita, he started to investigate Viktor's fate. The obliging Red Cross could not provide accurate data, but informed Heinz that it was quite likely that Viktor perished in Buchenwald, a concentration camp near Weimar, in Germany. The camp was liberated by the US military. Information was scant, but this was the last-known whereabouts of Viktor.

The officials shared with Heinz the fact that Rita was briefed about the known facts, but refused to accept them, persisting in her unfounded faith that Viktor would return alive. Like a woman possessed, she roamed the expanse of the camp daily, crisscrossing back and forth, searching for Viktor or some news of him. The officials pointed out that time was running out.

Theresienstadt would soon be returned for restoration to the Czech authorities and, should Rita insist on staying there, she would be forcibly transferred to Vienna and admitted to an insane asylum.

Far from being pleased or filled with malicious satisfaction, Heinz was deeply moved. This last piece of information transformed his unstable equilibrium into quick resolve. He felt that it was his duty to find Rita and help her return to reality. He could not just sit on the fence and let her wither in some medieval lunatic asylum. She needed help, and Heinz would do his damnedest to assist her.

The very next day he rented a car and drove at high speed to Theresienstadt. It was the third time he had come to this fatal town, each time a different man. The first time, he was a deeply worried, frightened inmate, uncertain of survival, even for the briefest of time. The second time, he was near death, apathetic, no longer capable of clear thought. Presently, he was a self-assured man with a bright future, well dressed, self-confident, and worldlier, a new Heinz, a man at his best.

Upon his arrival, a cluster of inmates still lingering around surrounded him. They admired the nice car, his smart appearance, and asked for money, never guessing that only a few short months ago he was in the same boat they were in at that moment. It took Heinz a while before he located Rita in her small cubicle, where she insisted on staying until Viktor's return.

Heinz found a different Rita, one he never knew nor imagined she could become. Both husband and wife looked at each other with considerable surprise, both aware of the vital changes in each other. Rita was a shaken, deflated and much-chastened woman. Gone was the cheerful, self-confident, assertive and, at times, arrogant Rita. That part of her old self dissipated during the long, painful stretch of time spent waiting, torn by the occasional euphoric hope and the more frequent despondency. This emotional roller coaster corroded her mood and spirit; even her looks had lost some of their crisp radiance.

Rita was very lonely in Theresienstadt. The other liberated inmates, still waiting for transfer to convalescent institutions, hospitals and sanatoriums, largely ignored her, but some insulted her at every possible opportunity. However, that did not matter to

Rita, for she was tormented by indescribable pain, gradually losing faith in Viktor's return. She was not concerned that many considered her a lunatic, who could not regain command of her reason. With every passing day more people became convinced that she was stark raving mad, a woman obsessed. Heinz impressed her as every bit the well-recovered man. She was still very much in the grip of her personal tragedy.

Heinz greeted Rita warmly, not revealing a hint of his shock at her physical deterioration. He embraced her and to his surprise, unlike previous occasions, she let him hold her. She did not push him away and, quite unexpectedly, put her head on his shoulder and began to sob. At first she just cried quietly, but as Heinz began to stroke her hair, she convulsed with a torrent of tears and moans, breaking down under the pressure of her sorrow, released by his silent, kind caring and patience with her heartbreak. She could not stop, as if his warmth unlocked some bolted gates that restrained a deluge of unhappiness and wretched despair. Heinz sensed that much time had passed since anyone treated Rita with any loving kindness, and her need for compassion and understanding broke through in his accepting, non-judgmental embrace.

Heinz let her cry for a long time. He did not move; he gently stroked her hair, which had grown back to a cute crew cut. The shaved, tarred and feathered state was long gone and perhaps partially forgotten. He caressed the bristles on her temples, and held her as if she were a heartbroken child. Only slowly and reluctantly her sobs began to subside, the spasmodic shaking began to lose some of its intensity; the release of her pent-up emotions was ending. Heinz did not press her to talk; they just sat, drained, looking at each other.

After a while, Rita began to speak of her love for Viktor, admitting that her hopes for his return were fading. No sooner did she suggest that she might never see him again, than her sobbing began anew, and her body began to writhe in agony. She could no more stop talking about him than she could stop breathing. Her love for him was all-absorbing and consumed both her mental and emotional worlds. She alluded in a roundabout way that she might not be able to or have the desire to carry on without him.

As she talked, more to herself, Heinz thought it strange to listen to her words; he knew all the emotions she was tormented with, for not so long ago he, too, was inundated by a similar gloom, when he thought of life without Rita. Finally, she said all she needed to and seemed to have found relief in letting go of the shut-in words and feelings. She fell silent, looking at Heinz with so much sadness that it nearly broke his heart. She sat quietly, seemingly resigned to her tragic loss, and Heinz knew well enough that there was little he could say or do to diminish her pain.

They sat in silence, interrupted by Rita's occasional sob. Then Heinz began slowly and gently to reveal his plan for Rita's return to Vienna. He offered to take her back to his comfortable and large apartment, where in much nicer surroundings she could wait, rest and investigate Viktor's fate. In Vienna, she could meet with people or retire to solitude. She would not have to live exposed to the rudeness and scorn of the other inmates who, still unforgiving, branded her the war mistress of von Biebow. Furthermore, Heinz was financially comfortable, and she could live in conditions she was accustomed to from her pre-war life.

Almost as an afterthought, he added that he had neither demands nor expectations; it was not his wish to force himself on her, and their marriage need not be consummated unless she would want to. They could divorce at any time or she could stay until she came to terms with the new realities and decided what to do with her life. He hastened to add that he was hardly ever in the apartment, working most of his waking hours, trying to advance his career. He paused and almost in whisper cautioned Rita to leave the camp as soon as possible, otherwise she might be committed to an insane asylum because of her peculiar behavior.

It was this last point that tipped the scales; Rita feared another enforced detention. She therefore accepted his very generous offer, reserving her right to privacy and informed Heinz that their relationship was to be a friendship only, without a chance of resuming a marital relationship. Heinz consented and promised to take good care of her, without demands or expectations. Gratitude not being one of her noteworthy characteristics and being accustomed to royal treatment, Rita somewhat fleetingly thanked him.

Before leaving Theresienstadt, Rita left several notes with the Red Cross administration and some remaining inmates, all addressed to Viktor and noting her new Viennese address, asking him to contact her immediately. Heinz watched her, deeply concerned; the tenacity with which she held onto her illusion suggested some detachment from reality.

Though Heinz encouraged me to keep in touch, somehow we became disconnected. We all were busy trying to re-establish a foothold in the post-war, ruined economy. We all had the best of intentions, as only a handful survived the nightmarish years, but as the saying goes, "The road to hell is paved with good intentions." Many a friendship became a casualty of our struggles and emigrations. In the early months after the war, I did not have a fixed address of my own, and so we lost touch.

Years passed, I left Europe, and then unexpectedly I received a letter from a friend who among other news told me about Rita and Heinz. According to her narrative, Heinz maintained his faith in the restoration of their marriage, but after some time it became obvious that this would never happen. Rita rejected his attempts at reconciliation, thwarting his hopes of her coming to terms with Viktor's death and resuming a life with him.

When Rita finally gave up her dream of a life with Viktor, she sank deeply into depression and refused to leave her room or take care of herself. She spent her days in bed, passive, unable to generate the energy to resume a normal life. Heinz consulted the best psychiatrist, who treated her without success. She remained despondent and with time became uncommunicative. In spite of Heinz's valiant efforts to fulfill her every wish, she remained unresponsive. No medication worked; her melancholy seemed incurable.

Her condition gradually deteriorated, her profound depressions worsened, and Heinz had to retain nurses to look after her physical well-being. She spent two years submerged in a deep gloom. Then, finally, she took her life. She overdosed on sleeping pills. These were used to treat her, and she hoarded enough until she accumulated the lethal dose, which delivered her from her earthly anguish.

Heinz grieved for a long, long time. He had many friends, but he could not find a romantic interest in any woman; none in his eyes could compare with Rita. To Heinz, Rita was in class of her own, unlike to any other. Eventually time healed much of his pain. He found some consolation in his successful, flourishing practice. He felt that he made up in some small way for his misdeeds perpetrated on those pathetic, helpless wretches during the insane times, back then, in Theresienstadt.

Some five years into his widowerhood, he met a woman whom he learned to love with a mature, normal affection, dissimilar to his one-time obsession with Rita. They married, and the last I heard was that they had no children, but lived in harmony into their old age in Vienna.

Fred: Informer

Barracks in a Concentration or Death Camp.
This degree of over-crowding was typical. Death from contagious
diseases was commonplace. A kapo brutally enforced the rules
and held power of life and death over the inmates. Each day
the prisoners were expected to put in a full day's labor
on what amounted to starvation rations.
Those who could no longer work were killed.

He was an acquaintance; we never bridged the twenty years age gap to form a truly intimate friendship. He hailed from a family much estranged from Judaism. Not only were his clan non-practicing, unobservant Jews, but they also dallied with conversion to Christianity. The fact that most of their friends and business associates knew them as Jews prevented them from taking the plunge. Even had they done so, it would not have made a scintilla of difference to their fates, as the Germans followed their own racial laws, refusing to consider baptism a saving grace.

The man I am portraying was named Alfred. Fred was his familiar name, commonly used by the sizable German minority living in his hometown of Cheb, Czechoslovakia. Society, though not philo-Semitic, was tolerant, especially of Jews who differed little from the rest of the population. Fred's family belonged to the new non-denominational group, the Neologs, who negated without exemption all that was metaphysical, and particularly rejected all religious affiliation, traditions and practices.

According to the mores of the rather patriarchal society of those days, the head of the household made all the important decisions affecting the family. Men of those times bore not only full responsibility for their kinfolk, but were for the most part the sole supporters. The wife was expected to comply, preferably enthusiastically, and assist her husband with his endeavors. The notion of deviation by the wife, in any direction from the course charted by her husband, ideological, financial or social, was then all but unthinkable.

Fred's mother would have been the last one to deviate from the smooth path of the traditional, dedicated wife. The plain and unpretentious Lora would never openly disagree with her rather despotic spouse, who had no tolerance for dissent of any kind, shape or form. Lora would not consider doubting the wisdom of his rulings and submitted willingly to all his demands. From early childhood, she had been prepared for the role of the compliant and deferential wife, one she shouldered willingly, almost happily. In her view, housekeeping, especially cooking, was the traditional domain for a woman, and in Lora's case one in which she was genuinely talented and interested.

Lora, like most women of her generation, was groomed to please the man in her life, uphold his ideas and promote, to the best of her abilities, all his ambitions. In turn she was assured of his loyalty (although not necessarily sexual monogamy) and his support for the family to the best of his abilities. She was sheltered from the need to stand on her two feet, find a job or advance her own career. Lora was pleased by her role; she was a submissive woman, who loved to putter around her home.

She was fortunate, in that her rather ambitious husband advanced to a high position as an executive of an insurance company, where he applied himself assiduously and tenaciously, successfully climbing the corporate ladder. Thus, he was able to provide handsomely for his family and still pursue his hobby of card playing, where he often lost an arm and a leg.

Fred was their only child, a gifted boy who not only studied exceedingly well, but also showed great promise in music, mastering several instruments without benefit of formal instruction. Even better, he not only excelled in interpretation of many scores, but he composed a number of pleasing tunes and songs. He was not an accomplished athlete, but did partake in some sports, if only to please his father who placed great emphasis on physical fitness and prowess. On his father's list of values, athletics was second only to academic distinction. Like most of the youngsters of his generation, Fred never dared confront his progenitor with opposition or resistance to his judgments, even on issues which affected only him, many of which he loathed or well nigh hated.

There were many subjects that Fred found himself on a head-on collision course with his father, albeit in a soundless, quiescent manner, never expressed openly. Not that Fred was such a well-behaved and compliant boy—far from it. He frequently cursed some of his father's outlandish rulings, muttering inaudibly under his breath words he did not dare articulate. Fred knew his father to be a stern, merciless disciplinarian, who chastised his son for any offense, even the most trivial one. Punishments were always meted out in the form of a whipping. Fred's father would administer hideous thrashings, often using his belt, inflicting not only pain but also a deep humiliation that troubled Fred even more.

Much later, Fred assured me that his father did love him. Only his voice was filled with such emphasis and insistence, that I was uncertain whom he was trying to persuade. His father was convinced of his own competence, of his duty to chart the course of his son's education and life, and he was prepared to enforce his will brutally, with Draconian measures if necessary. He was by no means an exception to the general prevailing philosophy of the day, which held that children were to be seen, not heard. Total obedience was the only expected and accepted behavior.

Fred's father was a tone-deaf, practical man who had no use for Fred's love and talent for music. To the contrary, he feared that his gifted son would spend too much time composing and playing his music, at the expense of his academic pursuits. Horror of horrors, Fred might forsake his academic studies in favor of a musical career! Most professional musicians then, with the exception of the few top talents, would live in dire poverty and the last thing old Mr. P. wanted was a life of deprivation for his one and only son. Fred was not an obtuse boy and probably would have understood his father's concern had the latter only bothered to explain his point of view and worries.

Fred longed to own a piano of his own and would have felt far less hurt if his father had made his motives clear, not dismissing off hand and vetoing any future discussions of the topic. Old Mr. P. said a simple, "No," period, end of debate. The same scenario repeated itself when Fred asked his father's permission to buy a bicycle from his saved money. In later years, the more mature and levelheaded Fred concluded that his father's ban of the bicycle was based on fear for the safety of his son. The streets of the town were narrow, filled with many horse-drawn freight wagons, and though there were only a few cars, the roads were unsafe. Although the traffic was not comparable to today's congestion, the narrow streets, constructed with large, uneven cobblestones, were potentially hazardous.

As a young boy, none of these arguments crossed his mind and, angry and frustrated, he interpreted the denial as the wish of a mean tyrant who wished to embitter his son's life. However, youngsters are imaginative and innovative, and Fred was no exception. He snooped around the house and the neighborhood, and soon enough he discovered that in the adjacent building lived a family who owned a piano. Fred promptly made it his business to find out who lived there and luck was on his side; the family had a daughter who was a reluctant student of music, showing little promise and even less enthusiasm.

This family also had a son, and Fred made up his mind to befriend the boy, who was roughly his age. Their daughter was not thrilled by her duty to practice daily, but she, too, could not contest her father's will or remonstrate with him. The lucky owner of the piano did the absolute compulsory minimum, and the instrument stood for the most part idle, orphaned, collecting dust. Soon Fred became a self-invited guest, and after some basic pleasantries, he would sit at the piano playing his tunes to everyone's delight.

Fred had another quarrel with his dad. He perceived him not only as the perennial despot, but also the ultimate miser. Perhaps he did not really hate his father, but Fred surely held in contempt that which the old man stood for and embodied, according to Fred's perceptions.

Fred had no problem with the religious dissociation from Judaism, though he had some friends among the Jewish youth. Most were from assimilated families of the so-called "three-days-a-year Jews." This sobriquet was based on the habit of Jews, distant from traditional observance, to visit their synagogue three times a year, namely on the high Jewish holidays, the two days of Rosh Hashanah (the Jewish New Year) and once on Yom Kippur (the Day of Atonement). Fred's family repudiated all trappings, symbols and expressions of their one-time religion. Even their last will contained the wish to be cremated, an absolute taboo for Jews of the day, irrespective of their estrangement to piety and traditional rites.

Fred had no quarrel with that; he was well aware that he was considered an apostate by most of his classmates, although in reality he was void of any religious affiliation. It suited his purpose; by not being thought of as Jew, he enjoyed wider acceptance, including by those who disliked Jews. His Jewish classmates did not detest him for his stance, though he was judged the consummate opportunist and envied by many a boy for his widespread acceptance and his abstention from religion classes. Fred believed that he had the best of both worlds, a fact he did not mind at all.

While Fred had little affection for his father, he harbored somewhat warmer feelings for his mother, but no matter how he tried, he could not generate respect for her. He was contemptuous of her passivity and resigned obedience to his father, though he knew in his heart of hearts that she could not assert herself even had she wanted to nurture some intellectual or emotional independence.

No matter how much Fred loathed his mother's open admiration and love for her husband, he had to admit that she seemed to be in synchrony with most of his decisions, except for the harsh strictness with which he treated their son. She had convinced herself of the appropriateness and duty of a father to discipline his son, and she believed that it was the mother's role to offset the strictness by showing warm, loving kindness to her child.

Fred's childhood would have been a lonely one, had it not been for his many friends and hobbies. Among his many diverse talents, Fred was able to make the best of any given situation, an attitude that made him very popular with his peers. Socially, Fred displayed only good cheer, a sense of humor and imaginative versatility in planning any enjoyable activity.

In due course Fred completed high school and enrolled in the faculty of law at Charles University in Prague. The choice of a career in law was the single decision on which father and son concurred. Fred was a bright and articulate young man, attracted to study of humanities, with no interest in the exact sciences or talent in the technical fields. He seemed to have been predestined for a calling in the legal profession, politics or journalism. Politics was soon ruled out; Jews had next to no chance of attaining prominent, highly visible appointments. Journalism, Fred decided, was an option he might consider, if his legal career did not take off.

He fulfilled all the requirements for admission and studied well for his chosen calling. Fred was not really a diligent student; he placed great trust in his rather formidable memory, which was well nigh photographic. The gods seemed to have taken a fancy to Fred. Once he outgrew the awkwardness of his teens and developed some polish, he became a handsome, if not virile-looking, man. His forte was his quick wit, his glib, smooth style of conversation and his appeal to the opposite sex. During his teens, he dated sporadically, occasionally becoming briefly infatuated, but no romance became serious or lasting.

In his senior year of high school, he fell in love. Ida lived in his neighborhood, almost the girl next door whom he initially considered unattractive, much younger and simply too uninteresting to be involved with. One day, he noticed that this tiny, plain looking, pimply-faced girl had metamorphosed into a lovely teenager.

Now Fred began to court her, using all his charms and relentless energies. Surprised, he noted her petite, dainty figure, her fine complexion, and her heart shaped face illuminated by two large brown eyes. Her coloring was exquisite; an artist's pallet could not produce a sweeter harmony of shades. Fred, being a self-centered young man, was also impressed and flattered by her adoring glances and her barely concealed crush. Her infatuation was written all over her lovely face, and Fred basked in her open admiration.

Before long, they began to go out together, frequently, under the pretext of shared musical interests. They would also share a game of tennis, more to fool both sets of parents who disapproved of an early commitment by their children. Additionally, the girl's family belonged to the conservative faction of the Jewish community, and they viewed with disdain Fred's estranged, irreligious family.

A timeless maxim teaches that young people rarely abide by their elders' guidance, particularly when affairs of the heart are involved. Fred and his sweetheart were hardly an exception. They met frequently, furtively altering their ruses and stratagems, often using their friends for cover. Most of their peers went along, lending their names as chaperones, but soon becoming bored with the amorous chitchat, leaving the couple alone, much to the lovers' delight.

Fred pressed the girl for more and more intimacy and in a little over a year their romance was consummated. Though initially reluctant, she finally agreed, more out of fear of losing him than from her own desire for sexual intimacy. Fortunately, Fred was not as naïve as many a young man his age and knew the ways of avoiding unwanted complications of sexual intercourse, and so his girlfriend quickly relaxed and began to enjoy the glorious fulfillment of a loving, intimate affair. Additionally, Fred was a sensitive and talented lover, who knew how to arouse passion and desire in her.

If only time would not pass so quickly—was the frequent wish of the young girl, who anxiously counted the days before Fred's senior matriculation, for soon he would leave for university, far away from her. More worrisome was the fact that once in the big city he would meet sophisticated, attractive, polished girls, who might have designs on her heartthrob. Though she was young, she was not naïve and nursed few illusions about his faithfulness. She was apprehensive that during the course of his studies he would meet a charming seductress who would readily outclass her, a small town girl. Exposed to temptation, Fred would not hesitate to fall into the arms of another mistress, forgetting that far away in the small town of Cheb was a girl who loved him with a devoted passion.

Time is the unyielding master of our lives; in due time Fred completed high school, capping his academic record with excellent grades. His final exams furnished him with a straight "A" report.

They spent a beautiful summer filled with passion and love, both not knowing the future, worried their romance might fade. Their lovemaking was colored with a tinge of sadness. Each time they embraced was potentially their last to relish the magic moments their bodies offered them. Even then, during the summer of their hot passion, Ida could not help but notice his roving eye. She saw that he made little effort to hide his womanizing inclinations and felt powerless to influence him, especially now that he was leaving for Prague.

From then on, they would meet only during school vacations, which might be very short, for he planned to find work in a lawyer's office to supplement the meager stipend his father allotted to him. They did not talk about this, but both felt a huge barrier rising between them, one they might not be able to surmount. Perhaps the feeling of the impending separation served as an aphrodisiac, and their bodies craved sex in ever increasing intensity. While Fred was stimulated by her newly discovered fiery rapture, Ida demanded his body with the fierceness of a drowning person clinging to a sinking raft.

When they made love, she felt that he was still hers, even if for a brief moment only. This was their summer of great passion; they made love whenever they were together, in Ida's home, in parks, fields, attics, wherever they could find a secluded spot, often risking discovery. They would cling to each other, finding new heights of ecstasy, their bodies set afire by their hungry and greedy love.

Nevertheless, all comes to a close, particularly good things, and at the end of August, Fred left for Prague. Their parting was teary and sad. More so for Ida, who was heartbroken and devastated by their separation. Fred knew he would miss her, but by the same token looked forward to new challenges and opportunities. He was excited with the thought of meeting people in a larger, more sophisticated setting than their small hometown. Only Ida, left behind, felt a deep sense of loss and sorrow for the potential loss of a man she loved above all else.

In Prague, Fred soon became the toast of the young crowd. He was well on his way to become a lawyer, was handsome, pleasant and in addition a talented pianist who was well versed in the social niceties. He cut a great figure on the dance floor, swam well and even mastered a passable tennis. What more could a young debutante want? Or her loving parents wish for their budding socialite daughter?

However, most of these girls were abstemious, preserving their virginity till their wedding day. They were far less forthcoming than his small town flame, Ida. Still, Fred was not starving for sex. He casually dated some of the less restrained girls and the ones who were not so marriage oriented, placing lesser value on their purity as a main asset for their future husbands. Indeed, Fred had a good time in Prague and only on occasion would reflect on the summer with Ida and feel a vague guilt for having nearly forgotten her. It was during those moments that he would sit down and drop her a line, blaming his long silences on a heavy study load and his part-time job.

Back in Cheb, Ida knew that he was not entirely truthful. He was an innate philanderer, who had perhaps all but forgotten her. Somehow she anticipated this happening and though she was hurting and heartbroken, she knew that it was in the cards and almost inevitable. At times, she would spend a doleful afternoon, shed some tears, but then pull herself up and carry on.

Soon she readied herself to accept the end and look around for a more suitable companion; perhaps one less accomplished, more down to earth and less fickle. She established a few contacts, but most of her dates bored her and only proved the point that Fred, in her eyes, was irreplaceable. Nevertheless, she forced herself to persist, accepted dates and went out with many men, becoming intimate with some.

There, of all things, she missed Fred the most. Her lovers seemed awkward, rather unimaginative in lovemaking, and the entire experience was often embarrassing. She did not feel a trace of the ecstasy and the magic that permeated her intimacy with Fred. The rascal, she thought, had crippled her sexual joy with his skillful, accomplished lovemaking.

Meanwhile, back in Prague, Fred graduated as a lawyer and was immediately drafted into the army. The deferment his military duty granted him extended only for the duration of his studies. Fred was not an enthusiastic member of the armed forces; rigors and discipline were not up his alley. He was fortunate, for as a university graduate completing basic training, he was upon completion conferred many advantages as a young officer in the service of his homeland.

As soon as Fred became an officer, everything began to look up for him again. Although he was stationed far from his hometown, he took pleasure in the less pressurized pace, the

carefree life, his smart uniform and the approving glances of the
local belles. As in every other place, Fred soon became the local
Casanova, bedding many women and breaking a few hearts in the
process.

Time was running out on Fred's paradise. All these pleasures
were short lived, for Europe slid rather quickly into the
apocalyptic nightmare of the Second World War. The Nazis'
aggressive and all-too-soon expansionist regime in Germany
played havoc with life on the European continent and in the world
at large. The Teutonic invasion swept through countries like a
wind-driven fire, leaving in its wake devastation and tears.

Initially many of the world's politicians dismissed the Nazi
phenomenon as a passing aberration resulting from the prevailing
economic depression and unemployment. Germany suffered from
rampant joblessness; the work force teetered on the brink of
despondency, all aggravated by menacing inflation.

The extreme right Nazi party promised a cure. The Germans,
the "master race," would assume their due place in the sun, occupy
territories for needed expansion and rule the other, lesser nations.
The Germans bought into this philosophy, hook, line and sinker.
They hailed their leader, Adolf Hitler, and they threw their lot in
with him, offered their support, their electoral votes and eventually
sacrificed their own lives for him. He in turn repaid their loyalty
by soiling and staining their reputation, as a nation, for all future
times of recorded history.

In 1938 the ongoing German aggression, which had already
engulfed several territories and states, extended its tentacles to the
southeast, towards the home of some fifteen million Czechs and
Slovaks. While the Czechoslovak populace watched the
explosively unfolding drama with grave concern, the Czech Jews
were seized with panic, grasping that Hitler's Third Reich was
sworn to Jewish destruction, indeed to the physical annihilation of
all members of the Jewish race.

Few Jews wanted to read the much derided and despised
book written by the crazed prophet of the Nazi movement, Adolf
Hitler, *Mein Kampf* (*My Struggle*). Only a handful understood the
"Nuremberg racial laws," omissions that later revealed the
victims' flawed judgment. The Nazi racial laws were to become a

tragic surprise to many for the delineation as to who was and who was not a Jew. These lines were drawn strictly along family lineage. For many an apostate or a self-hating convert, the laws were a rude awakening and shock. It turned out that not only the pious and devout Jew was a thorn in the eye of the Germans, but anyone having even a single Jewish grandparent, regardless of conversion or alienation, was considered a Jew, not fit for life, doomed like vermin to extinction. Some who for generations had considered themselves Czech patriots, were out for a nasty shock by their unexpected inclusion in the derided and endangered Jewish minority.

Fred, like many others, rushed to catch up, to fill in the gaps of his knowledge. He immersed himself into reading the prattle written by Hitler. The more he read, the more he became convinced that such sickly phantasmagoria could not take root and find fertile soil in Germany. Was he not taught that the Germans were the most cultured and educated nation in Europe, who gave to humanity many an illustrious philosopher, writer and artist? Was Germany not the home of men like Kant, Hegel, Beethoven, Schiller and many others who enriched humanity with their assorted talents, thereby lifting mankind to ever-higher spheres and standards?

Fred was not an artless simpleton, he was well aware of the many rabid anti-Semites the world over, Germany being no exception. Nothing, however, anywhere or at anytime prepared the European Jewry for the deranged harangues vilifying them in the Nazi press. Fred convinced himself, as did many others, that this was an unfortunate but passing phase of history, soon to blow over without lasting consequences. Surely, Germany was not a huge asylum where a raving lunatic could chart the course for the future world and generations to come? Once Fred reached this conclusion, he became somewhat more re-assured, but decided to monitor unfolding proceedings closely.

However, events often take on a life and speed of their own. Those who gave credence to Hitler's repeated pledges that he was only interested in unifying all Germans and that other nationals were of no concern, woke up to a stark new reality. Initially, the details of his design and the enforced extinction of the "lower races" were kept under tight wraps. Later it became clear that some "inferior races," like the Slavs, might be used for slave labor. In Hitler's New World, however, there was no place for the Jews; they were marked for summary execution and extinction.

By 1938, the Nazis were firmly established in Germany, which they expanded by the annexation of Alsace-Lorraine and of a willing Austria to the German realm. The next step was the dismemberment of Czechoslovakia. At the Munich conference in the fall of 1938, Hitler seemingly mesmerized the British Prime Minister Neville Chamberlain who, accompanied by his French counterpart Edouard Daladier, caved in to Hitler's threats and sacrificed the small nation in the heart of Europe. The Czechoslovaks were forced to cede their highly fortified northern region of Sudeten and in doing so Czechoslovakia became indefensible. The Czechoslovak army was soon demobilized and disbanded. The march of history was unstoppable, engulfing Europe in tidal waves of violence, accompanied by a continuous deterioration of security.

Fred was discharged to civilian life, where he could not find a job that paid a living wage. He decided to leave Prague and seek refuge in his hometown. There, too, he found little solace; his parents and friends were deeply worried, scrambling for any chance to flee the oncoming Armageddon.

Few found a haven. Most had nowhere to run, and no country opened its gates, even a small crack, to harbor the mortally endangered Jews. Fred explored daily for opportunities, hoping to find an embassy or consulate that issued visas to wannabe emigrants. He searched in vain, returning daily empty-handed; no visas were issued to the doomed Jews.

The trap closed in March of 1939. The German armies overran the previously dismembered Czechoslovak republic, occupied it without firing a shot, declared it a German Protectorate, and installed their iron fisted, bloody rule. The first and most affected were the Jews. At first, they were robbed of all they owned and, in rapid succession, the Nazis began to the implement expulsion of all Jews from the Czech lands.

Fred at that time returned to his hometown and eventually secured a minor job with the local Jewish community. This in itself testifies to some magnanimity of the folks there, for few forgot that, prior to the persecution, he and his parents had estranged themselves entirely from the Jewish fold. The Germans in turn channeled their orders through the offices of the Jewish communities, and so Fred became privy to first hand information earlier than most.

One day an alarming leak reached the office. A call up of able-bodied men was imminent. Fred rushed home to warn his father who, then in his early fifties and being healthy and strong, would fall into the specified category. His warning fell on deaf ears. The elder man believed himself better informed and a sober judge of the situation. He dismissed his son's warning outright.

All too soon, the hearsay turned into a frightening reality. A number of men between the ages of 15 to 55 were called up, ordered to be ready for deportation to the East. They were to spearhead a new operation by laying the groundwork for a new concentration camp to which their families will soon follow.

Fred's father packed his knapsack, attached to it a warm blanket (never admitting that he should have heeded the warnings of his son) and left the city for an unknown destination. His pride did not allow an admission of error although the circumstances of his departure were dramatic, much aggravated by the teary despondency of Lora, who was severely distraught on seeing her husband taken away. Fred remained at home. As an employee of the community, he was not a subject for removal, being temporarily exempt from deportation.

In his heart of hearts, Fred feared that he would never see his father again. The forced labor camps were rumored to be difficult places to survive, notorious for ill treatment and hunger, none suiting a man in his fifties unaccustomed to deprivation of any kind.

Fred was proved wrong this time; his father was a much tougher cookie than Fred gave him credit for. Moreover, he was endowed with the talent of adapting quickly to new realities and one of his great motivators was his genuine devotion to his. wife and son. Fred had difficulty conceding that his father was a man of such sterling qualities.

The initial plan called for the construction of a camp in Ceska Lipa. This project was eventually abandoned and some of the men,

Fred's father included sought to flee the forsaken camp. This happened in 1939, a period of construction of many concentration camps in the newly occupied Poland. At that time the Nazis lacked the experience to efficiently organize new prisons for numerous deportees. The loosely supervised group soon assessed the situation and concluded that the structure could lend itself to escape.

The burning wish to escape was prodded by the abysmal conditions. The work was backbreaking and most of the men were unaccustomed to manual drudgery. Jews were mostly city dwellers, members of the white collar middle class, not often athletically inclined and few were robust or muscularly built. Historically Jews cultivated hobbies like music or chess and if sports were their recreation, then perhaps tennis or skiing were the activities of choice. They were ill-prepared and unfit for the harsh labor demanded in any camp. In addition, the food supply was totally inadequate and erratic, leaving the men hungry and lacking even the barest essentials.

Ceska Lipa was perhaps the only camp which recorded numerous, successful breakouts. Most inmates traveled to the East, hoping to reach the part of Poland under Soviet rule during the brief interim of the German-Russian Non-Aggression Pact. In the flux of the fluid situation, many hoped to find shelter in Russia rather than remain under the Nazi boot. In 1939, the most dangerous place on earth for a Jew was within the realm of the burgeoning German Reich.

Fred's father weighed his options and decided on flight as well. He chose the opposite direction, back to Lora, about whom he worried, concerned that she could not manage on her own. He was one of the few who returned to the perilous west, into the rule of the Nazis, instead of joining the majority who fled eastward.

A few days later a knock on the door summoned Lora, who saw to her joy and amazement her husband in front of her, somewhat leaner, but none the worse for the ordeal he had just surmounted. Crying, she pulled him quickly in, overwhelmed with happiness and relief. The decision of Mr. P. to take the moral high ground and return to his wife may have been a gallant and noble one, but it later proved to be ill-conceived and extremely perilous.

The Germans were not the bunglers the botched Lipa experiment suggested. They learned all too quickly from their mistakes and soon consolidated the newly occupied Poland into a territory renamed the "General Government" and embarked upon a serious assault on the indigenous Jews.

The massive removal of Jews from all walks of life and their transfer to concentration camps started in earnest. It began almost simultaneously from the Czech Protectorate and occupied Poland and proceeded at a rapid clip. This time the lessons of Ceska Lipa were implemented, with construction of and transportation to concentration camps being carried out in the most organized, ruthless and deceptive manner possible. Few had a chance of escaping or hiding. They began their odyssey into the unknown, into indescribable suffering that for most ended in death.

Fred's parents were included among the early transports, leaving together, but without their son. Fred accompanied his parents to the gathering place, but took his leave some distance from the gates. It was foolhardy to approach the enclosed area, for the Germans were not only erratic and capricious but also vindictive, often including escorting family members among those marked for deportation. He kissed his mother, hoping against hope that she could muster the stamina needed to pull through her upcoming ordeal. His father offered a hand, which he pulled somewhat abashedly away, when he noticed that Fred was about to embrace him. Even in what was probably a long if not a final good-bye, old Mr. P. could not show his feelings. The deeply ingrained code of men's conduct did not make allowance for the display of sentiment.

This was indeed the last time Fred saw his parents. They did not pass "selection" by the odious Dr. Mengele at Auschwitz, who judged them too old and therefore unfit for hard labor. Mengele sent them to die in the gas chambers, where most of the considered Jewish detritus spent the last moments of their lives.

Fred's call came in the spring of 1943. At first, he was brought to Theresienstadt, by now a well-established transit and holding camp in Bohemia. His first compulsory work post was in the construction of new barracks, readied for the ever-growing numbers of new inmates pouring in daily from the four corners of

Europe. Soon Fred met some of his old buddies and made some new friends.

To his utter dismay, the persistently hushed rumors stated that an enormous, wholesale slaughter was in progress; that somewhere in the East mass murder of Jews was actually taking place and though it sounded inconceivable, the dogged hearsay never ceased. The call for removal from Theresienstadt spelled catastrophe for most, though few knew the full truth of what was in store. There was only one certainty: There in the East was looming a grave danger, conditions even more perilous than those in Theresienstadt.

There was only one way to prolong an inmate's stay in Theresienstadt: to arrange for work within the infrastructure of the camp itself. The rest of the inmates were bound for deportation: the destination, camps to the East. There, according to rumors, were huge installations working around the clock, an assembly line of murder, executing the arriving Jews. The rumors cropped up daily; "where there is smoke, there is fire." The anxiety and inner panic rose to hitherto unparalleled heights.

Fred, always a realist, initially dismissed the repeated whispers, unable to admit that his next stop might also be his last. Though he tried to dissuade himself and keep a distance from what he wished to perceive as panic mongering, he nonetheless worked very hard to stay at least for a while longer in Theresienstadt. He was not at all keen to find out if the incredible rumors were substantiated.

A few months later, sometime in the summer of 1943, his one-time love, Ida, was also deported to Theresienstadt, where they met again. Their puppy love, the infatuation of their teens, was behind them, eclipsed by his latter days' affairs and dalliances. Although men and women in Theresienstadt were sequestered in separate barracks and quarters, the former lovers met and, to the surprise of both, they experienced a resurgence of their one-time flame, rekindled under the strangest of circumstances.

During their long separation both dated others and believed their own affair had ended; stamped out by the many pressures of the stormy times and the disapproval by both sets of parents.

Within a relatively short time, they promised that in the unlikely event of their survival, they would remain together, perhaps even marry. Both were of one mind: The chance of outliving this onslaught was miniscule.

In September of 1943, several thousand inmates were deported from Theresienstadt and promptly sent postcards from the new camp of Auschwitz-Birkenau, describing their new home to be much like Theresienstadt. The cards kept streaming in, all sounding upbeat and re-assuring, but no one was certain if they were written freely, under supervision, or perhaps duress. However, Fred and Ida decided to believe and hope.

The next two months passed relatively quietly. Then came December and a new wave of expulsions began. Among those called up was Fred, whose valiant efforts to obtain an exemption came to naught. Before he kissed his little Ida good-bye, they made a secret pact. As soon as permitted he would write, and if the next camp was all that it was cracked up to be, he would let her know. Only in that case should she join him. To make sure that he wrote freely and with an unencumbered will, his postcard would be written in a secret code to which only the two were privy.

The code was simple enough; every second word was to be picked out and be combined in a sequence, forming the true message. The inmates were generally permitted to write up to 30 words. Thus, the fifteen words linked together would contain the naked truth. Only then, would Ida know the stark reality and so be in the position to decide if re-unification with Fred was possible.

Fred took a teary farewell from Ida, who was sobbing uncontrollably. Just when she realized that he was the only man she truly loved and began to hope ot having finally captivated him, he was leaving again and, even worse, for a hazardous place, where he might be put to immediate death. For Fred the past months had turned out to be a revelation. Suddenly it dawned on him that he could do without all the glamorous young ladies back in Prague. They were mostly the female versions of "fair weather Charlies." When times got tough, Ida was the ideal partner, down to earth, practical and shrewd; she would be a suitable life mate for good and bad.

While taking leave of her, Fred felt genuinely sorry for the time lost, the many missed opportunities, his infidelities and his deprecatory judgments of her. He regretted his lack of understanding, and was pained to see his much-tried love so heart broken. To comfort her, he assured her of his love, devotion and as early a communication and reunion as possible.

Following their heart-wrenching parting, he picked up his backpack and walked quickly towards the barracks designated as the gathering place. Behind the building lay railway tracks, where already the train was prepared for boarding.

The wagons were soon tightly packed, and still the SS insisted on squeezing in more people. Czech sentries, who in turn took out their frustration and displeasure on the men responsible for the smooth loading of the transport, assisted the irate Nazis. Bedlam was the only fitting word for the mood reigning in the courtyard. Shouting, screaming and jostling made the whole scene surreal. The wagons were quickly packed to capacity and bolted. There was no space to sit; all had to stand tightly pressed to each other. Those who fainted remained upright as well, for nowhere was there an empty space to place them in a horizontal position to allow some comfort. The wagons were submersed in near darkness, the only light coming in through the cracks of the small, wired opening near the ceiling of the car.

Fred observed all with an uneasy feeling of sinister foreboding; he reasoned that little good could be expected at the end of a voyage with such a nightmarish beginning. It seemed that all pointed to disaster at the end of the two-day and three-night journey. To compound the misery, there was no way to relieve oneself; only one overflowing pail stood in a corner of the car, the inmates being allowed to empty it only on the rare occasion the train came to one of its halts.

The air in the wagon was unbreathable; a mixture of unwashed bodies, sweat and excrement aggravated by sordid crowding produced a stench that lay like a heavy blanket on the unfortunate people. Some fainted. Others died or went mad, screaming and cursing. Other began to sing, or recite prayers. Some of those who were once devout and pious began to curse the Almighty, screaming that there was no God and if He did exist after all, He was a murderer and a criminal just like His favorites: the Germans.

Few retained their sanity and ability for cool reason. One of those who did, though, was Fred, who forced himself to dissociate his mind from the prevailing confusion and concentrate on preparations for the next station of his life, should there be one.

He received the answer soon enough. The train jerked and came to a sudden stop. The bolted wagons were torn open. For a moment Fred, along with the others, was blinded by glaring, stabbing floodlights, brightly illuminating the ramp and the previously darkened wagons. Fred's eyes, dazzled by the brilliant glow, began to tear, and he squinted in search of a firm point of reference on "terra firma."

The frosty night was unusually cold, even for this part of Poland, where in December the frosts are merciless, plunging the mercury frequently way below the freezing point. All the newly arrived were dressed inadequately and suffered from exposure to the chilly air. Fred was bewildered by the oppressive presence of armed SS men. Most had guns at the ready, while others clutched leashes, restraining snarling dogs. The animals tugged wildly, trying to free up and pounce on the newly arrived captives.

Fred saw a unit of men, scrambling to and fro, obviously helping clear the transport from the ramp. They all wore striped slacks and tunics with a matching cap. They went about their work in a hurried, grim silence, looking surreal, like apparitions from a nightmare or a horror movie. He could not understand why the men had yellow triangles affixed on the front of their uniforms.

The longer Fred looked around, the more shocked he became. He could not fathom where fate had tossed him. While nobody could accuse the Germans of lacking in savagery at any time, here at the unloading train-ramps noise, blows and sheer brutality were the order of the day. The thought occurred to him that perhaps he had died and was entering hell, but he soon dismissed his fantasy, chiding himself for being such a big fool.

His attempt to pull himself to earth suffered another jolt when he began to notice a peculiar stench that permeated the entire ramp. He sniffed again at the air and decided that the curious smell was a mixture of burning flesh and hair. Seconds later he noticed the tall chimneys belching black smoke along with orange-red flames darting into the night sky. What was this inferno? Was it man's or the devil's handiwork?

Fred had little time to consider the flood of his anxious thoughts. Unfortunately, he was not just an observer; he was prey on the hook looking for a loophole out of this hell. The frightening impact of this scene slowed him down for a second, a major crime in any Nazi concentration camp, but a sudden blow from one of the striped men stunned him to his present state, and he moved quickly, to get away from the brutal inmate. Others, weakened, remained lying on the frozen ground. Those who did not have the ability or the presence of mind to jump up and join the crowd, those unfortunates remaining stupified even for a minute or two, were quickly beaten to death on the ramp by one of the zebra-like men. Alternatively, they might be lucky and a passing SS man might deliver the coup de grace: a shot to the nape of the neck. This was, alas, the routine in the infamous camp known as Auschwitz-Birkenau.

None of the newly arrived was allowed to take their luggage, which they were ordered to leave on the platform, to be delivered later. The men in the striped uniforms yelled at the top of their voices for the new arrivals to keep close ranks and advance in an orderly manner. These exhortations notwithstanding, many could not keep up. Some gave up, dropped down and could not get up; others fainted, and most of those were summarily dragged to nearby-parked lorries, marked by large Red Cross signs. The familiar symbol offered some comfort; the presence of an organization dedicated to humanitarian causes provided a semblance of legality and compassionate care.

Soon Fred smiled a bitter grin, rebuking himself for his hope-filled naiveté. Nothing was easier than to paint the insignia of the Red Cross and thus conceal an ulterior, sinister purpose. At that moment, Fred suddenly recalled that in Theresienstadt someone told him that under no circumstances should an inmate admit that he was unfit for work or unable to march. Any transportation provided was to be avoided at all costs. Those who needed to be driven or carried were considered useless, a condition making an inmate automatically unfit for life, by Nazi standards.

Suddenly amongst the crowd a shadow brushed by him; it was Fred's old class chum, now an inmate in the striped uniform. Both men flashed a wordless sign of recognition, and Fred heard these enigmatic words whispered quickly in his ear: "Report that you are a hospital attendant!" Having said that he vanished, within a second merging into the moving, crazed mass of people, pushing ahead in an unknown direction.

Fred was still somewhat dazed, uncertain if all this pandemonium was not Dante's lowest circle of hell. Moreover, he could make no sense of the advice just received. In spite of his bewilderment Fred decided to follow the whispered tip, though he did not have the foggiest idea why and to whom he should misrepresent himself to be a hospital orderly.

As the column inched ahead, a clearing came into sight, revealing several impeccably uniformed SS officers. Fred, once so particular in the care of his wardrobe, became painfully aware of his own grimy, squalid and tattered appearance. The Nazi officers wore perfectly pressed uniforms, with razor sharp creases. The sharp contrast between the perfectly groomed SS men and the filthy, squalid Jews massed on the platform was painfully depressing to Fred.

Fred trembled, barely able to control his shivering, his teeth chattering, only partially because of that icy December night. Fred became aware that he was frightened; indeed, he was petrified. He feared death by beating or torture from one of the savage Kapos. He feared death by starvation or raging epidemic diseases or other unknown killers.

He brought his tremulous body under control; he clenched his teeth tightly, trying to appear calm. He pulled himself upright to his full height, wishing to retain some dignity. Fred, the perennial atheist, began to pray with all his heart and power. It dawned on him that no man could extricate himself from this gruesome hell, that only the divine might be able to perform this miracle.

Fred scrutinized the large crowd awaiting instruction. The nightmarish scene included the very old, parents huddled with crying children, and some who lay prostrate on the ground, unconscious or in the throes of death. It was a pitiable crowd of doomed human shadows.

Orders were shouted to climb into the large lorries marked with the Red Cross at double time. Many of the old, the weak, and the very young could not comply. After the near three-day horror on the train, most were too spent to accomplish this feat. The speed was too slow, and the incensed Nazis ordered the commando assisting the newly arrived inmates to beat the daylights out of the procrastinators.

Thus, the loading on the platform proceeded, drowned in a noisy pandemonium; the striped prisoners went into action yelling, cursing and beating the half dead mass of helpless people. The commando of men responsible for the expeditious processing and loading the lorries could not manage to organize the transfer of the new inmates. If the supervising Nazis were dissatisfied with their underlings' brutality, they could get angry and shoot them right along with those they supposedly failed to brutalize with sufficient cruelty. Nothing ever seemed quick enough.

Fred bit his lips till they nearly bled. He didn't want to make a sound as the thought entered his consciousness that his parents passed on this same painful road, some time ago now, at this station. Fred quickly pushed aside this destructive rumination, a luxury he could ill afford.

This night, Fred's first in Auschwitz, was one he would never forget nor entirely recover. Nothing ever seemed the same to him following this experience of a descent to harrowing depths that normal men and women can never entirely fathom. Later Fred recalled that he forced himself to disbelieve the mass gassings. He wanted to convince himself that those who could not work would be allowed to subsist somewhere else; they would not be outrightly murdered in cold blood, would they? Then he pondered that the entire expanse of the camp was covered in black smoke, which curled from the tall chimneys saturating the air with the distinct and pungent stench of burned flesh and hair. What was this nightmarish Hades? Why did the orange-red flames rise to such heights into the darkened skies? Did so many die here, every single day, to make such massive cremations imperative?

There was no one to ask, talking was forbidden. Fred was one of the last to be ordered onto one of the repeatedly returning lorries. In the camp itself, women were separated from men, each being sent to a different hall and ordered to take off all their clothes. That done, they were ordered into showers. Fred held his breath as he looked at the showerhead above, wondering what was going to rain down, water or gas? To his relief, large drops of water trickled down, temporarily calming his fears.

Once the inmates regained composure, they began to scrub themselves in the running water, which alternated from boiling hot to freezing cold several times. That accomplished, they were ordered to run to another barracks where they received some rags to wear. Most were remnants of other prisoner's garb although some received civilian clothes. All was dirty and torn and Fred caught a pair of pants soiled with dried blood, and a torn tunic. The clothes were threadbare, worn out, without buttons, but that was all he could get. It was better than nothing. Nobody was issued any undergarments.

Another order was barked: to run to the next barracks where they would remain for the rest of the night. Dead tired, they dropped off on the bare floor. It was dark and cold; the number of men packed in the barracks far exceeded its usual capacity. It was permeated by a sour stench that added to their discomfort, but little bothered the exhausted men, grateful for a moment's respite, the crowding providing some warmth. Most fell instantly asleep.

Fred dozed off; the ordeal of the train ride and the traumatic scene at the ramp had drained him. He was jolted from a deep sleep by the shrill sound of a whistle. All was dark, and the barracks was bitterly cold. Fred warmed his stiff fingers, the humidity of his warm breath bringing some relief to his sore joints.

Then everything accelerated into a mad rush. It was time for roll call. Fred scampered after the other men trying to move quickly and join those already lined up. It was a raw, brutally chilly morning. The obligatory count of the inmates was completed, and then they were marched to an empty barracks where other inmates tattooed numbers on their forearms. All was done quickly, displaying the efficiency of experienced men who routinely performed this task on newly arriving inmates. Once the indelible ink was etched into their skin, they were returned to the same barracks where they had spent their first frosty night.

Fred's transport left Theresienstadt in December 1943 and joined the "family camp" in Auschwitz. A similar group had departed Theresienstadt in September. Both transports were an anomaly in Auschwitz's routine, in that none of the deportees had their heads shaved, and they continued to wear civilian tattered rags confiscated from previous arrivals.

Both transports were settled in without "selection" and lived in the family camp, isolated from the other sections and treated with unprecedented leniency, for Auschwitz. The strange notation that accompanied the transport lists of the both of the special groups was "6M S.B." Only the underground resistance movement in Auschwitz could decipher the enigmatic abbreviation. S.B. stood for *"Sonder Behandlung"* meaning gassing after a six months stint in the family camp. Fortunately, the spent inmates did not have the foggiest idea of what was in store for them.

On that first morning in Auschwitz, filled with apprehension about this new camp, they began to examine their surroundings. Before they could get very far, the thunderous voice of a large man shook the barracks. He informed them that he was the *"Blockaelteste,"* the man in charge of the entire block, clearly a powerful person in their bizarre new world. In his resounding voice he informed the quivering men that they were in the concentration camp called Auschwitz, that they were expected to work very hard and obey all his orders and those of his proxies: the Kapos. Failure to comply would result in the most severe of penalties.

Then the *Blockaelteste* began to question them about their skills and Fred, recalling the whispered admonition, declared that he was a hospital attendant. The big ogre nodded and ordered him to report to the sick bay.

Fred was relieved to leave the presence of the huge and intimidating man. He quickly rushed to his assignment, quite anxious because he knew little of hospital work, felt a strong revulsion when exposed to any malodorous, purulent discharge, and was repelled by bodily afflictions. He loathed pain, any suffering, and the decline that accompanies old age. He feared detection, for anyone with a minimal familiarity of hospital work could within minutes expose him for an impostor, for he knew nothing about the medical profession. Fred reached the sick bay barracks gasping for air, overcome with a feeling of doom, the pit of his stomach knotted in a thousand tangles.

As soon as he entered, he realized that his chances had not yet run out. It was one of the most fortunate moments of his life. He soon learned that he was to be saved by a stroke of sheer luck, the one most important variable in the life of any inmate in a Nazi camp. The head nurse to whom he was to report, to his surprise was an acquaintance; indeed, it was an old flame from bygone days. Theirs had been a brief affair, eternities ago, now buried under the weight of persecution and threats which overshadowed their previously normal, carefree lives.

Helga instantly recognized the man with whom she had once had a fling. Fred felt uneasy, deeply embarrassed, aware that his looks were pathetic and ridiculous. His soiled tattered rags hung loosely around his torso, giving him the appearance of a scarecrow, bearing little resemblance to the dapper man he once was. Helga, being one of the camp's "old-timers," was almost neat.

She followed camp etiquette strictly, not revealing a hint of recognition, and assigned him immediately to a room filled with dying female patients, most of them unconscious and moribund. Fred's initial reaction was one of anger. It did not seem that she did him much of a favor. He felt disgust in obeying her orders to wash the incontinent women and clean the room to the best of his abilities. The stench of the tormented, decaying, death-bound bodies permeated the entire room, nauseating Fred until he could vomit no longer.

Only later did he fully grasp the wonderful favor Helga gifted him. To begin with, when the main meal of the day arrived (a thin soup) more than half the women were unable to consume anything at all. Most of the fare was then split between the two orderlies who were assigned to this ill-fated ward. By mid-day Fred was famished, having had nothing to eat since he left Theresienstadt, and discovered his ability to separate himself from his environment. He ate heartily, overcoming his disgust and nausea at the sight and smell of the desolate, decomposing bodies surrounding him.

There was yet another advantage to his assignment. The SS men and even the Kapos shunned the ward of the dying women. They made a wide detour rather then get near the sights and stench of death. Therefore Fred found himself receiving additional rations of soup and also being sheltered from the wrath of the many snooping SS men and Kapos, who often prowled about venting their fury on innocent men and women who had the ill luck to be in the wrong place at the wrong time.

Other inmates in different commando units slaved outside the camp and labored under the continuous scrutiny of brutal and dangerous supervisors where no rest or procrastination was allowed. Fred could afford both. In his isolated ward, he worked at a leisurely pace and on occasion took a discreet break, though always wary of being obvious or noticeable. Once Fred understood the dynamics of the *Revier* (sick bay) and the camp, he understood and appreciated the enormous help offered by Helga. The room for those nearing death was the most coveted work appointment of the entire sick bay. Those assigned there were considered inordinately lucky, and Fred owed his one-time girlfriend.

A few days later, already well into his routine, he was called to present himself to the surgery where Helga was in charge. There she ostensibly ordered him to clean the many dirty instruments most used to incise the many carbuncles and abscesses of that day's patients.

While they worked as always in silence and at high speed, she took the opportunity to whisper a few instructions, imperative for survival in Auschwitz. She informed Fred that she would gladly help him for as long as she could, but little was stable or predictable in Auschwitz. Life hung by a thread, all was volatile and fluid. Any day, Helga continued, she could be removed, demoted, sent to another camp or be gassed. While life always hung in a precarious balance in any camp, Auschwitz was amongst the most perilous of places on the face of the earth. Therefore, if an opportunity presented itself, Fred should try to transfer to any other camp.

Helga spoke hurriedly, fearful of being overheard and concluded by advising the continuation of the pretense of not knowing each other. This particular jungle, said Helga, had many predators, most of them evil, hungry or jealous. Then she vanished, not giving him the chance to thank her. He returned to the room of the dying, filled with gratitude for having met his one-time girlfriend Helga.

Fred reported daily to his post and after working a full month, began discreetly to look for a way to be included in a transport to another camp. There had to be an exit out of the death factory of Auschwitz. Again, fate favored him. His old chum, the very same man who whispered the life saving advice on the ramp, looked him up and explained that the very next day men would be picked for a labor detail. The selection would take place in Fred's barracks and 500 men will be sent to another location. The forced labor camps did not have gas chambers, and Fred should try to put his best foot forward, to appear strong, clean and healthy. The 500 men were sorely needed in an important war production plant.

Fred scrubbed and cleaned his clothes and himself, looking his camp's best. He was nearly spic and span, considering the limitations and squalor of Auschwitz. He hoped passionately to impress the selecting SS man that he was a good prospect for hard labor. Fred's chances were good; he had not lost much weight, thanks to his plentiful supply of soup. His clothes were relatively clean, for Fred could wash and hide them at work, a place shunned by most. Fred followed every suggestion of his friend; silently marveling at how well-informed he was about every impending action. Later Fred discovered that his knowledgeable but circumspect friend was a trusted member of the underground resistance movement in the camp.

It was indeed time for Fred to leave Auschwitz, for the entire transport of men, women and children who arrived with him in December of 1943 was in grave danger.

Helga, now in the full swing of teaching Fred all the ropes, explained that his transport was preceded by a September transport also from Theresienstadt. They, too, were treated differently; families were allowed to live together, retain civilian clothes, their hair was unshaved, and they were not subjected to selection. None of Auschwitz's rules and routines seemed to apply to this privileged group. The Czechs were cloistered in the only family camp ever established in Auschwitz, and they received their belongings. They were even granted permission to teach their children, but their only peculiarity was that strange mark: "6M S.B."

The only people who refused to believe the meaning of the ill-omened three letters and a number were the inmates of the family camp. They would not believe that they were doomed to die in that short a time. Besides, it made no sense to delay the execution by six months. After all, if they wanted to murder them, why not do it right away, upon their arrival, as was done with so many others?

However, there was a system to the madness, after all. Rumors of the wholesale murder of Jews began to seep out and reach many regions of the outside world. To refute these allegations and assuage the increasingly restless people within and without the camps, the Nazis decided to sequester a special group of families and order them to write postcards, most quite postdated, to prove that they were alive and well.

These postcards would reveal to the entire world that the ugly rumors of mass murder and genocide unfolding in the East were false, they were merely nasty attempts by the wicked Jews to malign the Nazis. The postcards were to include a description of their general well-being, that their families were living together and that the existing conditions were good, and all enjoyed good health. The cards had to be postdated up to three months and the explanation provided was to allow for potential delay of delivery due to wartime censorship. Few worried about such trifles at the time; only later did most understand its sinister significance.

Within days, the members of the December transport were issued postcards, and all were ordered to write their relatives or friends. Fred was eager to write Ida and warn her, using their code, about the naked truth of Auschwitz. The *Blockaelteste* ordered them to put emphasis on the camp's good living conditions, their togetherness, and a host of other lies all written in less then 30 words.

Fred wrote Ida, and on the surface there was only praise for his new station in life. As agreed his message was coded; every second word was to be read for the correct message that testified to the full truth. Though awed by the responsibility of sending the right warning, he composed a succinct note. When read as intended, the message woven into the platitudes transmitted the ominous warning: "Do not follow, I will die soon".

Fred was confident that his message would be properly interpreted and acted upon, if possible. He experienced some relief, glad that he had discharged his duty to warn Ida. The down-to-earth, practical Ida would understand that he was near death and put up a valiant fight to avoid deportation, no matter the cost.

Though he felt better after warning his girlfriend, he could not help but become more depressed with each passing day, fearing for his own fragile existence. He saw his diminishing odds of survival. His days spent in the company of the dead, and dying did little for his morale.

He was submerged in the nauseating stench of the ward. He never knew which was worse—the stench of the decomposing bodies inside or the air outside saturated with the unmistakable smell of burning human flesh and hair. The hellish horror was punctuated by daily beatings and selections, all against the backdrop of tall chimneys continuously belching dark clouds of smoke. The dismal scene drained his spirit and hope, and he began to contemplate suicide. The best and only available method chosen by those at the end of their tether was a run at the high power electric wires. More often than not the suicidal inmate did not reach the charged fence, for the SS men on duty in the watchtowers shot any inmate nearing the forbidden perimeter, thus preventing the desired electrocution.

Now, the information of a potential transfer with a work transport out of Auschwitz offered Fred a beacon of hope.

The next day, the entire barracks was ordered to remain standing at attention for selection. It soon became evident that only young, healthy appearing and able-bodied men were being picked. Fred certainly qualified and, to his delight, he was soon singled out. Though no one knew a thing about this next camp, all were confident that there could be no worse place than Auschwitz.

As soon as Fred saw his number jotted down among those destined for departure, he was overcome with feelings of such intensity that it resembled happiness, Auschwitz style. He could have cried for joy. There, in the middle of the largest murder

factory invented in the history of mankind, he experienced a flash
of elation. He was convinced that he was given a stay of
execution.

From that moment events moved quickly. They were ordered
to collect their tin bowls and spoons, that represented all their
worldly possessions, and were sent running to the train stop, where
they quickly jumped onto freight cars. Before long, to their
delight, the train chugged away from the site where humanity lost
its sanity, all its senses, its thin veneer of civilization, and where
the inscription *"Arbeit macht frei"* ("Freedom through Labor")
was only one more abhorrent lie.

Fred's transport reached Schwarzheide. The badly damaged
synthetic oil plant was in desperate need of manpower. The slaves'
turnover in Schwarzheide was swift. The toil was so savage that
many obliged the Nazis and dropped dead, or those somewhat
more resilient but no longer able to toil, were returned to
Auschwitz for their rendezvous with death. The modern day
Jewish slaves when worn out became dispensable and disposable,
replaceable by others with some strength left. They all appeared
emaciated with sunken cheeks, the typical appearance of the long
term *"Katzetniks."* Why should the Germans feed, house or treat
humanely their vassals, when they seemingly had an inexhaustible
supply of Jews who could be worked to death and, when required,
readily replaced? It was cheap, convenient and made the bottom
line look better than ever.

The new arrivals were ordered into a barracks, where they
found three-tier bunks. Their new Kapo instructed them about the
commando unit they were to join the very next day. The Kapo was
a middle-aged man, a habitual criminal, who in civilian life had a
long record of sadistic murders and violence of the worst kind. His
speech was short, delivered in the gutter slang used by street
rabble. It contained the usual threats of beatings and death to those
who would not work efficiently or comply to the letter with all the
rules and regulations. This was old stuff. Most eyed the Kapo,
trying to assess him, pondering the potential damage he could
inflict.

Fred hardly bothered with the Kapo, he was transfixed with
another sight. Next to the Kapo stood an inmate in a prisoner's

uniform and, behold, it was another friend, a professional musician with whom Fred had spent many hours practicing their favorite tunes in the good old days. This man, Martin, seemed fed and clothed better than the ordinary rank and file inmate. According to the camp's precautionary code, neither man flashed a sign of recognition.

Fred searched for the opportunity to meet his colleague and, as usual, the best location was in the outhouse, where logically there was the least German supervision or likelihood of their presence. The only threat was the possible proximity of a snooping inmate, but few took an interest in anything but their own immediate survival. Nobody trusted anyone, except perhaps if they knew each other from the days they lived in civilized society.

Fred lurked around the latrines till he got his chance, but to his disappointment, his one-time friend brushed him off with a curt: "Later." That "later" materialized the very next evening when most inmates dropped onto their bunks, dead tired from the day's work. They fell asleep almost instantly, some snoring loudly in a haunted, restless slumber.

A boy summoned Fred, who later learned that the teenager was the much feared and privileged boy-lover of the chief Kapo. Now he readily followed the boy to a secluded corner where Martin bunked. When an inmate had a bunk all for himself, it was a sign of some distinction. The boy left them alone and hurriedly left for the room he shared with the Kapo.

Martin opened the conversation in a muffled voice, speaking so rapidly that not only was he quickly out of breath, but some of his words were garbled, mumbled and unintelligible. It took a few moments for Fred to adapt to his speedy murmurings and make sense of the monologue of his highly nervous friend.

Martin let Fred in on the secret of the handsome boy that fetched him. He was the much-pampered favorite of the pedophile Kapo and had to satisfy every sexual perversity of his sadistic master. In return he did not have to work, was given every luxury he could wish for, and shared the private room of the Kapo. The living quarters of the twosome were quite spacious, furnished, and equipped with a small stove, where the youngster cooked their daily meals. The boy possessed a wide choice of nice clothes, scented with expensive French perfume. He had soap and towels and scores of toiletries and fragrances, items the rest of the men long ago had forgotten existed.

Most inmates felt deep contempt for the farcical relationship, but were deathly afraid of the savage Kapo, and they treated the princeling with a show of deference. Nevertheless, the boy was not slow on the uptake; he was cunning and well-versed in the ways of the street. He knew that he was held in contempt, and he retaliated in his own way. He spied and squealed on the men, and they in turn tried to avoid him, fearing the wrath and jealousy of the brutal Kapo. There was not a man in the barracks who would not try to placate the capricious, mean and pathetic boy.

The Kapo, whispered Martin, had a peculiar ambition. "He continues to perfect his skill of killing an inmate with a single blow to the neck." He kept count, carefully recording the number of "successes," and he practiced frequently to upgrade his deftness. After the SS, the Kapo was the most powerful man in the camp.

Fred sat in silence, much troubled by the revelations of Schwarzheide. Clearly, the undercurrents here were just as deep, murky and dangerous as in other Nazi camps. They whispered in Czech, cautious not to be overheard. Fred mouthed his words silently: "What's this camp all about and what is your position?" Martin, well adapted to lip-reading, said that the work in the commandos was brutal, the amount of food parceled out was less than minimal; both were designed to bring the inmate to his knees within several weeks.

As at all other camps, Schwarzheide operated on the premise that inmates should work for as long as their strength held out and then perish in one of the many ways provided for in camp life. Replacement with new inmates presented no difficulties, for Auschwitz sent as many men as the commandant requested. Those in turn would toil for the remainder of their short life span, in due time becoming emaciated, and so on and on, in the perpetually moving merry-go-round, applied by Nazi economics, driven by thrift and cost effectiveness.

Why feed slaves, if more and more could be had? After all, it was cheaper to exploit and starve them to death. Voila, said

Martin, "This is the Nazi economic miracle, their road to prosperity and the financing of the costly war."

Martin shared more details of the camp's secrets and perils, and then shifted to his personal bondage to the mighty Kapo. Although their relationship was not sexual, Martin provided an essential service for the Kapo. Hesitating and searching Fred's eyes, Martin began to elaborate that the Kapo was no fool, he knew that desperate men toiling all day long and starving to death were desperate and prone to organize an open revolt or sabotage the all-important production at the synthetic oil plant. Any rebellion or deliberate damage would end his lifestyle, indeed the very life of the powerful Kapo.

It did not require a great deal of imagination to understand that desperate men do desperate things and might plan a doomed uprising or design a risky plan to sabotage the plant to avenge their suffering. They had nothing to lose and could go down with a last hurrah! The Kapo, a street-wise man, knew his boy-lover would not be privy to important conversations of the regular prisoners. When the angelic looking boy came within earshot, all whispering came to an abrupt end. The Kapo needed another, less conspicuous man and that was Martin's role. His privileges were by necessity far less obvious, such as a bunk separated from the others by a few planks that he pretended to have stolen. Of more importance was that he was rewarded surreptitiously with some bread and margarine at night.

Martin devoured his life-sustaining food right away, never revealing that he had more food than the others. However, with time, his unchanging appearance, surprising longevity and somewhat less worn uniform cast a suspicious shadow over him. Everyone knew that the only way to obtain extras was through doing infamous deeds. The inmates were well aware that the Kapo was a pedophile and that his sexual preferences did not include homosexual relationships.

The men's mistrust fell on Martin, resulting in his being ostracized. Martin feared that his time was quickly running out and, to prolong his usefulness, he concluded that he had to find another man who would collaborate with the same scheme, rewarded with a portion of the bread Martin was receiving. He had to solicit the Kapo's permission, which was willingly given, for it was as much in the Kapo's interest to forestall any serious mishap, which would infuriate the Germans.

Martin, in desperate straits, began to scout the latrines, to spot a man despondent enough to betray his fellow inmates and snoop for stirrings among the men. Now Martin had decided to present this offer to his one-time friend, Fred, who recoiled as he listened to the proposition.

Martin continued, perhaps understanding that at that moment this proposal sounded abominable, but it would give Fred life; it would be his only ticket for survival. His role as a stool pigeon would net him extra soup and an occasional piece of bread. This food would make the difference between life and death.

Martin's nervousness was rising with every passing word, but he pushed on with growing urgency. He suggested all that Fred would have to do: "Prick up your ears, and if you hear something out of the ordinary, bring it inconspicuously to my attention." Martin did not give Fred the opportunity to indignantly refuse his offer. Instead he told him to go about his duties, observe all carefully, and return to him after he had experienced a few working days while sustaining himself on ordinary rations.

Fred quickly took his leave and returned exasperated and drained to his bunk, unwilling even to consider the proposition, let alone accept it. After all, he was not a wretched scoundrel and even this wicked place would not push him over the precipice to perpetrate so base and deep amorality. He only wondered what happened to Martin, once such a decent and unswerving man, to sink into this morass, propelled by the desperate will to live at all costs.

The next day Fred joined the commando unit as they marched to the synthetic oil production plant. He was given an order to carry heavy crates to a loading station. The crates were not only weighty, but the wood was not finished properly. Soon, Fred had many splinters driven into his bleeding hands. His hands and back were afire and he could have sworn that someone hammered into his body thousands of hot burning needles. Fred was hardly used to manual labor, nor very adept at lifting and depositing the crates, so much of that day was unmitigated suffering. The many blisters covering his palms began to tear open and bleed. His back ached, and he could hardly stand straight. His feet were sore as the wooden clogs, his only footwear, ripped open his soles and drew blood from his tormented feet.

Fred breathed a deep sigh of relief when the shrill sound of a whistle announced the mid-day break. A few large cauldrons were brought to the work site and each inmate received one ladle of a thin, watery soup. Fred was famished, but even worse, his entire body ached, and all he wanted to do was put his head down and sleep.

He gulped down the soup and, as if by coincidence, his thoughts drifted to Martin and his offer. The thought occurred to Fred that he could pledge co-operation while only pretending to do so. He would not have to denounce his fellow inmates, but could promise to be on the lookout and in this way receive his reward of transferring to an easier commando work unit and additionally improve his food supply.

Now he understood Martin's reluctance to accept an answer immediately. He wanted Fred to experience the rigors of a regular commando detail and, only after having a taste of this hell on earth, first hand, to make up his mind.

Fred carried on for a few days. Perhaps destiny prodded his final decision. This, at least was Fred's interpretation of the sudden outbreak of bloody diarrhea in the camp. Many men died, dropping like the proverbial flies, victims of a highly contagious bacterial infection.

Fred fell victim on the third day of the outbreak, suffering painful cramps and quickly became so feeble that he thought his end was near. He had enough experience of camp life to know that without medication, food and a few days' rest, he was doomed. If, come tomorrow, he could not stand up on his own two feet, he would be clubbed to death at work. Even if he could, by some miracle, drag himself to the work site, he could no longer generate the strength needed to carry the heavy crates.

That very evening, near physical collapse, he signaled to Martin by the prearranged sign that he was ready to deal. He repeatedly tilted his head to the left. Martin understood. He had been watching Fred every evening, returning more and more wretched from his day's suffering. Martin was waiting impatiently, fretting, for his position was becoming very shaky, and his last hope was Fred's co-operation.

At nine o' clock, when the one naked bulb suspended from the ceiling was turned off and the barracks fell into semi-darkness, the boy came for Fred, who could barely crawl, his weak, shaky feet no longer able to carry his meager torso. He dropped at Martin's bunk and confessed that he was done, willing to do anything to live. His bowels were running, he was weak, at the end of his tether. Martin nodded pensively and, reaching under his pillow, handed Fred a swig of a medicine, which was supposed to clear his inflamed bowels.

Fred spent a relatively quiet night. The very next morning he was transferred to another work unit. This commando unit was charged with fitting some mechanical attachments to metal parts. They were allowed to sit, and this by itself was a major improvement. Fred felt much better, perhaps because the medicine cleared his cramps, and he was indoors, no longer running and carrying heavy crates while exposed to the bitter winter frost, barely protected by threadbare rags.

As Fred's health improved, his will to live became ever so much stronger. Soon he resigned himself to this only option for life, to be a stool pigeon, the ears and eyes for his one-time friend Martin. He stoically admitted that he had become an informer who bought his life by spying on others. He only prayed and hoped that he would never overhear any plots or plans of sabotage, flight or rebellion.

Luck was on Fred's side. The men were much too weak and worn out, dying in droves and unable to organize any meaningful action against their oppressors. This situation remained unchanged until January 1945, when the camp received a new and different batch of prisoners. This particular group of men was evacuated from Auschwitz before it fell into Russian hands and was comprised of veterans who had survived the worst of hells. They had extensive experience managing their continued existence and were well aware that Germany was losing the war. The long pined-for liberation was at hand, in only a matter of a very short time. They decided to flee, unwilling to die in the last throes of this horrible war.

Fred overheard their plans. Where else, but in the latrines? The new men, five in all, had no reason to suspect a fellow inmate. They hammered out in considerable hurry the details of their getaway. Fred was well within earshot, but they were not bothered by his presence. He was not suspected of being a squealer. They never thought of including him in the escape, but Fred sensed that his hour of truth had arrived. Either he would let them flee, or report their plan to Martin.

Either way, he feared he would pay with his life. Though he could pretend that he never overheard the conversation, a successful escape would have the furious Kapo kill him anyway. He was kept alive and rewarded for one reason alone: to be well-informed and keep abreast of all conspiracies hatched by the inmates.

Fred was torn by monumental indecision. The longer he pondered his options, the more he was filled with naked terror. His stomach was in knots, and his heart pounded as if it wanted to jump from his chest; he trembled, covered in cold sweat. He, an innocent, was caught in the iron vice of a moral, life-and-death dilemma foisted on him by his savagely cruel captors: a position in which no human should ever be placed.

Fred was well aware that by pretending ignorance he would pay with his life irrespective of the success or failure of the escape. Even if they were caught and shot, he would die right along with them for failing to inform the Kapo of the impending escape. On the other hand, if he would report to Martin all he overheard, he would become the real scoundrel, actually acting out the part for which he was commissioned. Fred shivered realizing that the time to pay—for all the extra bread rations, the additional bowls of soup, the warmer clothes and the lighter work assignment—was at hand.

Time was short, there would be no turning back nor opportunity for second-guesses. Fred did not want to die, especially now, when according to most the Nazi defeat was near and inevitable. He was desperate to return to freedom, his hometown, his Ida and all his interrupted plans. He longed to sit at the piano and compose his music, to restart his law career, in short to take what most consider their inalienable rights, so easily taken for granted. Fate seemed to take malicious pleasure in denying him all, because he was a Jew, for whom the Nazis held a raging hatred.

Fred squirmed as he pondered the unfairness of having to deal with this momentous and unsolvable dilemma, to select from options that were all heartbreaking, to save his life at the expense of others. Even during those moments when he pretended to contemplate his next move, he knew that he wanted to live, badly enough to do anything and everything to save his own skin. Fred felt like the legendary Dr. Faust, who sold his soul to the devil, only Fred did not do it for the fancy of knowledge and power. All he craved was his bare life. Was it a crime for a man just thirty years old to want to live? He had only one night to agonize over his "indecision." If the escape were to be aborted, he would have to make his move the very next day. Their escape was timed for the early night, right after lights out in the locked barracks.

Fred lay awake the entire night, weighing his very limited options. The whole time he knew, subconsciously, that he would betray them, for he could not contemplate his own demise at the hands of the savage Kapo.

Fred was certain that the infuriated Kapo would also murder Martin, the primary informer. For a moment he mocked his own hypocrisy, for in his heart he realized at the time there was not a shred of concern for Martin. He was not all that noble to truly worry about anyone but himself. All he could feel was the naked panic of his vulnerability to the frenzied rage of the violent Kapo. Fred tossed and turned all night long in his narrow bunk, at times covered in sweat, moments later shivering with cold, knowing his nerves were shot.

The next morning Fred followed Martin's every move and as soon as he noticed him heading for the latrines, he followed at some distance, in no obvious hurry. Once there, he used the previously agreed sign signaling that he had urgent news. Not a word was exchanged; Fred rubbed his right eye, the signal for Martin to arrange an urgent meeting. Both men chose different paths and times to return to the barracks.

Shortly, the Kapo emerged from his quarters and announced that a few men were to stay behind, that the floors of the barracks had to be scrubbed. That in itself was not startling, for the Kapo was known to make a fetish of cleanliness, often forcing inmates to scrub the corners of the hall with their fingernails. He was frequently overheard boasting that his barracks was always spic-and-span. He handed new brushes to some of the men in order to wash the floor. As if by chance he picked Fred, the last of the group of four. No one gave a second thought to the cleaning detail, it would not be the first nor likely the last time the Kapo would follow his maniacal obsession.

As soon as the other men marched off to their daily drudgery, the Kapo dispatched the rest of the men, except Fred, to clean the latrines. The Kapo yelled at the top of his coarse voice that Fred should have a head start at scouring the floors since he had stronger fingernails that the other three. When all were gone, the Kapo sent away his young lover, and with Martin began to interrogate Fred.

Fred fleetingly wished to be buried by an avalanche, or drowned in a tidal wave. He could no longer turn back; he had to conclude this messy affair, have it over with and then try to forget it all. Little did he know then that this particular morning would remain indelibly and vividly etched in his memory for the rest of his days, tarnishing every joy and pleasure, every frivolous moment, every unencumbered delight in his future life.

On that fateful morning, he stood at attention in the Kapo's room and quickly reported the words he overheard, identified the five men, and reported the time set for their flight. The Kapo listened attentively, his darkened demeanor slowly lifting. At the end, he seemed relieved and, judging from the large piece of bread he handed Fred as a reward, he was very grateful.

Certainly, Fred's information was of immense importance; it spared the Kapo the brunt of the SS commandant's ire he certainly would have dished out had the five succeeded in escaping. Though he mumbled unintelligible obscenities, he had the appearance of a man savoring a situation. In his sadistic mind he already visualized pouncing on the fugitives as they scampered in the darkness, on the first leg of their carefully prepared flight.

Martin was ordered to stay with the Kapo, while Fred, feeling worse than Judas, was ordered to scrub the floor. The others would rejoin him as soon as they completed the cleaning of the latrines. To keep up appearances, the Kapo planned to inspect the condition of the outhouses and only if he found them satisfactory, would he release the men to their floor-washing chores in the barracks.

In the meantime, Fred experienced a new phenomenon: He, who was in a state of chronic and ravenous hunger, suddenly could not swallow the chunk of bread, the reward for his betrayal. Clearly, Fred was not so hardened or ruthless to deliver five men to their deaths and then stuff himself with a traitor's booty. Nevertheless, he knew that he had to gobble it up, if only to hide it, for if anyone noticed, it would all add up tomorrow, identifying him as the informer.

The sudden windfall had to disappear. Fred had to gulp it down, even if he were to choke and it killed him. Of course, it did nothing of the sort, but he felt dreadfully low as he stuffed himself with the blood payment.

Soon the rest of the men returned, knowing their work was more or less redundant since the barracks' floors were always immaculate, but they were grateful for that day's much lighter toil. They had no idea of the infamy to which they owed the day's concession. Fred was the only one who had to feign joy for the unexpected good fortune of an easy day as he continued to be tormented by his deed. Never, even in his worst nightmares, did he think himself capable of something as vile and ugly as placing other men in jeopardy of their lives. The one thing he did know was the stronger motive: his will to live and his dread of torture and death.

The rest of the day lingered uneventfully. Time hardly passed as Fred prayed it to stop. Finally, late that evening, the commandos returned in the dusk of the fading day. The routine of the camp's evening unfolded with the distribution of soup, after which some inmates made futile attempts to clean themselves; deviating little from the day to day drudgery. Most inmates returned to their bunks, dead tired, trying to rest and conserve some strength. The light flickered out at the regular time, only one naked bulb cast some shadows on the sleeping men huddled in the narrow bunks.

The five men retired along with the rest. All was designed to look very normal, not to arouse suspicion. When all fell silent in the barracks except for the snoring of the men, the conspirators began their carefully planned decamping. One by one, they crawled soundlessly out of their bunks waiting for each other in the rear of the barracks. All seemed to go smoothly, without a hitch.

What they did not know was that only few steps away lying in wait for them were several armed SS men and the Kapo, who had conceded that he could not single-handedly subdue five determined fugitives. Armed only with a truncheon and his fists, in the darkness he could apprehend one, at best two, but the rest would escape.

As soon as the men squeezed through an opening prepared by loosening a few planks in the wall, and began to crawl in the snow, all bedlam broke loose. The two SS men opened fire with their automatic weapons, killing all five men at close range. The fugitives had the chance of a snowflake in hell.

Inside the cabin, the men were startled from sleep and, seized with panic, they listened intently in the darkness to the bursts of gunfire shattering the still night. The salvos rang in their ears, and they knew that someone was caught trying to run. The pandemonium and echoes of violence terrified and outraged them.

Just as suddenly as it began, all fell silent. It all lasted a mere minute. The men lay dead on the frozen ground, the white snow around their lifeless bodies beginning to discolor with dark red blotches as their blood seeped from their many wounds. They died: Executed. The SS ordered the corpses be left as they lay for 48 hours, a warning to those who might entertain similar plans.

Few slept the rest of that appalling night. Fred did not shut an eye, squirming with guilt, shock and revulsion at his own deed.

The next morning's roll call was different. Not only were the inmates counted, but the Kapo delivered a thunderous harangue. He roared and threatened that a similar fate would befall any man who would try to emulate the five, whose treacherous escape was thwarted by him, the ever-vigilant Kapo. All who dared to challenge the commands of the camp would meet instant death.

Fred stood at attention but could not help staring at the five sprawled corpses with their wide-open mouths and glassy eyes. Fred felt certain they were staring accusingly at him, voicing a silent reproach. He was their murderer. There was no doubt in his mind that he, and only he, was responsible for the night's massacre. Fred was sure that he was going insane, believing the five would yet take their revenge on him. He shivered and trembled seeing the enormity of his crime, and feared that he might cry out and confess his guilt.

This roll call seemed to last forever; his body felt pierced by pins and needles, and he thought that any second he would scream out and be shot on the spot. He did not let out a peep; suffering in silence, grating his teeth, his entire body shivered. Then the thought occurred to him that if it were not the five frozen bodies in front of him, it would be his and Martin's lying in a pool of blood. They would not have been offered the quick exit of a bullet; the Kapo would have clubbed them to death for failing to report the escape plan.

The Kapo droned on about the merciless fate awaiting those who would choose to disobey, but Fred could no longer listen. The sight of the splattered blood forming geometric patterns transfixed him. The red splashes on the blinding white layers of snow and ice formed a surreal contrast. Fred was nauseated, certain that he would vomit.

Then, to his relief, it was over. The Kapo barked sharp orders dismissing the inmates to fall into formation to march back to the barracks, in preparation for the new day's work.

Fred hoped that now he would have a reprieve to restore his balance. However, fate took yet another detour. The inmates marched to the plant, looking gloomy, sad and angry. Fred, much depressed and wrapped up in his own thoughts, paid little attention to the world around him. As usual, he worked at a machine with the same small group of men who were some distance from a larger party of inmates who huddled around another mechanical devise. The men were much agitated by last night's tragedy and whispered in outrage to one another. They were preoccupied with the haunting thought that there was an informer among them. There had to be a man who knew of the fugitives' plan and betrayed them by informing the Kapo.

Fred did not pay attention to anything else but his work and guilt. Consumed by his misery, he failed to notice the daring whispers of the grim and embittered men. The only thoughts tormenting Fred were his repeated analysis of his handling of the situation. Was there a path he could have taken, that would have let him avoid this carnage? Did he really have to stoop to this level?

Finally the day ended, and the men marched in sullen silence back to the camp. The customary routine followed: the distribution of soup, followed by washing of their tired bodies and then bedtime. Fred almost managed to fall asleep when suddenly he was alerted by the rustling of a few soft, almost inaudible steps of several men, hurrying past his bunk.

In the dim light of the barracks, Fred could recognize a few of them as they rushed in the direction of the corner cubicle, to Martin's bunk. Fred's sense of danger was honed to precision, an ability acquired by necessity during his lengthy incarceration. He became immediately alarmed. He was in mortal danger! It was not difficult to extrapolate from the unfolding scenario that the inmates had decided to punish the traitor. They made up their minds as to the identity of the culprit, sat in judgment and now were about to deliver the camp's swift justice.

The prisoners' secret tribunal decided that Martin was the collaborator and for a crime of this magnitude, only one punishment was fit. Fred also knew the retribution would be carried out swiftly. The understanding and deliverance of justice in any concentration camp was based on the Old Testament's dictum: "An eye for an eye and a tooth for a tooth." Fred was certain that unless these men were exceptionally good Samaritans, Martin was going to die.

Fred, lying in silent panic, began to sweat and quiver, seized by sheer terror. What if Martin, in an attempt to divert suspicion, pointed to Fred? He might try to cling to a crumbling straw, hoping to clear himself by incriminating Fred. Would the men grant Martin time to utter a word or would they gag him forthwith and keep him silent?

What if the men already suspected that he was Martin's collaborator; they were known to be compatriots. What if Fred's relatively less emaciated body gave him away as the aide of the Kapo's scribe? Would it not be a walk in the park to guess that Martin supplied his friend with additional soup or bread for services rendered? Perhaps he was a suspect already, after all, the men would remember that he was kept behind with the Kapo in the barracks, while the others scrubbed the latrines. Was this to be his final hour? Was he going to be beaten to death now, so close to liberation, in spite of all his valiant efforts? Would death come quickly or would his release from this earthly existence take long?

Fred knew he must not move. There was nowhere to run or hide and, even if he tried, any trace of doubt in the minds of his judges of his guilt would only be removed; he would succeed in incriminating himself and setting the men on him. Nor could he count on the Kapo for help; these beasts never protected their informers. Even if he could reach the Kapo, the men would beat him to death later, probably in the latrines. In any event, he would have to pass Martin's bunk, where the men were in the process of killing his comrade. His only option was to keep still and pretend to be fast asleep like a man with clean conscience. His only hope was that he might not be targeted for retribution; he always made a point of lying low and being as inconspicuous as possible.

The execution of Martin was indeed swift and silent. The men asphyxiated him, gagging him before he could utter a sound. The last thing they intended to make was any noise that might awake the Kapo or his crafty lover.

Once done with Martin, they covered his lifeless body with his blanket and tiptoed away. Fred listened intently in the darkness as their steps paused near his bunk. He froze, recognizing his moment of truth; now they would pounce and break his neck or else choke him to death. Now he, the atheist, began to beseech the Almighty to grant him deliverance, a painless death. Lying still, holding his breath, waiting for the blows to come, he heard a whisper: "He might or might not have been involved. Let's beat him till he is black and blue, but not kill him. He deserves the benefit of the doubt. We'll catch up with him in the latrines and whip him harshly."

These words were music to Fred's ears. Though he realized that he was out for a major thrashing, he was grateful that he would live. Though he dreaded physical pain, he valued his life much more and hoped to survive the upcoming ordeal. He will live and that was all that mattered, at least for the moment, on that fateful night.

Over the next few days, Fred pretended that nothing had happened. Though he was in a high state of anxiety awaiting the execution of the verdict, he hid his fears and inner tensions. The morning after the murder of Martin, he showed little emotion as the body was carted away after roll call. The Kapo exhibited little interest in the death of his long-time barracks clerk. Though Fred mourned Martin, a man much like himself who wanted very much to live and to that end sold his soul, he could ill afford to show any sadness. He, too, was a traitor and an informer; the only difference was that he might have better luck.

Several days after the execution of Martin, Fred entered the abysmal latrine, when he noticed three men dawdling around. It took but a moment to realize that the hour of his punishment had arrived.

Losing no time they jumped him and rained blows to his head and body. They could have killed him; Fred never knew when they let go of him; he lost consciousness right after several blows struck his head and genitals. He remembered that he was filled with terror that the men would drown him in the pools of excrement, as sometimes happened to inmates who incurred the wrath of their fellow prisoners.

He pleaded that he was innocent of all wrongdoings and pretended not to understand being singled out for this violent attack. But one of the men hissed into his ear: "Shut up, you asshole, you are being punished if for no other reason, than for your poor choice of friends, one of whom we had to execute in total silence because of the proximity of the bloody Kapo."

Such was the law of the camps, where justice was meted out by the strongest and toughest. Even these men had only a marginal likelihood of survival and needed an inordinate amount of luck to succeed. Fred survived the trashing, albeit with a lot of pain, partial loss of hearing on one side and a broken collarbone. He sported black and blue hues for some time. While he tried to cleanse himself, washing his badly soiled uniform, he looked absurd, his eyes grotesquely swollen, black and blue, his nose broken, several teeth missing and countless open wounds. One of his ears was nearly torn from his head. All this healed gradually and very slowly.

The men ignored his appearance. Only the Kapo asked, full of malicious solicitude: "Well, what happened to our Fred, did he have a falling out with some of his many friends?"

Fred swallowed back all the humiliation; he sacrificed his pride, dignity and self-respect, all to preserve his life. The next weeks he spent in self-imposed isolation, avoiding people, answering questions directed at him only in monosyllabic grunts, no longer wanting to justify or explain himself.

Sometime during the deep frost of February, the camp received orders to evacuate as the American armies were drawing near. All the prisoners were ordered to form columns and set out on a march towards lands still under Nazi domination. Each man received half of a loaf of bread and a piece of sausage. Thus supplied, accompanied by several SS men prodding them to march faster, they proceeded. Many stumbled, dropped to the ground and were shot by the heavily armed SS men. Those who could not keep up were executed, resulting in thousands more deaths. These were the last "glorious" days of the murderous Nazi hordes; their license to kill at will was expiring.

Fred marched and staggered on the frozen highways of Europe. He suffered from frostbite, hunger and loose bowels, but he persevered. He kept the day of liberation as a guiding star. Towards the end, he could barely walk, but on he plodded, reaching Theresienstadt, barely alive, with a handful of men whose stamina and will power matched Fred's. Half dead, starved and ill, he arrived only one day after the Russian army liberated the camp. There he was re-united with his previous girlfriend, Ida, who had managed to avoid deportation, forewarned by his cogently coded message from Auschwitz.

Ida had to make some questionable decisions of her own; few could survive with their honor untainted. Ida, after reading and re-reading Fred's letter, decided to give up on him; after all, he wrote that his life was ending. She then hooked up with another man, whose power and collaboration with the Nazis saved his and her life as well.

Ida was not only pretty, but also cunning and calculating, and their affair served both their interests. Few survivors could live upholding a high code of honor, walking the moral high ground. The shame and guilt rested entirely on the shoulders of the Nazis and the world that empowered them to debase innocents to their most primitive instincts in the human struggle to live for yet another day.

Fred and Ida married, left Europe, and spent their lives together. However, their union was not made in heaven. Ida was headstrong and manipulative, and Fred perhaps never really resolved his traumas of the war years. Rather, he pushed it all into the background, never coming to terms with the damage the years spent in hell had wrought on him.

Later, when I met him again, on another continent, some twenty years after the end of the war, he confessed that he still lived with his guilt. Many of his nights were haunted by the image of glassy-eyed, frozen corpses, sprawled on brilliantly white snow painted with congealed, dark red blood.

Marianne: Kapo

Newly arrived inmates undergoing selection.
A lucky few might eventually make their way
into the camp system itself to work as slave laborers.

Marianne was a distant relative who, after the war, chose me to be her confidant. She was ten years my senior, a fact that made her almost unreachable for she, the self-respecting teenager, would not chum up with an unsophisticated child. Therefore, before the war I could only admire her from a respectable distance, wondering about the swarms of admirers attracted to her like moths to a light.

Marianne's mother was my mother's cousin, a woman of considerable charm but of somewhat questionable reputation. Whenever the conversation drifted to this distant relative, the adults hushed and we, the children, were sent on an errand on a rather flimsy pretext. We idealized her to be an enigmatic, enchanting figure that we wished to know better. Marianne, her daughter, was the spitting image of her mother. We called her Nan, a childhood, endearing pet name.

Nan had many friends, for she was companionable, cheerful, and attractive. She loved good times and good cheer. Her crowd was not troubled by serious issues; even the clearly nearing storm, soon to engulf all Europe, remained on the back burner. She surrounded herself with youths from affluent families, the "spoiled brats," who thought that life was one big party, filled with dance, sports and other recreational activities.

Marianne's family lived in a city near the Czech-Polish border, so we met only during summer holidays or some other school recess. Later, after the deportation of the Czechoslovak Jews, Marianne and I were interned for a while in the same camp, Theresienstadt. Her story serves as an extreme and poignant example of the lengths to which some people went to cheat their executioner.

The calamity, which befell Europe in general and the Jews in particular, demanded the utmost struggle with absolute evil, which sometimes required the abandonment of the values of normal life. Those seeking to survive dealt with the worst of humanity on earth, the Nazis, who were armed to the teeth and sworn to the annihilation of all Jews.

The human animal, confronted with such peril, reacts in different ways. I am often vexed by sanctimonious comments and observations voiced by those who have never shared similar experiences, and who dispense expert opinions on how we, the inmates, should have coped while fighting for our lives. They resemble Monday morning quarterbacks who have—with hindsight—20/20 vision. Having said that, I have to admit that the means chosen by Nan were out of the norm. Few would have wanted to or been able to pursue the measures to which Nan chose to stoop.

She was born in 1920, the second child of a middle class family, totally submerged in a German-Jewish background. Nan's father was a gifted journalist and editor-in-chief of a German daily, widely read and popular in the area. His position was a prestigious one and, as editor-in-chief, he was well paid. The couple already had one child, a boy of four. Little Marianne completed their family; a son and a daughter were all they wished for. Nan's father was a serious, scholarly man, greatly respected and admired for his work. Her mother was quite a different person. She was a pretty, vivacious and flirtatious woman, uninterested in most serious topics. She intrigued her husband. She could afford ample domestics, which relieved her of the drudgery of domestic chores, the maintenance of a large and elegant house, and the care of their two toddlers.

Free of the many traditional duties of a housewife, she found ample leisure time, which she mostly spent on the tennis courts or in some social activity. She devoted an inordinate amount of her day to care of her appearance, which she correctly considered her main asset. At no time did she believe that her intellect first attracted and later kept her husband's affection. She was indeed an alluring woman: chic, elegant, lithe and sexy. Her movements were catlike and graceful with just a hint of sway in her hips; just enough to give her an exciting touch without suggestion of vulgarity. Her face was unusual, more engaging than beautiful, dominated by two green eyes, set far apart, all of which reinforced the predatory air about her.

A little over a year after Nan's birth, the marriage of her parents began to falter. Her mother was bored with life in the provincial city and grew tired of her sedate husband's dullness. She felt unfulfilled by the run-of-the-mill pleasures of everyday life, and even worse, the local housewives made no bones about their contempt for her. They patently omitted to include her in their tea parties, where they gossiped freely about their marriages, children and servants, and exchanged recipes, all of which was quite tedious for the frivolous Mrs. B. She was young and vain, and craved the admiration of men. She was contemptuous of women wishing to excel in cooking for their man; she drew the opposite sex with her feminine magnetism.

Most local men noticed the attractive, fickle woman, and might have been tempted to engage in a dalliance, but nearly all were married, so all they could offer was some clandestine rendezvous. Such a diversion would repel Mrs. B., who deemed such an affair below her dignity, a pastime for the domestics. While she had no objection to making a cuckold of her husband, she would not share her lover with his wife, especially none of the plump, homely housewives, who for most part gave her the cold shoulder.

She flitted from one distraction to another, uneasy and unfulfilled, searching for something, though not quite certain what. She joined the local tennis club and showed some talent, eventually turning into one of the better players. Her husband was not oblivious to her discontent and emotional malaise, but could not come up with a solution. He tried to involve her in his work, but had to give it up, as she loathed all academic pursuits. In this, she did not differ from many women of her generation; very few partook in their husband's concerns.

It was almost the rule that each followed his own life, sharing mainly the physical aspects of marriage: the table and the bed. Mr. B was a sedate, set-in-his-ways man, who had no idea of how to satisfy his wife or find her a suitable diversion. He hoped that given time she would settle down, take more interest in their children, join some local clubs, and learn to appreciate the lifestyle he offered. With some travel thrown in for good measure, she should count her blessings and stop complaining. But fate had plans of its own.

The provincial town and its tennis club welcomed a new member. The new addition was a young and very single dentist, who had just moved to the community and opened his practice in this under-doctored town. He was confident he could attract a large, if perhaps not so illustrious, clientele. His appearance evoked a tumultuous stir. He was handsome and pleasant in demeanor and soon became the toast of the local social life. Many a family with a daughter of marriageable age thought him a godsend.

Before long, the young dentist was inundated with invitations to all kinds of gatherings. Some not-so-virtuous local socialites, bored by their flat, stuffy, matrimonial life, may have hoped for a brief fling to add some spice to their bored existence. All these wishes and expectations came to naught the very moment Mrs. B ran into the newly arrived dentist.

She had heard about him and his outstanding serve. Rumor had it that he was one of the best tennis players the town had ever seen. When they first met, he was smitten by her appearance; her tall, attractive, slim figure, clad in snow-white shorts and blouse stood in stark contrast to the rest of the local fair sex. She, in her hungry state of mind, did not require much encouragement to engage in a minor flirtation. Only developments raced ahead of their initial plans.

As the affair became more intoxicating and enrapturing, so inevitably they became conspicuous. The local tongues were wagging, as the lovers became less careful, throwing all caution to the wind, giving way to their passionate infatuation. They met daily at the tennis club, hit a few balls as a twosome, and quickly left for his office adjacent to his living quarters.

They seemed to live only for each other, dismissing and ignoring the world around them. However, their surroundings did not reciprocate. They stirred anger, jealousy, disdain and curiosity. The small town was not accustomed to a lover's triangle. Soon the local tattlers began to wag their tongues, slinging mud at the entire family.

Mr. B was well informed and knew about the blatant infidelity almost from the very start. First he noticed her different demeanor; she became unresponsive to all his overtures for lovemaking, which was quite a change from her normally passionate disposition. Her frequent complaints about the drab, humdrum life-style of the town suddenly ceased. The affair became her focus and soon Mr. B reached the conclusion that something had to be done, for his continuous tolerance of his cuckoldry threatened to reach the ears of their children.

Never one to jump to conclusions or be precipitous in judgment, Mr. B waited for a while, secretly sustained by a flicker of hope that the passion might burn itself out and cool reason might prevail. However, the passage of time did not affect the situation. As both children were gradually reaching the age of comprehension, they became frequent targets of ridicule and remarks they did not yet understand. Their playmates parroted the many slippery innuendoes and insinuations overheard from the adults, leaving Nan and her brother bewildered and hurt.

In spite of his love for his wife, Mr. B was ready to give up on his marriage, which had once given him great happiness, but gradually had turned into a humiliating soap opera. Mr. B thought for a long time about his plight, his children and their potential trauma of a broken home, and arrived at an idea that might diminish some of the over-all suffering and offer a peaceful solution.

Armed with this plan, he was ready to confront his wife and her paramour. The meeting of the trio bore little resemblance to the raging passions of Othello; rather, it proceeded like a business meeting, in a low key, polite and civilized form. All three had a stake in finding a tolerable compromise.

Mr. B was willing to accept their relationship, for the sake of his children. He would allow them opportunities to meet, on condition that these meetings followed his dictates. Then came a thinly veiled threat: if his stipulations were not adhered to, he would file for divorce, name the dentist as a correspondent, claim the custody of the children and deny his wife any financial support. Mr. B concluded the meeting by giving the couple two days to consider. At the door he remarked casually that in case of failure to comply, he would insist on the lover's moving away, for surely his practice would collapse if he were cited as a correspondent in divorce proceedings. After all, he would be a man who broke up a family, engaging in an affair with a married woman.

In the end, it was the fiscal argument that tilted the balance in favor of Mr. B's suggestion. The young dentist, just a beginner, had sunk all his money and a large bank loan into his practice. He carried a precarious credit rating, and a move would play havoc with his shaky financial stability and plans. Moreover, he feared the stigma of an adulterer who had destroyed another man's marriage, an offense not taken lightly. It might mark his name, with devastating effects on his future career.

Few husbands would openly condone a wife's meeting her seducer. Officially, the lovers stopped seeing each other. They met, with the consent of Mr. B, in a small apartment rented by the B family. Additionally, to hush the local idle chatter, the dentist became a frequently invited guest in the family residence, a kind of a family fixture. He was presented to the children as a devoted family friend and their warm, loving uncle.

Both men began to cultivate what was farthest from their minds, a friendship, forced out of shared needs. They would meet in the local club, where they would engage in a game of cards or chess. Eventually they developed an almost benign association. Time, the grandmaster of healing, did its work; the burning passion began to peter out and the hurt of the betrayed husband began to heal. The once lovelorn pair and the hurt husband assumed a routine that was quite satisfactory to all and lasted a number of years.

As the years went by, the now middle-aged dentist's passion cooled off towards the woman he once thought he could not live without and, somewhat disillusioned, he concentrated on his professional career. No longer infatuated, he often wondered at and felt somewhat embarrassed about the arrangements of the threesome. He took pride in his flourishing clientele and occasionally toyed with the idea of leaving, for the affair bored him and he conceded that he had behaved like a fool, wasting his best years in a soap opera.

As the love story lost its radiance and charm, he regretted not establishing a family of his own, never having children—and all because of his intoxication with a rather shallow woman. As her beauty faded and wilted, he often felt disgust with himself. The prior love story turned into a connection of habit and duty. Moreover, the sobered up dentist felt that he hardly had the energies to revolutionize his life at its halfway mark. Times were difficult. He felt that he did not have what it took to start all over again.

Still, he could not help harboring bitter feelings at his self-inflicted degrading role of a rival for the love of a vain woman, in whose family he was considered an unusual sidekick. He was never quite permitted to partake in the intimate emotional richness, as an authentic link in the family chain. The more he felt the empty void, and the greater grew his desire for a family of his own, the harder it was to continue his chosen role. However, he was all-too-aware that it was too late to change the course of his life. As his feelings turned to indifference, he looked at Mrs. B without desire and only wished to escape from his servitude. Nevertheless, here, too, fate tied his hands.

Nan and her brother grew up in a home where a ménage à trois was a fact of life. They knew little else and for many years they believed their home an ordinary household. They were well-sheltered youths from an affluent home that featured loving parents and a generous uncle who was, for the longest time, considered a blood relative. Their homes provided a stable and calm environment; only later, on occasion, they might overhear malicious gossip, whispered by some domestics.

When Bert, Nan's brother, reached his teens, he began to understand the cryptic jeers. Suddenly he looked at his parents with a different set of eyes, embarrassed and contemptuous of their strange arrangement. Though, while children, they never lacked care, love and material goods, during their teens their respect towards their parents was destroyed and slowly the home atmosphere became saturated with bitterness. Bert felt especially irate. He greatly resented the frequent double entendres aimed at the risqué circumstances, the dubious reputation of his mother and the less-than-heroic stance of his father.

Nan had a different take on their home life. When she fully understood, she was neither embarrassed nor resentful. She developed into a cool, calculating and self-centered girl, totally wrapped up in herself. She not only bore a close physical resemblance to her mother, but her personality and character were also analogous to that of her role model. During her teens, she was often mistaken for a younger sister of her mother, a comparison that flattered her mom enormously. Nan was, in all aspects, a chip off the old block, as close to a clone as one can get while being a generation apart. Nan's father adored and pampered her, fulfilled her every wish and whim unconditionally, always keen to make his little girl happy. It seemed as if he transferred all his tender feelings, once invested into his wife to her near replica, little Nan.

Early on, Nan knew that her father was softhearted and that she could influence and mold him to her wishes. She cultivated this weakness from early on, exploiting him, becoming cunning and deceitful while appearing coy and loving. Nan was infrequently given to gratitude and while she liked her dad, deep in her heart she felt contempt for his unbridled emotional dependency on her. He was her first and perhaps most ardent fan, later joined by many men who for other reasons could not resist Nan's charms.

The only person Nan really respected was her mother. She looked up to her and considered her the prototype of the successful woman. That is not to say that they did not lock horns on many occasions, for Nan, particularly during her teens, tested the will of her mother and the boundaries set down by her. All the time she was learning to emulate her mother's guile and manipulation of men and the art of handling people to her best advantage. Both women shared the belief that men were put onto this earth to take care of, indulge and cater to beautiful women. It goes without saying that they included themselves, perhaps rightly so, in the category of the most exquisite and rare examples of feminine perfection.

Filled with a somewhat inflated self-esteem, Nan reached the age for dating. She seemed always surrounded with a throng of young admirers, who tried to woo her while competing for her favors. She became popular, flirting with and teasing many of her wooers, much to the chagrin of her father, who belatedly recognized that his darling was shallow, flirtatious and selfish. Nan would do next to anything to cater to her own vanity and popularity.

Finally, much to her father's comfort, Nan seemed to settle into a more serious relationship with the youngest son of a respected local family. Though few of the local notables held the proposed match in high regard, the family of the young man did not voice disapproval. John was much too much infatuated with the attractive Nan to listen to the voice of reason. Even though she seemed genuinely fond of him, she still engaged in a few more or less serious flings, which was not lost on the backbiters. The city burghers nodded their heads, whispering discreetly the time-tested axiom: "The apple does not fall far from the tree."

Nan relished her dominance over men and used her spell over her boyfriend to the fullest measure. The longer she dated, having the pick of the crop, the more she believed that most men were weaklings, meriting only contempt, albeit well-concealed and veiled in professed affection. Nan had few deep emotions, save self-love and greed. Most of her young suitors never unearthed this part of her personality, for she always presented a masterful front of a soft, loving and gentle girl, one in search of her "Prince Charming." Though nearly engaged to John, she often whispered thinly veiled hints to another prospective suitor that if he could live up to her demands and exceed her boyfriend's qualities, she might reconsider.

While this mini-farce unfolded, a real tragedy was in the offing. Initially few ascribed any significance to the budding Nazi party and its perverted platform. The deranged Nazi dictator, Adolf Hitler, advancing swiftly in his quest for world domination, inaugurated his campaign of expansion, straight in the direction of Czechoslovakia. A powerful tremor shook the Jewish communities. Most were well aware that the Nazi ideology called for nothing less than total annihilation of all Jews under their domination. Jews scrambled for refuge, but few found a sanctuary. No country wished to admit the dispossessed and impoverished exiles. Most nations paid lip service of disapproval to Nazi inhumanity, but no meaningful action was mounted against the barbaric master plan of the new German leadership.

The Nazis embodied their racial policy in a body of laws called the "Nuremberg laws" that outlined in minute detail who was considered a Jew and spelled out the future ostracism and expulsion of Jewish life from the "Third Reich."

This plan initially called for the stripping of all the victims' rights and worldly assets. The second step called for large-scale relocation to concentration camps, and the final station for the unfortunates was to the killing fields for their physical destruction in the death camps. In the northeast of Moravia, the initial action called for the deportation of able-bodied men to a newly established labor camp in Nisko, located in western Poland. Their alleged assignment was to build the barracks and roads for a new camp, which would house families.

The opening of the Nisko camp came at the crucial point in history, on the heels of the bloody defeat of Poland by the Nazi forces. Hitler invaded Poland in a ferocious military attack, thus starting the Second World War. The violent aggression all but paralyzed the ill-prepared Poles, who retreated in disarray. Though fighting valiantly, they were soundly defeated in just under three weeks.

Nan's father and brother were among the men who toiled on the construction of the Nisko camp. All suffered terrible deprivation struggling with the marshy ground without proper equipment, food or shelter.

During the confusion caused by the swiftly advancing German armies, most of the Nisko inmates escaped. Some returned to their families in the Protectorate, straight into the arms of their archenemies the Germans, but most fled East, hoping to join partisans and fight against the Nazi oppressors. Nan's father wavered, torn between his wish to join the partisans and his perceived duty to return to his wife and daughter. His son, Bert, convinced him that return was a preposterous idea. Besides, there was male help present. The dentist was still very much in the picture, and Nan had her boyfriend at her side as well. He could be counted on to bend over backward to do all that was possible for her.

Bert's convincing argument won the older man over, and both joined the many refugees trying to reach the Soviet border. The battle over Poland was over; the non-aggression pact signed between the Nazis and the Soviets ushered in a brief lull. The Soviet action was dictated by the need for a buffer zone before the advancing Germans. For that very reason they allied with their archenemy and were awarded the eastern half of Poland. This unexpected partition was a windfall for many Jews, not only those from Nisko, but to many from western Poland, now under the German yoke. Although the journey to the border was filled with peril, it offered the best and only chance to escape the clutches of their demonic, implacable enemy: the Nazis.

The countryside was in disarray; some units were still engaged in skirmishes, mostly German units engaged in mopping up operations. Random shooting and stray ammunition were a hazard. The roads were littered with the dead, the wounded and exhausted, co-mingled with many animal carcasses. Many horses of the cavalry, the pride of the Polish military, lay amongst dead livestock, victims of the many aerial bombardments. The air was filled with the stench of putrefaction, which only intensified the apocalyptic mood of impending danger, compounded by groups of roving partisans searching the countryside to fight and kill some of the German invaders. Every minute of their flight was potentially the last. Their road out of bondage was fraught with lethal perils.

As they hurried, Bert had to reduce his pace to conform to his father's slower steps. The older man seemed to fall behind, tired and on the brink of collapse. Later Bert tried many times to re-enact the last moments of his father's life. He remembered being a few steps apart, his father trailing, when suddenly Bert heard a dull thud amongst a volley of bullets. He spun around and saw his father keeled over on the dirt road, a small trickle of blood flowing down his left cheek. Bert fell to the ground, attempting to avoid the bullets around them. Once the attack was over, he tried to lift his father's head. Mr. B lay prostrate and lifeless. A stray bullet had struck him in his left temple. Filled with shock and panic, Bert's first impulse was to run for his life.

Though Mr. B was not a lucky man while alive, he was fortunate in his death, which came to him in an instant. He was fifty years old. For a moment, Bert wavered, uncertain what to do. His first instinct was to bury his father's body, but he quickly reconsidered. Time was short, the German units were advancing quickly, and every moment could be the difference between life and death. Amongst the flying bullets, he could not take the time to perform the pious act and filial duty; he had to run. Moments later when the volleys slowed, those still alive moved on.

In later years Bert was troubled by the thought that he left his father's body on the dirt road, the slow trickle of blood soaking the dust, his glazed eyes wide open. The final sight of his father accompanied him for the rest of his life, during his troubled days and even worse nights.

Meanwhile the two women still living in the provincial town began to feel the pinch of the drastically changed times. Life became hard, filled with shortages of all kinds as the German overlords restricted Jews to less and less. Their prohibitions and regulations were tailored to isolate and deprive the unwanted Jews of most of life's necessities. Most of their assets were invested in stocks and bonds, all of which immediately became inaccessible. The two women subsisted, relying on the odd opportunity to barter some of their concealed jewelry for daily necessities. Even when possible, this was a modest and unreliable source, scarcely sufficient for their basic survival. Gone were the days of luxury, taken for granted only a short while ago. The sad truth began to sink in: the good old days of affluence and carefree existence were gone.

The only man they could count on, the family fixture, the dentist, was mired in deep trouble of his own. He lost his source of income, his office, and his residence. A less successful colleague quickly jumped on the bandwagon of anti-Semitism to take advantage of the seizure of Jewish ownership. He was granted possession of the practice of the man he envied and whose prosperity he begrudged. Indeed the office was a plum, equipped with state of the art instruments and gadgets.

The local Gestapo gave the Jewish owner two weeks to vacate his office and home. The time was so short that all he could arrange was a small room in a nearby Jewish boarding house. His property was sealed and awaited someone the Nazis deemed meritorious. The previously well-off man hardly had any money left; even paying the rent for the tiny room became a problem.

He would have been better off to move in with his former sweetheart, but propriety prevented him from making this practical decision. Most people in the dark year of 1939 and 1940 still kept up appearances and hung on to hypocritical middle class mores, still uncomprehending that they stood on the precipice of an abyss.

In turn, the Germans, the methodical people that they were, never lost sight of the time and their highest priority program: the total annihilation of European Jewry. The spring and summer of 1942 targeted the Jews of northern Moravia for expulsion. Jews were ordered into transports, which generally consisted of about one thousand people. The first station of the journey into the netherworld was Theresienstadt.

Of the three remaining protagonists of our story, the first to be summoned was the dentist, who at that time was almost 50 years old. He could not know that his age placed him in the category of those having a slim chance of pulling through the rigors of the Nazi camps. A few weeks later the two women were ordered to present themselves for deportation and resettlement, bringing the standard 120 pounds of necessities deemed adequate by the master race for the subhuman Hebrews. The packed train slowly chugged ahead, crammed with frightened Jewish families, uncertain of their future. Though they were tightly squeezed together, had hardly air to breathe, and the cars were filled with the agonizing stench of the many bodies, they managed reasonably well as the journey lasted only several hours.

They reached Theresienstadt, once a garrison town, now converted into a concentration camp. Once there, Nan set out to secure their existence, to ensure a bearable niche for both of them. She applied her best assets, the timeless feminine attraction to the opposite sex.

Upon arrival, Nan scanned the young men processing the new inmates and realized that luck was with her. One of the brawny lads noticed the sexy blond and attached himself to her, efficiently tending to her and her mother.

On reaching the women's barracks, following a brief stint in quarantine, Nan did not miss a beat and set out to familiarize herself with the new environment. Soon she found an acquaintance of sorts, employed in food distribution, who looked at her with much admiration and intimated his readiness to supply more soup, sparing them from starvation, if only Nan would bestow her favors upon him. Never having been particularly fastidious or restrained in her love life, she consented immediately and though the food provided was not tasty or even fit for human consumption, nothing else was momentarily available, and it spared both women from Theresienstadt's scourge: starvation and its painful consequences.

Mother and daughter shared a bunk and only on infrequent occasions where more women squeezed in with them. For three or four women to share the narrow space was added hardship, forcing them to cling together in a filthy, hard wooden bunk, but revolting as it was, it still was far from lethal.

In Theresienstadt, Nan managed to secure an assignment with an indoor work detail. This provided immeasurable advantage, for she was sheltered for the entire twelve-hour workday from the biting cold that tormented the commandos who toiled in the open air. The backbreaking work, made more perilous with sub-zero temperatures, overcrowding and poor nutrition, brought about upper respiratory illnesses, which quickly turned into pneumonia, finishing the suffering of the afflicted.

Very few old timers in the camps had warm clothing. Most were stripped from them when screened upon arrival, but even those who somehow dodged this bad piece of luck lost them to some brazen, thieving inmate, or at times the owner bartered it for a piece of bread, succumbing to the pangs of hunger gnawing at his innards. Such imprudence compromised short-term gain for long-term pain. Indoor labor also protected the inmates from frostbite, for whatever footwear was available was always falling apart. The soles were paper-thin, and the many holes exposed the skin. In the long run, hardly any inmate was spared from severe frostbite. Inmates assigned to indoor commandos won a windfall of comfort and a much better chance of survival.

With time, Nan arranged and enjoyed most of the desired privileges attainable in this camp. Additionally, she secured for her mother a cleaning job, scouring the floors of the barracks. As for Nan, she maneuvered for a long time, ultimately succeeding in transferring to the best detail, the one sorting clothes confiscated from arriving transports. Soon Nan mastered the skill of stuffing, in an opportune moment, some item under her skirt or blouse, which could be smuggled into the camp and readily bartered for some food.

Clearly, conditions of the two women surpassed those of most other inmates, compliments to the cool, crafty shrewdness of the perky, seductive and attractive Nan. Nevertheless, this almost comfortable existence in detention was to be short-lived. All Nan's valiant efforts to reverse the decision of the Council of the Elders fell on deaf ears. Both women had to present themselves for deportation East. Nan was not accustomed to this kind of major defeat. Both were shocked and silently apprehensive. Nan was the first to regain her old spirit, trusting that no matter where they would be sent, she would find the ways and means to improve their lot.

The journey to Auschwitz was rough and lasted a few days, without food, drink, or provisions for basic hygiene. The journey of the freight train was not smooth, the logistics of the war were complicated, and the tracks were filled with the many trains used by the German army. The transport of the doomed was subjected to frequent halts, during which the inmates sat in the dark, desolate cattle cars, despairing over their fate. With every passing hour, more and more people fell into an apathetic stupor, resigned to their imminent death. Suddenly the train jerked to a stop and some strange looking people, dressed in striped uniforms, ripped open the car doors.

A line of SS men stood behind them, with their guns poised. The zebra-like men screamed at the top of their lungs for the newly arrived to get out, on the double, or else. Some used whips or truncheons, indiscriminately hitting at the half-blinded people squinting to see after leaving the twilight of the wagons, suddenly exposed to the floodlights of the ramp. They scrambled as fast as they could to leave the train. Though stunned, they understood that they had arrived in hell itself, and this particular one was called Auschwitz.

The Jewish ramp, flooded with dazzling, blinding lights, offered a surreal impression. In the distance, clearly visible were tall chimneys, exuding orange-yellow flames, soaring and darting into the night skies. Sharp floodlights, glowing fires, and belching curls of gray-black, wreath-like smoke dominated the entire expanse. The air was saturated by the sickeningly sweet stench of burning flesh and hair. Its pungent smell blanketed the infernal monstrosity.

Nan was not only able to retain her presence of mind, she even recalled the warnings whispered in Theresienstadt, that people deemed unfit for slave labor would be poisoned by noxious gas. Nan grasped that she was face to face with the confirmation of what she had considered panic mongering. There was little time for thought. Both women were pushed to join the long queue, slowly moving forward in the direction of a young SS man, who seemed to separate the newly arrived into two distinct groups. Most men, women and all children were directed to the right, only a handful sent to the left.

Nan sensed those on the left were chosen to live, for most were young and stronger looking. She leaned towards her mother and in an urgent whisper instructed her to claim that she was thirty years old and a seamstress by profession. She should stand tall and look upbeat. Nan had little to worry for her own fate; she had full faith in her attractiveness. Even now, soiled and disheveled from the long ordeal of the terrible journey, she felt confident in the power of her appeal.

The line crawled ahead, but soon the moment of truth was upon them. Nan looked up at the tall SS officer and flashed a timid, innocent smile, conferring on her a girlish-sweet look. The officer seemed genuinely surprised, and it appeared that he would return her grin, but at the last moment, he regained the stern mien of an SS man facing a lowly Jewess. Though he put on a serious frown, Nan knew that she prevailed, winning herself a stay of execution, at least for now. As the officer motioned her to the left side, Nan took her mother's hand, as if by reflex of a little girl, and walked with her in a most natural way in the appointed direction. The man in charge of the selection was still under the spell of Nan's smile, thus failing to voice objections to her leading her mother.

However, if Nan was anything, she was smart and cunning. She understood that her momentary accomplishment was just that, the first among many hurdles she would have to vanquish to elude death. All her senses on high alert, she grasped that it would call on all her smarts to dodge the angel of death in this most efficient homicidal factory called Auschwitz.

Still on the ramp, but sent with those destined for forced labor, they were ordered to undress and were pushed by some rough men into a barn-like, tumbled down shack, where some crude hands pulled them by their hair, tearing and cutting it with blunt scissors, till their heads were completely bald. Nan noticed a trickle of blood on her mother's face, slowly dripping down, prompting her to touch her own baldhead. She fingered a thick, warm layer of blood, slowly congealing and covering the many cuts and tears inflicted by the rusty scissors and the crude hands that wielded them.

Stark naked, they were driven into another large room, where all noticed the ceiling dotted with faucets. For an instant, all stopped breathing. Frightened, they stared at the ominous installation. This was the moment of truth. Would these taps discharge water or the lethal Cyclon B? Suddenly the hiss from the ceiling signaled some activity, and all eyes turned upwards. Some prayed; others stiffened with fear. When the first large drops of water began to form and drop down, the relief was beyond description, almost palpable, an all-encompassing appreciation for life and the reprieve from death. Many women continued their prayers as the water co-mingled with their tears and blood streaming down their haggard faces.

The comfort that they had once again avoided death, prevented them from feeling the extremes of the seething and icy temperatures of the water. They washed themselves without soap or towels. Then someone shouted an order to hurry, still wet, to another room. During their run they were tossed some rags, which they caught in mid-air, mostly torn and dirty, their only future clothes. Among the tatters thrown were no underwear or anything warm. They just simply put on what they caught. Another order was shouted to line up for tattooing. Each had to stretch out her forearm to several working inmates who tattooed numbers on the newly arrived. These numerals would be from now on their new identity. The inmates who etched the marks on their forearms worked quickly and dexterously, obviously much experienced. All was done in a hectic hurry, but this last filthy procedure signaled the end of the day's ordeal. The terrified women were driven to an empty barracks, their home for the time being.

They were allowed to lie down on the cold, bare floor, where they bedded for the rest of the night. No straw or blankets were provided and the women huddled together for a little warmth and rest, hoping to mitigate the icy draft wheezing through the building. Right then, during the first abysmal night, Nan decided that she had to work very quickly to find help, lest her mother or perhaps even herself fall prey to such infernal, inhuman conditions. As she fell asleep, jaded and cold, she resolved to find it and live, irrespective of the cost.

It was still pitch black when loud screams and shouts woke them from their fitful sleep. Dawn seemed ages away when they filed into columns for morning roll call. Nan was surprised to see a well-dressed and well-fed woman enter the barracks, deferentially accompanied by a younger inmate. She swung a whip, beating down mercilessly on the slower inmates who were not fast enough in following her orders. While most of the women were bewildered and shocked by such unwarranted brutality, her warm, clean clothes and a well-groomed exterior impressed Nan. She stuck out like a sore thumb among the filthy, no longer human-looking bunch in the barracks.

The woman yelled at them, telling them that she was their Kapo, in charge of the barracks, and if they knew what was good for them they would obey every one of her orders. Nan listened, full of admiration. Here was a role model! Clearly a prisoner herself, this woman had worked her way up to the upper echelon, in charge and handsomely remunerated, not wanting in any essentials. Not only was the Kapo impressive looking, she even had long hair, pulled back into a knot. Her entire exterior was fetching; her high boots were polished to a glossy luster, and Nan noticed that she wore a wristwatch; a luxury even Nan lost many months ago. The longer Nan watched the imperious woman, the more she wished to join the ranks of those privileged ones, who obviously traveled in a different orbit, closer to the standards enjoyed by the SS men.

Later Nan learned that the word "Kapo" was derived from "Kameradschafts Polizei" which loosely translates into "police of peers." That was, of course, a misnomer; nothing could have been farther from the truth. Almost all Kapos were habitual criminals, felons whose rap sheet was long established. In addition, most were loose cannons, cruel, brutal, and frequently sadistic perverts, who curried favors from the Nazis, often surpassing them in brutality and inhumanity.

Immediately, Nan began to investigate her odds for attaining the position of a Kapo and soon discovered a few snags. Most of the Kapos in Auschwitz were of pure Aryan lineage and had an arm-long criminal record, almost a prerequisite for such an appointment. Nan happened to be Jewish, a blemish that automatically disqualified her. There were but a few Jewish Kapos and the only way to work one's way up, as a Jew, was to exceed the professional criminals in bestiality and so earn the qualification for this task.

Nan would not concede defeat. If need be, she would use any means to advance the cause of her survival. On that first morning, she made up her mind to pursue her exploration stealthily and persistently until she reached her goal. Nan was impressed with the ease with which the Kapos swung their canes, it seemed that those canes were the badges of honor of those entrusted with such high office. The mostly black canes, some hewn and embossed with silver decorations, were the insignia of power, much dreaded by the inmates who were on the receiving end of the Kapo's violence. Most Kapos lashed out mercilessly at their charges, prodding them to ever-increasing speed at whatever task was at hand.

Nan hoped that her chance would come and, when it did, she pounced on it like a beast of prey, with all her energy and desperate will. It came in the form of a male Kapo, who visited his mistress, the woman in charge of the barracks where Nan and her mother were housed. Though she had already worked a few days and felt the full impact of the starvation diet, she was not yet reduced to one of the emaciated, sexless forms, trailing their legs in the camp. As the powerful man entered the barracks, Nan made sure to show up and, however improbable, she still radiated her feline sensuality and attractiveness, much in contrast to the rest of the women. The man could not help but notice.

Risking all, Nan attracted his attention and then gave him her famous glance, a mixture of sexy flirtation and demure shyness, one that always impressed the men around her. It took a great deal of courage to prance in front of the lover of the woman who could have killed her with one swing of her cane. Quickly she noticed that he was not only an Aryan, but also a professional criminal. All inmates in Auschwitz had color-coded triangles attached to their tunics. The one on the chest of the burly man was green, indicating that he was a felon, beyond the possibility of returning to society. However, no Jew was allowed to approach members of the "master race," criminal or not. Nevertheless, Nan was playing for the highest stakes: her and her mother's lives. Underneath the seductive smile teetered a fearful, almost panicky heart.

However, Nan's luck had not run out. The huge, ogre-like man ogled her with a lewd and lecherous expression, and Nan, an expert at appraising men, knew she had won. Franz, the man targeted by Nan, was a long-time lover of Hertha, Nan's Kapo. He not only noticed the young woman who unmistakably flirted with him (one of the most powerful men in the camp), but he liked very much what he saw.

Matters were helped along by Franz's weariness with Hertha, whose moods and excessive demands annoyed and bothered him. Nevertheless, Franz was a career felon and an Auschwitz veteran; a man well-versed in the written and unwritten laws of the camp. He knew he had to tread softly. Any Aryan caught in violation of the Nuremberg racial laws, prohibiting sexual contact between a Jew and an Aryan, was guilty of a capital offense and put to death. Franz had long ago taken measures to cover his hide, for the eventuality of falling out of grace. He built an impressive dossier, gathering and documenting evidence of transgressions committed by other Kapos and many of the SS officers. To ensure his safety, particularly from another Kapo, perhaps jealous of his success, he accumulated damning evidence that he intended to use later to enforce his will.

In all concentration camps the SS officers and the Kapos used their position to enrich themselves. They were, almost without exception, engaged in black market operations, handsomely lining their pockets. In Auschwitz literary millions in multiple currencies passed through the hands of the SS and Kapos, who kept busy building for their post-war nest eggs. It did not detract from the zealous diligence with which they murdered thousands of Jews. Priceless diamonds, precious jewelry, hard currency, gold and much, much more was smuggled by the inmates with the desperate hope of ransoming their own and their families' lives. Instead, they were stripped of all rights on arrival.

These treasures were officially confiscated by the camp administrators to be delivered to Berlin, but much of the plunder found its way into the pockets of the executioners and their helpers, the Kapos. The men in power who knew their way around this infernal camp became quickly and unimaginably rich. Franz was the expert in thievery and the camp's machinations, and was the master of the unwritten etiquette of Auschwitz. He knew who, and with what, to bribe and who to remove or kill, and how. Though he was a rough brute, his senses were sharpened and honed to the fine details needed to survive in the unnatural, man-made jungle that was Auschwitz.

Nan had little in common with the crude, lewd and ribald womenfolk: the majority of the incarcerated Gentile females to which Franz was accustomed. To Franz she seemed ethereal, at once refined and sexy. She had cat-like appeal, her green eyes illuminating her finely chiseled features as she maneuvered about in a deliberately seductive, almost gyrating gait that teased and provoked the male predator in Franz. The longer Franz scanned her, the more he liked what he saw. Even her repugnant, foul-smelling rags could not hide her unique attractiveness. He was drawn to her by a magnetic power and, in spite of the risks of dealing with a Jewess, he could not stay away or free himself from Nan's magic spell.

Searching for a solution, he decided on a desperate gamble; he would engage Hertha's help. She might turn on him and lead him to disaster; but then again Hertha was no fool. Moreover, she had one intrinsic weakness, much stronger than her vanity or affection for Franz. She was pathologically greedy for gold and most other valuables. Franz, the street-smart thug, trusted that Hertha would not cut off the branch she sat on, too. Therefore, Franz confided in Hertha about his intoxication with one of the women on her block, a fact she had noticed already. He asked for her understanding and help, suggesting that he would be very generous.

Hertha was ready for his request. She wanted to strike a bargain; she demanded an astronomical sum for the juicy tidbit for which he pined. The Jewess, Hertha decided, would become Franz's costliest caper. He consented to pay a nearly ruinous amount in gold, but knew that he could make it up, and such an outlandish windfall soothed Hertha's ruffled feathers. Hertha was too smart to jeopardize their association; she could never manage or succeed without Franz.

As a Kapo, Franz had a small room of his own, where Nan became a frequent visitor. Soon she was a fixture, known as Franz's mistress, thus untouchable and inviolable. She was officially assigned to a cleaning commando, but never showed up to work. Even her mother was freed from serious drudgery. Mrs. B. had to make a nominal attempt pretending to sweep the barracks and scour the floors.

Nan relished the many luxuries Franz lavished on her. Her meals, often shared with her lover, consisted of exquisite delicacies. Nan wore elegant, stylish and warm clothes. Her toiletries were even of finer quality than those she used in the pre-war years, and she always exuded the scent of a fine French perfume. Franz proved to be a grateful and generous lover. He inundated and overwhelmed her with incomparable jewelry, the likes of which she had never seen or even knew existed. He supplied all Nan needed for her mother as well, for if she was anything she was a devoted daughter, perhaps one who could not respect her mother, but who nonetheless loved her. The elder Mrs. B was not left wanting either.

All this took place in the very shadows of continuous flames shooting high from the tall chimneys, consuming human remains day after day and night after night. The skies were always cloudy, the air thick with black smoke. The air reeked of burning flesh, the breeze carried small particles of ash while the bulk of the silvery, gray residue, the last remnants of the cremated Jews, were shoveled into large sacks for some later use. Only those who could dissociate themselves from the horrors of the gassings, the shootings, and the stench of human flesh burning on pyres, stood a chance of living a while longer.

Nan would have signed her soul to the devil, following Dr. Faust's example, and in a way she did, "Auschwitz style." Nan had a passion for life; no cost seemed too high. She was well aware the price was steep, but she was more than willing to pay. Always practical, she was a mistress of intrigue, which she cultivated to new heights. Nan also had the uncanny talent of inflaming the passions of her lovers who then became enslaved and dependent on her favors.

Now she applied all her skills on Franz, who soon was wrapped around her little finger. That is not to say that Franz was not a master of similar abilities and that he did not feel occasionally humiliated by his servitude to a pretty Jewess. In his more sober moments, he was confident that he would get her out of his system, would grow weary of her and then rid himself of this bondage. He had done it many times before when he no longer desired a particular mistress. To his chagrin, with every passing day he seemed to desire and need her more. She was to him all he had yearned for and had been denied all his life.

Nan, in turn, was a practical soul. She was well aware that nothing lasted forever and that the day might come that Franz would either want or have to rid himself of her. Nan would not sit tight waiting for that day. She had to secure her Auschwitz existence, independent of Franz. To that end, she began to work on Franz, to arrange the position of Kapo for herself. Then she would have power and a position of her own, free of servitude, independent of the whims of a benefactor who might lose interest.

Initially Franz attempted to talk her out of it, but Nan remained adamant. As bait, she reminded him that if she were to become a Kapo, she would have a cubicle of her own, and he would not be endangered by her visits to his room. He risked much less by visiting a Jewess in her barracks than by having her in a men's barracks, where she was highly visible to the many inmates. The argument was not fully logical, but Franz could not resist, for in his heart of hearts he wished to be convinced.

It was not to be a great challenge for the powerful Franz. All he had to do was to pull a few strings, and place some bribes in the proper hands. A few day later Nan and her mother moved to a different barracks, where Nan became the uncontested ruler. Thus began a new era in the life of the ambitious and now ruthless woman. For the first time in her young life, Nan experienced the intoxicating sensations of wielding enormous power. Precious little from her past prepared her for the wise and judicious use of such might.

In her new position, Nan became the mistress of life and death, answerable only to an SS officer, who rarely corrected a Kapo who abused the inmates. In the eyes of the Nazis, the Kapo who treated his inmates humanely was quickly disqualified and would soon get removed. For the most part, the members of the SS contingent wanted everything to go smoothly. The number of inmates should be tallied; the barracks were to be clean and the work commandos to toil at their maximum capacity. Little else mattered to the master race. If the Kapo chose to beat the daylights out of an inmate, brutalize, maim or murder him or her, so much the better. No Kapo was ever called to answer for any barbarity. Indeed, it was expected. The more violence and torment inflicted by the Kapo, the happier the SS. There were a lot more Jews still.

Initially, Nan justified her remorseless treatment by the fact that she, a Jewess, had to be doubly efficient, but later she conceded that she enjoyed inflicting pain. She was surprised at the degree of pleasure she experienced while flogging or clubbing inmates. She stopped at nothing. The terrified expression in the eyes of her victims gave her a feeling of great satisfaction, and she became addicted to power and sadistic behavior. Before long, she became infamous for her savagery. She caned her charges, reducing some to broken skeletons. Before long Nan accepted the fact that she was a sadist, that her inclination was most probably suppressed when such behavior was deemed repugnant and punishable by law. However, in the camps all decency fell by the wayside.

Nan would pull aside some inmate, with or without a pretext, savoring their panic, relishing their vain attempts to mollify her just to avoid the inevitable: the blows administered with her elegant, black cane. Few recovered from her vicious beatings. Many lay there in the dust or mud, bleeding, mutilated by her savagery. Often she continued hitting long after her victim lost consciousness or died. Nan lost count of the many killed by her brutality; all were simply included with the many other casualties of the day.

Nan's mother was shocked and appalled at her daughter's behavior, but she was much too scared to reprimand her. She only hinted carefully at the inadmissibility of Nan's conduct. Even Franz warned her a few times that she was becoming notorious for her excesses, advising her to cool it. In all probability, something snapped within Nan. She could not stop; if anything, with time she became more and more ruthless, craving the perverse pleasure of causing bodily harm and inflicting pain. In just a few weeks, she was the most hated and feared Kapo in Auschwitz, surely a dubious distinction to be the worst among the many supremely evil, criminal women.

Many of the female Kapos looked the part they played. A number of them were lesbians, the "Butches," but Nan's exterior defied the stereotype. Nan had the deceptive guise of a chiseled doll, refined and dainty. At times she alone would wonder what it was that gave her such pleasure when she saw other women fear her, squirming at the mere sight of her, followed by the height of satisfaction when she inflicted pain.

These thoughts crossed her mind on rare occasions. Nan was not given to introspection and never experienced the sensation of guilt. She carried on unchecked and unrepentant for many long months. All around her death triumphed, taking its gruesome toll. The Auschwitz inferno, here on earth, was many times worse than the one of Dante's imagination. The smoke and stench of decomposing bodies no longer repulsed Nan. She became used to it, almost oblivious to the nightmarish scenario, besotted with her power, craving luxuries and concerned only with her own safety.

Franz never tired of her. He was obsessed with her, flooding her with gifts, doggedly hoping against hope that she might learn to like him. However, time was his worst enemy, and it was quickly running out. The war was drawing to an end, and the impending defeat of the Nazis had a sobering effect on the couple. Before long they realized that their heydays were all but over and that the time for reckoning might be at hand. The louder the rumble of approaching Russian artillery, the faster the impudence and spirits of the two Kapos sunk.

January 1945 finally ended the most shameful pit on the face of the earth, the slaughterhouse of millions of innocent people, Auschwitz. The most-wicked of symbols of the Third Reich was brought to its knees, leaving mankind wounded and its faith destroyed beyond reconstruction. In the death camps perished many religious beliefs; trust in one's fellow-men and confidence in a bright tomorrow died, right along with the millions of Jews.

When Auschwitz tumbled down, partially demolished by the Germans who erected this freakish, monstrous camp, Nan, her mother and Franz were all long gone. When the Russians entered the compound, the only living creatures were some Musselmen shuffling about, all near death. The camp lay in ruins; only the evidence suggested at what transpired there. The piles of shoes, glasses, and luggage bore silent witness to their murdered owners. Some of the barracks and parts of the crematories were deserted intact; the SS men did not have enough time to finish the obliteration of Auschwitz with the Russian armies approaching much too quickly. So it happened that much incriminating evidence of the wholesale murders remained behind.

The perpetrators fled for their lives as the Russian army approached. With the roar of the Russian tanks, rumors spread like wildfire that the Russians executed all members of the SS elite Nazi units and their helpers. Hearsay had it that the Russians did not take any of these captive; they shot on the spot all those having their blood group tattooed under their left armpit, the sure proof of belonging to the Waffen SS. Ironically, it was the SS who facilitated their own incrimination with the tattoo, which was mandatory for all SS men. All that the victorious Russians had to do was to cast a cursory look during routine physical inspection. The Nazis and their helpers were swept by panic. Petrified, they scattered, running for their lives, mostly westbound, trying to reach the American lines.

This moment marked the parting of Nan from Franz. While he was unhappy, Nan was quite relieved to be rid of him, since he was now useless. Franz had to run west, while Nan and her mother joined a transport marching inmates to the southwest. They hoped to reach the Czech border quickly. Nan was not at all alarmed or burdened by her nefarious activity in Auschwitz. Was not she after all a victim, too, incarcerated in the worst place on earth?

Although the end of the war stripped her of the power she coveted so much, she trusted that better days lay ahead.

Nan did not consider, even for a moment, that she might be called to task, to answer for her behavior during her heydays in the camp. She was glad to shake off Franz, who asked her for a possible alibi, which she flatly refused. She would not acknowledge his help, now that he was a burden and a potential liability. But Franz genuinely loved Nan and saw in her a woman from a different world than his, supposedly more refined than his, which was filled with crime and drunken orgies.

As they parted, the final act of the European tragedy began to unfold. Franz and Nan were mere understudies to the main protagonists of the drama that was concluding. The Nazis were left on the run, scrambling for safety, hoping to escape the Russian reach. Most followed the same routine; they discarded their fine uniforms or clothes; some even donned the striped prisoner's garb and joined the death marchers. The nefarious odium of the Nazis ended!

Nan and her mother marched for what felt like an eternity. Time merged into a gray, cold and hungry stretch of days with little hope of reaching a safe haven any time soon. They were plagued with hunger, frostbite and diarrhea. One day, Nan noticed that her mother began to wobble, weak and unsteady on her feet. This was an ominous sign; exhaustion and death were at her heels. Nan knew that she had to act. Already many others had escaped, taking advantage of a favorable moment. The SS guarding the evacuees slacked on supervision. The only time they shot an inmate was when she fell and could no longer rise. The rest of the marchers who could keep their wits about them could hide and vanish without a trace.

Nan, always alert, found the opportunity in a barn where they were ordered to stay overnight. She covered her mother with straw and crawled next to her. The next morning the SS men ordered the inmates to get up and form columns of five. The next command called on them to resume the march. Nan and her mother didn't stir; they remained lying quietly, hoping not to be noticed. The plan worked. The farmer put on a poker face, pretending not to see the twosome, nestled under the straw.

They rested for a day or two and then Nan, with her mother in tow, continued more or less at their own pace, hiding in the forests or with consenting farmers. Soon they fit in with the rest of the shadowy masses of humanity, stumbling towards some still unknown place hoping to find rest and help. Most moved unsteadily at that stage, hanging onto life with their quickly fading strength. Eventually some of the lugubrious procession reached Prague; by that time, both women looked every bit the same as the pathetic rest. Nothing singled out Nan from the other victims of the crazed, Nazi-invented "Final Solution."

Nan thought that all was well, that her nefarious past was dead, buried and under the rubble and ashes of Auschwitz. Slowly she recovered from the ordeal of the death march and embarked on restoring her life. She found an apartment and began to date a young man, who fell madly in love with her and within weeks proposed marriage. Nan accepted, and it seemed that her physical rehabilitation was nearing completion.

One day, a woman she didn't recognize stopped her on a cobble-stoned street in Prague. Nan looked uncomprehendingly at the elegant young woman whose angry frown focused on Nan's physique, particularly her abdomen slightly bulging now by her advancing pregnancy. However, the unfamiliarity was one-sided. The woman recognized Nan beyond any shadow of a doubt. In camp Nan never looked like the rest: sexless, gray, skinny creatures, covered in tatters. There, as the mighty Kapo, she was well fed and even better dressed, while the woman confronting Nan belonged to the rank and file distorted by their hairless, shaven heads, making them all look alike, almost invisible. Nan stuck out like a sore thumb then and was easily identifiable now.

The irate woman began to scream, right there, out on the street, that Nan was a murderer, who had to be brought to justice. She spat at Nan's fine fall outfit and ordered Nan to follow her. Nan wanted to quell the uproar, hoping to disappear from the growing crowd of curious onlookers, who began to form a circle around them.

Nan feared being beaten to a pulp by the inflamed crowd, whose memories of Nazi atrocities were still fresh in their minds. She obediently joined her accuser who marched quickly to the offices of the already re-established Jewish community. There the woman entered the office of the acting chief and forced him to listen to her charges. She needed help to bring Nan to justice, for she was a Polish national, temporarily residing in Prague and on her way to Australia. She was charging and wished to testify to the violence and beatings committed by Nan. She was one of the many victims of Nan's brute cruelty and atrocities, crimes for which she wanted Nan to atone by a lengthy sentence.

The secretary of the provisional council as well as his assistants recoiled with horror. They dreaded to comply with the woman's demands. To bring an indictment against a Jewess, a brutal Kapo and a despicable, abhorrent collaborator, was next to impossible. They needed time to settle the issue. They agreed with the accuser, soothed her anger by promising to work on the case, and asked her to return within two weeks time. By then, they would have retained lawyers to prepare the lawsuit.

That was said to pacify the woman. In reality, the community dreaded any such trial in an open court of law. They hoped to defuse the potentially explosive situation and gain some time to deal with it discreetly and intramurally. Their quest to quash such a high profile court case was based on a logical foundation. The Czech population, historically latently anti-Semitic, had become badly contaminated with the virus of Jew hatred and discrimination. During the six long years of Nazi occupation, the poisonous seeds maligning all things Jewish fell on fertile ears, resulting in an intense anti-Semitism throughout the land. The small remnant of Czech Jews did not want to incite the frenzied mob by feeding it horrible facts of Jewish collaboration with their persecutors.

The few returning Jews often faced hostile acceptance, especially by those who hid or appropriated Jewish assets and were asked to return these to the rightful owner. Many accepted the convenient Nazi propaganda and hoped to keep the valuables entrusted to them years ago by Jews sent to their deaths. After all, the Nazi propaganda masters spewed their vitriolic lies, charging that only because of the devious and parasitic Jew, the diligent and hard working Gentile had to live in penury, exploited by the foreign Jewish element. Indeed the tolerance for the handful of survivors was in question; few embraced the living ghosts emerging from their Gehenna (the Hebrew word for Hell).

The board of the Jewish council decided not to pursue the accusation. When Nan's accuser returned, she was told that she could not press charges because other witnesses did not corroborate them. Few if any would believe her incredulous story. In reality, some of the officials had grave doubts about the veracity of the accuser, but they would not risk a search for potential witnesses who could validate the charges. As it was, so few Nazi victims survived that it was unlikely to find one. Fear overruled their sense of justice and outrage. Nan escaped unscathed and delivered a healthy baby girl. Motherhood initially gave her a euphoric happiness, albeit a short-lived one, for soon she became restless and unfulfilled again. To silence her inner demons she returned to a life of dissolute promiscuity and profligate affairs, all of which her husband preferred to overlook. He chose to live in denial and silent tolerance of his wife's escapades. In that sense he resembled his late father-in-law, a man he never met.

The run-in with her previous inmate much affected Nan's disposition. Gone was her carefree, happy-go-lucky attitude. Nan began to worry. At times, she was depressed. She often avoided meeting people, perhaps fearing recognition. Gradually she developed mistrust of all around her, with the exception of her mother.

Matters came to a head when Czechoslovakia's political fortunes changed. The legally installed government was driven out by a Communist coup d'etat. Nan realized that the new system would not hesitate to prosecute her, and none of the underlying finer objections would stand up in court to quash the charges.

Nan's luck came to her rescue. Several hundred Jews were permitted to leave for the newly established state of Israel, an opening Nan and her family jumped at.

There, in the hot and barren Middle East, chaos, poverty and unemployment reigned. The family endured much hardship, and to complicate matters, it seemed that Nan was singularly unfit in adjusting. She could not buckle down and learn the language or fit into the diverse circumstances. She wept often, blaming her disconsolate sorrow on the deaths of her father and brother during the war. For the longest time Nan hoped Bert would return, only to finally receive official notification that he fell in the battle at Dukla Pass. Another hope shattered, the family now consisted of Nan, her husband, their little girl and the resilient Mrs. B.

Finally, after months of struggle to find some livelihood, things began to look up. Nan's husband joined a new venture in the food industry, which quickly picked up and turned into a prosperous business.

Just then, when all began to turn rosier, fate struck again. On a trip to Tel-Aviv Nan was confronted and identified by yet another of her past victims. This time Nan was in a pickle. Not only was the Israeli judiciary willing, even keen, to prosecute, but the legal code singled out Nazis and their helpers for the harshest penalties of the new state, this being the only crime punishable by death in Israel.

The family became alarmed by the grave crisis and retained a law firm with an excellent reputation. The lawyers initiated a tug of war, trying to convince the accuser that it was in her best interest to withdraw the charges, alternating threats of lacking credibility with the promise of a sizable financial reward if an out-of-court settlement could be reached. The woman would have none of it. She was not willing to let Nan off the hook.

Then she was bulldozed by a legal maneuver, which devastated the charges. Mrs. B was brought forward to testify that the indictment was a pure fabrication and a slanderous libel. As Mrs. B was the only other eyewitness, she would invalidate the charges against her daughter. Following some legal haggling Nan went, one more time, unscathed. There was no press coverage and the grieved party accepted the pre-arranged financial compensation.

Life went on for a while, seemingly on an even keel. Then fate caught up with Nan. Not quite 40 years old, she developed breast cancer. She had to subject herself to a radical mastectomy, followed by radiation and chemotherapy – in those days treatments comparable to medieval torture. The disfigurement of her most prized commodity, her body, was a devastating blow to Nan. She reeled under the impact of watching her beautiful figure mutilated. She cried over the loss of her blond hair that fell out following the chemotherapy; she had difficulties tolerating the drugs that were supposed to stop the spread of her malignancy, all to no avail.

I spoke with Nan during her brief remission. She was deeply depressed. She began to turn to religion and at times seemed divorced from reality. She speculated openly if all that had befallen her was divine retribution and, while she escaped man's justice, she pondered... in the judgment of the Supreme Power, would she be found guilty? It was the first time I heard acknowledgement of the many crimes she had committed. She was concerned that she had wronged her husband, engaging in her licentious lifestyle. Regrets and fear of what was in store after her passing tormented Nan. She talked incessantly about the brutality and carnage of her past, about the many victims she killed in cold blood with her very own hands. Her last days on this earth were spent in torment, panic and dread.

The spread of her illness could not be stopped. The malignant growth invaded most of her body. Towards the latter stages of her disease, she came to believe that the cancer that ravaged her body was the penalty for her evil behavior in the camp. All her torment, fear of death and the hereafter, the disconsolate anguish over the ugliness of her surgical scars and her disfigurement, reduced her ability to accept her rapidly approaching death. Close to her death, Nan lost her sanity and in an unobserved moment, no longer able to walk, she crawled on her hands and knees to the backyard of her house. There she lay curled by a rosebush, scratched and bleeding from the pricks of its many thorns. It seemed that she attempted to embrace the rosebush, then in full bloom. Her husband found her and gently carried her lifeless body back to bed. Finally, she was at peace and perhaps had met her maker. Her much tried and loving husband planted a rosebush next to her tombstone.

Years later I had an opportunity to talk to the elder Mrs. B, then a woman in her eighties. She still insisted that her daughter did only what she had to, to survive the Nazi terror.

Bobby: Death Marcher

Crematories and remains of inmates
at the Majdanek death camp.

H is given name was Harry. This name appeared on all his official documents, but had anyone called him Harry, he would have turned around looking for some other boy. For some inexplicable reason he was known to everyone as Bobby.

The good fairies that deliberated at his cradle showed poor insight. First, their timing was off, for Bobby was born in 1928, a year in itself that was not particularly ominous, but which foreshadowed catastrophic years ahead for the newborn. In 1928, the troubled waters of Europe's economy were choppy and murky, marred by the slow onset of an economic depression. However, these woes hardly touched Bobby's home, at least not at that stage. Though the unemployment figures were growing by leaps and bounds, it was still unimaginable what fate had in store for the rosy, fair infant.

Reckless fate dealt another injustice to this plump baby; he was an unexpected and generally unwanted addition to a middle aged couple. They were set in their ways, believing that the coming years would be filled with leisure, as their other son reached the age of 18 and left to study in Prague. The middle aged couple was not only disconcerted to return to parental duties, they were reluctant and frankly unhappy about their perceived burden and the ruin of their comfortable middle and later years. Fortunately, the couple had reached a certain financial stability and could afford domestic help, which reduced Bobby's arrival to a mere nuisance.

Bobby's teenage years coincided with the Nazi occupation of the Czech lands and the subsequent outbreak of the Second World War. The advent of Nazi domination over much of Central Europe gave rise to an explosive anti-Semitism, exceeding all previous eruptions of this perennial scourge. The unfolding cataclysm impacted all Jews enormously. Those who endeavored to survive needed strength, ingenuity, versatility, craftiness and a lot of good luck, a looming challenge for adults, let alone a boy who had barely reached his teens.

Bobby hailed from the mining town of Ostrava. It was an unappealing town, with a sizable Jewish community. The economic situation of most Jews was secure, resulting in a congenial and sociable climate.

Moravska Ostrava was also the nearest large city to the Czech-Polish border. Many Jewish families from Poland opted to relocate into the more benevolent Czechoslovak republic, glad to leave the strained and intensely anti-Semitic political climate of Poland.

In the aftermath of the First World War, newly established democratic Czechoslovakia practiced human and civil rights across the board, readily accepting, at least officially, the Jewish minority. Many Polish Jews took advantage of this policy of tolerance and relocated to the otherwise unattractive border town, bringing along their business acumen, diligence and profound gratitude to the young state. The latitude of the federal government greatly benefited Ostrava. The city experienced rapid economic growth, expansion of trade, and cultural and social development – all of which helped to lift the otherwise drab city above the usual standards of a typical mining community.

Bobby's home was no different from most middle class families. Although his father was only marginally involved in Ostrava's communal activities, his financial success depended heavily on the prosperity of the local citizens. He was a self-made man who had carved his career in the relatively new and initially rather unpopular insurance business. His hard work paid off; within a few years he had secured a top position earning an impressive income, providing a rather lucrative standard of living. He was a typical self-made man, determined, driven by an ambition to succeed, focused on popularizing the hitherto unknown concept of insurance and securities. He pushed himself and his subordinates, aware of his ambition to reach the top.

In those days, information and knowledge were disseminated at much a slower pace. Popularizing the purchase of insurance and investments was a painstakingly slow and gradual process. The fact that it was an innovative approach to securing a family's stability did not help a great deal, for people were rather suspicious of all things new and not time-tested. Slowly, his sales pitches resulted in a better understanding for the many miners, laborers, craftsmen, small businessmen, and petty bourgeois of Ostrava, and Mr. P began to reap the benefits of his doggedly persistent efforts.

Bobby's mother, Ella, was a typical middle-class Jewish housewife, fully compliant with the traditions governing her era. As expected, she was matched and married to a man who provided for her and took responsibility for the care of the family. In turn, he demanded compliance, respect and accommodation to all his decisions, whims and interests.

In those days, most Jewish women were, from childhood on, indoctrinated with the belief that it was their mission in life to please, satisfy and comply with all their husband's desires. Ella was certainly one of the many cast into the traditional mold. Better yet, for as long as Bobby could remember, she seemed to enjoy her role in life. She prided herself for her unique talent and skills in culinary creativity, which she cultivated, improved and perfected over the many years, till she reached almost artistic standards. Elegantly prepared food was one of her husband's top priorities, and Ella responded in an exemplary fashion, exceeding all expectations. Perhaps it is fair to suggest that Mr. P was a benevolent despot, though neither he nor his wife would ever describe him as such, for he, too, conformed to the generally prevailing and accepted norms.

Bobby's much older brother, Henry, studied law in Prague, and was a rather rare visitor to his parents' home. Bobby felt strangely intimidated and alienated from his sibling, who treated him with a contempt bordering on derision. Bobby was fond of his quasi-single child position. He was never excessively sociable and didn't like to share with anyone else the little attention his parents extended him.

When it came to his sons, Mr. P showed little patience and tolerance. He was an autocratic man, an exacting, strict disciplinarian with the final word on all matters affecting his family. If compliance was not forthcoming, he did not hesitate to resort to corporeal punishment. During Bobby's early youth, children were disciplined by physical chastisement; it was a generally accepted and applied maxim, "Spare the rod, spoil the child." Bobby liked to relate an episode of a trivial disagreement between Mr. P and his older son, by then a university student, who offered what the older man considered a boorish answer. Without batting an eye, he slapped the face of his grown up son and did not think that he was abusive or had trespassed the limits of propriety. I shudder to think how many charges of abuse such behavior would engender nowadays, in our so different times.

There was a footnote to Bobby's ill-timed arrival; besides inconveniencing his parents, he greatly embarrassed his only brother. On that day, Henry returned from school, where he had been teased and taunted about the exceptionally late fertility of his parents. He placed a perfunctory kiss on his mother's cheek and quipped, "Congratulations, Mother, did you really need all this and, if so, why?" The salutation is quoted verbatim; his brother oozed caustic acrimony in relation to the untimely addition. Clearly, such feelings did not bode well for future fraternal ties.

There were no enthusiasts applauding his belated arrival, but these questions notwithstanding, Bobby grew and developed well. He became a rather lonely wolf, frequently pugnacious and moody. His parents had poor tolerance for his stubborn antics, his roguery, all to attract attention. He reached a stage of rebellion long before his teens and relished annoying his elders at every opportunity.

School was no joy for Bobby. He was not interested and did not excel in any of the compulsory subjects, nor was he at his best behavior while attending lectures. He used every opportunity to cut classes, ignore assignments and generally sabotage all activities related to school. Playing the truant was risky business, for occasionally the school would inform his father, and then all hell broke loose. The old man, faithful to his disciplinarian philosophy, would chastise the boy mercilessly. This educational method did little to enhance Bobby's affection for his father.

Bobby's growing up under the clouds of such a solitary, rigid and punishing atmosphere resulted, perhaps not unexpectedly, in a distrustful man. He maintained few close friendships, trusting only in his own cunning, and although he loathed his father, he emulated, perhaps subconsciously, his abrupt, impetuous conduct and manner. He pulled pranks, mainly on adults, relishing in shocking and frightening them.

He shared with me one such practical joke, which struck me as childish and silly, but which to Bobby, even with the distance of years, seemed uproariously funny. This anecdotal event took place on Yom Kippur, the highest, most solemn day of the Jewish calendar. On this day Jews fast strictly, engage in soul searching, rededicate themselves to repentance, and direct their thoughts to atonement and self-improvement. Bobby chose this awe-inspiring religious highlight for a playful jest. He persuaded several of his non-Jewish classmates to join him at sunset, right as the congregation was leaving the service. They took up positions in full view of the worshippers, each ostentatiously devouring a large wiener wrapped in a bun. The shock and disgust of the constituents, mirrored in their faces, entertained the young rebels. The crowd of the faithful interpreted the display of gluttony as a sign of disrespect and mockery. Bobby and his pals scored a direct hit which, of course, met with the disapproval of his infuriated parents.

Nineteen-thirty-nine marked the outbreak of the Second World War, but on a more personal level, it also initiated Jewish deportation from Bobby's hometown of Ostrava. Immediately upon the completion of the military campaign against Poland, the German administrators of the Protectorate, inspired by Hitler's rabid anti-Semitism, conceived the idea of expelling all the Jews to Poland. To that end the Jewish community of Ostrava was ordered to provide volunteers for a retraining camp somewhere nearby in Poland. Men ranging in age from seventeen to seventy were encouraged to come forward, and when the initiative fell on deaf ears, the needed numbers were simply rounded up and forcefully brought to the local riding school. Only one concession was offered: The "volunteers" could return home and pack some warm work clothing, blankets, and food for three days. Each man was granted permission to also take 3,000 crowns.

Among those herded to the departure site was Bobby's father, then a man in his mid-fifties. During the lamentable October and November of 1939, three transports of Jewish men were dispatched from Moravska Ostrava to the retraining camp in Nisko, near the river San. All the disseminated falsehood of retraining and resettlement was one of the many hoaxes perpetrated by the Nazis to manipulate their defenseless victims.

Few, if any, of the men who arrived in Nisko were engaged in building barracks. Most were gathered in groups and ordered to run East towards the Russian territory and, to prod them into to faster movement, the Germans first shot in the air and later at the backs of the men running for their lives. Even so, a great number survived. Some returned to Ostrava, mainly those who left families and were tormented by anxiety of their loved ones' peril.

Those who reached Soviet territory were only too happy to turn their backs on the Nazi fury. Most of these men were single, but even the occasional family man was relieved to be in Soviet captivity, which though rough, offered a greater margin of safety and probability of survival than the volcanic denouement shattering the Czech lands. The conditions prevailing in the Russian prisoner of war camps were by far less perilous to life and limb than those under German rule.

Bobby's father fled Nisko and reached Russian-held territory, but then became overwhelmed with concern for his family and decided to return. He had serious doubts about his wife's abilities to cope without his guidance. After all, he reasoned, she was never on her own, even in the good old days, let alone when every move was dangerous and potentially lethal. In just a few months, this decision proved fatal, even though at the time it gladdened his wife.

The domineering and autocratic disposition of the men of his generation had another side. They shouldered full responsibility for their families; their women were ill-equipped by the many years of reliance on their husbands' decision-making, unprepared and untrained in independent thought and self-help. One afternoon, an unexpected knock on the door summoned Ella, who cautiously glanced through the peephole. Within seconds she turned ecstatically happy, for the silhouette in the hall was that of her husband. She threw all caution to the wind and screamed for joy. She quickly pulled in a much thinner version of her husband, who appeared sound, none the worse for his ordeal. For a short while life returned to normal, if only barely so.

Mr. P could hardly believe the changes which had taken place during his relatively short absence from Ostrava. The conditions governing Jewish life had deteriorated markedly. The day-by-day existence was encumbered by many restrictions, prohibitions and orders, which curbed the mobility and crippled the social, financial and work life of every Jew.

Bobby hated all these restrictions, except one; he welcomed the law banning Jewish youngsters from all centers of learning. He felt liberated from the hated school attendance, where he only found trouble. He disliked most of the material, achieved below average grades and was never able to excel academically or socially. No subject tickled his fancy, and he could muster no will power to apply himself more diligently.

His results channeled him into vocational training, but that, too, was not Bobby's idea of a professional pursuit. He lacked manual dexterity and curiosity for any of the offered courses. He remained undecided, and just then the order came to expel all Jewish students irrespective of their scholastic standing. Bobby was relieved; the need to make up his mind was removed from his shoulders, and he was free to leave that seemingly dead-end of school attendance. He had only one regret on leaving school; he had to abandon his place on the school soccer team, where he excelled and was much appreciated. He knew he would miss the only activity and sport he loved, and there was no substitute. The Jewish community had no comparable team to join.

Bobby also found it exceedingly difficult to adjust to the new ordinance, which made it compulsory for every Jew to wear the Star of David, the yellow six-pointed star stitched on his outer garment. He felt humiliated, like a branded cow. He would occasionally hide or remove the hideous, much-hated yellow patch, needless to say at enormous risk to himself and his parents. The Nazis always punished collectively; the family was included along with the culprit, irrespective of their awareness of the out-of-line transgressor.

Nevertheless, in time Bobby began to mature, his insubordination and defiance giving way to more adult behavior. He came to understand that the Germans were a different kettle of fish than his strict father, and that the consequences of his mutinous conduct would hardly be settled with one of his father's notorious punishments. He made up his mind, and lived up to it, that he would never become embroiled in a serious conflict with the regulations enforced by the Nazis.

Mr. P. made some half-hearted attempts to arrange an apprenticeship for his son with one of the local electricians, but all for naught. The Jewish artisans were winding down their businesses, and their Gentile colleagues had to obey the ban on hiring any Jew.

Bobby loathed the entire stretch of time from September 1939 through 1941. Time stood still. It felt like one unbroken span of boredom, an endless time of empty idleness. In the fall of 1939, his father had vanished, swept away by the tidal waves of transports to Nisko. Bobby was relieved. He did not pretend to miss his father, his rigid rules and harsh inflexibility. The only shadow which his father's absence cast on his newly gained freedom was the obvious unhappiness and lack of independence of his mother, who could not learn to cope with life without the powerful presence of her resolute husband.

It goes without saying that the sudden return of Mr. P. gave rise to discrepant feelings. While Bobby felt the old feeling of oppressive dominance, his mother was elated, happy to be reunited with her partner. The parents discussed daily, in hushed tones, the dimming prospects for an escape from Europe. Their elder son had completed his education some time ago and somehow, with a stroke of luck, he found employment with the local Jewish community.

The P.'s, like most other Jewish families, were at their wit's end. No one knew of an escape route or foreign sponsors to help the family flee the perilous trap of Europe. The devious Nazis designed a system that kept Jews on a frenzied run; mindful of the ever-expanding restrictions, they had to carefully hustle for food to supplement the inadequate rations allotted to Jews. Even the most basic maintenance made greater demands on their time and energy.

In later days, Bobby would reminisce about this period of his life, and he would rather caustically quote his father, whose wisdom in the P. household was never officially contested, as saying, "The Germans are an educated, cultured nation. This strange Nazi anomaly will vanish from the otherwise illustrious history of this most avant-garde nation of Europe. After all, a nation who gave to the world men like Beethoven, Brahms, Kant, Nietzsche and many others is not comprised of barbarians who will perpetrate atrocities, infuse dread and sink to the level of common criminals. The Nazi aberration will blow over soon and the order loving, respectable German nation will bring into line these initial excesses."

Bobby's lips would curl in an ironic sneer while paraphrasing his progenitor. Meanwhile the world seemed comprised of nations who thirsted for Jewish blood and those who slammed their gates shut, preventing escape out of harm's way. With passing time little changed, the atmosphere remained tense, filled with deprivations, each day looming with obvious signs of the impending apocalypse.

Before the turn of the Jews from Moravska Ostrava came, their brethren from Prague and adjacent localities began their circuitous journey to their deaths. The first transports went to Poland, Belarus, and Ukraine; all these regions were dreaded and the camps there were rumored to be incompatible with preservation of life. Then, to marked relief, a new place, Theresienstadt, was designated as a camp for evacuated Jews. Once a family was picked out for deportation, they were duly notified and instructed which items they were allowed to take with them for the foreordained change.

The deadline for the Jews of Ostrava was set for September in 1942. The first circle of hell, or rather the first stopover, was in Theresienstadt.

The deportees from Ostrava were subject to the same stringent rules as the rest of the Jews targeted for removal from society: 50 kilograms (120 pounds) of personal belongings, a blanket and a mess kit. That was all they could keep back from their past lives. All else was to be left behind, confiscated by the occupiers and their helpers. Bobby and his parents carefully planned and packed all they could take, only to have most of it taken away right upon their entry to Theresienstadt, the anteroom to hell.

The family was immediately split and sent in three different directions. Mr. P senior was ordered to a large, shabby and unclean barracks which housed men of all ages. Ella was assigned a bunk in a wooden shack, home to several dozen women.

Bobby was more fortunate, only he did not define his right to sleep in the boys' home as a special privilege. He had just the opposite reaction. He ascribed his forced lodging with other teenagers to bad luck. At the time of his deportation, he was just fourteen years of age, and any inmate younger then sixteen had to live in the youth home. This offered many advantages, because the incumbent Elder of the Jews, Jacob Edelstein, decided that no matter how gigantic the Jewish catastrophe, it had to be mitigated for the youth, the potential future, should there be one for the Jews.

All distributions and allocations were carried out in compliance with this conviction. Not only were the young ones housed in the best available barracks, but also their clothing, blankets and, most importantly, their food rations were markedly augmented at the expense of the older, doomed and written-off inmates. Although the children eventually became, in due course of events, malnourished, they suffered less intensely from hunger, cold and disease. The little medicine that was smuggled into the camp was immediately earmarked to the home of the youth.

For as long as the Jewish children were cared for by Jewish attendants, valiant efforts were mounted to prolong their survival and delay their deaths for as long as possible. The caregivers took great pains to assist in their physical development and also paid attention to their schooling, not to mention the attempts to simulate somehow an almost normal environment. The incarcerated youngsters were provided with rudimentary instruction, mainly in reading, singing and drawing. The Germans caught on quickly enough, turning their hatred towards the Jewish future, designing a program for extinction to blot out any potential continued Jewish existence.

Upon arrival, Bobby was brought under one roof with other teenagers his age. At first it hardly seemed all that bad to him, in spite of his constant, ravenous hunger; indeed, he still thought that the worst was the boredom of this uninspired camp existence.

As we know, from his past days, Bobby always hated scholastic instruction. In Theresienstadt, the youth had to study as if in regular classes. Though the Nazi overlords forbade it, the appointed instructors followed almost normal classroom teaching materials. All youngsters had to study, draw, sing and become proficient in material pertinent to their age and levels of advancement. They were being prepared for a future productive life, which most never lived to reach, losing their lives in the gas chambers of Auschwitz. The Elder of the Jews was not a fool. He knew well enough that only a fraction might live to see the new dawn, but it was on these few he pinned his hopes, to carry the banner of the Jewish nation and religion. He had no illusions that he or his wife and 13-year-old son had any chance of slipping through the cracks, but he insisted that his boy study along with the rest of the youthful prisoners.

It was an ironclad policy of the Germans to execute every incumbent Elder and his Council after several months of service. The Nazis feared that any Jewish official whose term allowed sufficient time to learn the mechanics of the German implementation of the Nazi "final solution" would be a threat. These camp administrators might weaken and spill the beans, divulging to the inmates their inevitable fate.

The Nazis dreaded an insurrection by the inmates and believed that its prevention could be achieved by removing the leadership, the Councils, on a regular basis. To this end, in all camps their terms were limited; they were usually accused of some trivial infraction, followed by their immediate dispatch, with their families, to the gas chambers. Their fate was a given. The only variable was the time they would serve as Council members. The Nazis determined the date for their disposal, but in the interim they lived in better conditions than the rest of us. They did not starve, were better housed and clothed, and wielded, for a brief moment in history, enormous power over the life and death of their fellow inmates.

Meanwhile back in the boys' barracks in Theresienstadt, Bobby remained one of the least involved students, but his insolence did not land him in hot water. The youth home in the camp did not have rigid discipline; it only had a program of scholastic subjects and required regular attendance. In Bobby's case, it was largely a passive presence only. The teachers and instructors of the home were more concerned with the emotional well-being of their charges, and they mounted valiant efforts to lift their spirits.

Singing was much encouraged, plays rehearsed, all with uplifting content. Even a children's opera was studied, just to divert and occupy the minds of the incarcerated, doomed youth. In all those plays Good ultimately defeated Evil, suggesting that in the end all would be set right again.

Slowly, Bobby began to feel more comfortable and began to participate in the life of the home. For the first time in his life, he began to feel that he was accepted and belonged to the large group of youth. Cautiously and slowly he stretched out feelers to form relationships. With time, he made a few friends, and he was elated; he felt included and liked. The continuous company of peers was a joyous revelation to a boy who never had a real friend and was accustomed to fitting into the company of adults in a highly rigid, structured home. Bobby spent a few happy months in this setting, quickly maturing in the harmony hitherto unknown to him, denied to him during his rebellious, tempestuous formative years.

Bobby would occasionally call on his mother in her barracks, but would rarely visit his father. He disliked those meetings; he could not help but notice how swiftly they were deteriorating, showing the signs of wear and tear of an elderly camp inmate. Both lost a great deal of weight, but it was more striking on his father, who in the pre-war days was a hefty man with a protruding paunch. His skin hung loosely around his one-time stout torso, and with his withered appearance, his overbearing attitude vanished. He looked sad and skinny. His once well-groomed, tailored elegance was suspended around his frame, loosely hanging around his midriff, somehow pointing to the dramatic changes, making him appear sad and pathetic. His pants were held up with a string, which could easily have been wrapped twice around his shrunken waist.

Gone too, was his imperial manner, his self-assurance, which usually bordered on arrogance. The unapproachable, conceited man was replaced by a pathetic apparition, which Bobby liked much better. He could not help but notice that his tone became conversational, not commanding, almost addressing Bobby like an equal. This was totally new and only a short while ago quite unimaginable.

Bobby had never had this experience with his father before. It came as a surprise that he felt almost fond of his changed father, in spite of their past painful kinship. Suddenly, Bobby was sorry for all those years of discord, the fear and disdain he once felt for his father. Finding profound empathy for the defeated and worn man, he saw him in a different light. Cut down to size by suffering, Mr. P looked and sounded like an ordinary inmate.

Even more painful to Bobby was the sight of his mother, who seemed to be fading into thin air, losing weight, strength and the will to live. She was no longer the well-groomed, elegant lady. Ella was unkempt and deeply depressed due to her separation from her husband, her "pillar of her strength." Only around him did she seem less apathetic and heartbroken.

Moreover, she was not accustomed to any deprivation. She had been taken care of and provided for her entire life and, as a result, she developed a submissive personality and could hardly be expected to emancipate herself now that she was in her fifties. She did not have the courage to struggle and improve her lot; she was totally lost in such rough, primitive conditions.

Bobby's older brother was also deported to Theresienstadt and from there, further East sometime in December 1943. The family received only one card written in his hand, but the reassuring content seemed strange, definitely not in his usual style, more as if composed or dictated by someone else.

Bobby found a niche for himself in this new environment in Theresienstadt. This situation did not change until May of 1944, when his parents were ordered to a transport leaving Theresienstadt to the East. An unalterable German policy stated that the entire family was to leave together; therefore, Bobby was included in the deportation order.

In May, one of the loveliest months in central Europe, the three remaining members of the P. family were gathered in the barracks dubbed the "sluice," behind which the railway tracks ran. There stood the empty train, a row of boxcars, into which they jammed the deportees. All proceeded with a Swiss-clock precision, smoothly and expeditiously.

The family P. embarked on one of those gruesome journeys endured by so many Jews before and after. Conditions in the boxcars were appalling. Bobby estimated that there were about 80 people to a car, squeezed into a narrow, dark space, unlit and airless. There was a small opening high on the wall enclosed by grilles, but the amount of air penetrating was completely insufficient. They could stand only in an upright position, body pressed to body, with no space to sit; before long, some fainted, swaying lifelessly. The journey, lasting two days and nights, was a continuous nightmare, which Bobby tried unsuccessfully to erase from his memory. During the entire time, no food or water was provided.

Terribly embarrassing was the need to relieve oneself; each car was equipped with one pail in a corner, which overflowed within hours of their journey's start. As they set out on their route, their physical needs caused mortification to the still-civilized people, who had not yet shaken off their social taboos. At first, everyone trying to make the complex way to the pail came to an end discreetly, but with passing time and growing agony, most consideration was abandoned. Most feelings were blunted; no longer did any care about humiliation. Soon those attempting to make their way to the pail were regarded with wrath, hostility and disdain. Some time later, they were cursed as if they were the reason for the wretchedness in the wagon.

The Nazis permitted them to empty the pail only on the occasional stops, letting one man near the door of the car pour out the contents. The stench emanating from the excrement-covered, unwashed bodies, and a few already decomposing corpses, aggravated the stifling atmosphere, making breathing nearly impossible.

The crammed-in men and women were nervous and apprehensive. Nobody dared speculate what waited at the end of such a road. No man could possibly design such torment; it was the handiwork of the devil himself. Bobby's parents, like most of the older folk, did poorly. Mr. P leaned on the next man, stooped, near collapse, and his wife seemed impassive, at times perhaps not quite conscious. On occasion, she would complain about being thirsty, but mostly her eyes were shut, her head hanging as if near death. Bobby did not disturb her. He thought she was better off when removed from this reality.

After what seemed an eternity, the train came to an abrupt halt. It had to be late evening or night, because when the sealed doors of the car were flung open, the first image to hit Bobby's eyes was a brightly lit rail platform, filled with frenzied activity. He squinted; two days in near darkness made it difficult to discern into the piercing illumination stabbing his eyes with a sharp discomfort.

Gradually his eyes became accustomed, and he distinguished moving shadows running to and fro, in an area barricaded by uniformed SS soldiers, armed with submachine guns. Some of the SS restrained snarling Alsatian German shepherds. Strange individuals dressed in the most peculiar fashion puzzled Bobby. Never before had he seen these prisoners' garb of striped trousers and tunics, topped by similarly striped caps, which they snatched down every single time they passed an SS man. These zebra-like people were in a hectic frenzy performing some task.

No sooner were the doors of the cars opened, than orders were shouted for all to exit on the double. The hoarse voices yelled orders to leave all suitcases behind. Those, according to the loudspeakers, would be delivered later at the new camp. In addition, the dead and dying were to be left as they lay; they, too, would be transferred later. The newly arrived gathered their last ounce of energy and rushed out. No matter how hard they tried, they were never fast enough for the impatient SS, who beat them, prodding them to ever-faster speeds.

Amidst the pandemonium, Bobby tried to help his parents out of the car and for his filial efforts he was awarded a few sharp blows to his neck by a passing German officer. Bobby remembered a warning, which he received from a friend, when still in Theresienstadt. The unsolicited advice, which at the time made no sense, was never to admit that he was less than 16 years of age and always to claim to be an apprentice to a locksmith or a carpenter. The same man cautioned him never to accept a ride on any truck offered by the Nazis and always join those who could

march, irrespective of the distance. Moreover, it was a good policy
to stay away from the sick, older folks or children. Even if unwell,
he should vigorously deny all suspicions that he was not in perfect
health.

While in Theresienstadt, Bobby listened to these suggestions
and thought the whispering man to be slightly deranged, confused
by his lengthy incarceration. Now, on the brightly lit platform in
Auschwitz, it all began to make a horrible, nightmarish sense. For
Auschwitz was a unique hell, where one had to adapt quickly to
incomprehensible rules in order to live just a little longer.

As these thoughts flashed through Bobby's mind, he was
pushed into a forming column that moved slowly ahead. Bobby
maneuvered deftly, joining his parents, who moved in a daze,
paralyzed by the shocking experience. He gently prodded them to
move along, lest some SS man beat them for falling behind the
milling crowd. At the end of this long queue of human misery
stood an SS man, holding a short riding crop in his white-gloved
hand. He motioned to the majority of people passing in front of
him to move to the right side and only on a rare occasion, he
would pause, look at some young person, and ask a question.
Infrequently, he would point his crop to the left where a small
group of relatively good-looking young individuals waited.

Unexpectedly Bobby picked up some Czech words. He
pricked up his ears and sure enough, the whisper came from one of
the zebra-like men, scampering around. Bobby perked up and
heard as the man hissed quickly and almost silently, "Say that you
are eighteen years old and a construction worker." Before Bobby
could make out a face, the man was gone, engulfed by the teeming
sea of people crowding the ramp.

The task of the inmates responsible for the orderly movement
of the newly arrived was all but impossible. The exhausted people
barely staggered along, stepping over the bodies of those freshly
fallen, left for the time being on the platform. The SS men
screamed at the top of their hoarse voices, instructing those unable
to walk to step aside. All who could not walk would be motored to
the camp proper. Bobby caught sight of a few trucks parked
nearby, marked with insignia of the Red Cross. The sight alone
infused some hope; perhaps the humanitarian organization, the

Red Cross, took care of the feeble and old. Nevertheless, the lingering warnings made him suspicious and cautioned him not to be gullible.

Deeply worried, Bobby decided to follow the admonitions from Theresienstadt and the anonymous zebra. Additionally, Bobby whispered almost inaudibly to his father, "Dad, tell him that you are a construction worker and forty years old." Mr. P gave him a look of disbelief; was his son stark raving mad? He did not merit the advice with a comment; he never uttered as much as a word in reply.

The long queue advanced slowly; before long, Bobby could discern the silhouette of an SS man at the end of the line. Bobby was struck by the marked contrast of the immaculately attired SS man and the disheveled prisoners passing by for his assessment. He was positively ill when he compared his appearance to the SS man's smart, clean uniform with its razor sharp creases, the shiny buttons on his tunic, the high boots polished to a radiant luster all complimented by snow white gloves. All in all, the SS man was an example of the perfectly groomed officer, whose immaculate exterior only emphasized the wretched he was dividing into two groups.

The much larger group on the right consisted mainly of older folk, women, children and many sick, barely standing. The others on the left were a few young men and women, who, though grimy, seemed more vigorous and sound. Bobby knew that the moment of truth had arrived for him. Though an unbeliever, at that moment he sent a fervent prayer to the Supreme Ruler, who had brought him to this evil place. He stood face to face with the officer, who was to pass judgment on him: Death now, or life for a little while. If only he could be deemed promising material for forced labor. Later someone told Bobby that the dapper SS man was Dr. Mengele, a medical doctor, adding a new dimension to the German understanding and application of the Hippocratic Oath.

The officer glanced briefly at Mr. and Mrs. P and, without batting an eye, pointed his riding crop to the right. When Bobby's turn came, the boy stopped breathing briefly. The smartly dressed officer paused, as he looked Bobby over. Then he barked a curt question: "How old are you?" Bobby replied in a firm voice, stretching the truth, "I am 18 years of age, sir." Bobby hoped that his marginal command of the German language, enunciated with a marked Czech accent, did not offend the sensibilities of the Nazi officer. However, clearly he did well, because the next question followed on the heels of the first query: "Do you have a skill?" Bobby again replied with as firm a voice he could muster, "I am a construction worker, sir."

There was a pause, which to Bobby seemed to last an eternity. Bobby stood there concentrating on controlling a tremor, which threatened to become obvious. Bobby wanted to believe that his rather sturdy physique provided the edge, convincing the Nazi that he was a potentially useful cog in the faltering German war machine.

The officer glanced again at Bobby and motioned to the left. In later times, Bobby would say that no one truly knows what a reprieve feels like, unless he has awaited a death verdict and been given a last minute stay.

Bobby breathed an almost audible sigh of relief and with a few smart steps joined the small, silent group attentively watching the unfolding drama. Not a word was uttered, most were in shock trying to make some sense of their feelings in this infernal experience. Bobby was searching for his parents' faces, but they were drowned out by the steadily growing crowd of men, women and children who did not pass the scrutiny of the dapper doctor. Then selection ended, and all those on the right were ordered to climb on the waiting lorries with the comforting Red Cross signs. The impatient SS screamed for faster speed, prompting the zebra inmates to ever-rising brutality as they recklessly tossed prisoners, just to fill the truck and have it moving to its final destination.

Bobby felt sick, but luckily his group was ordered to march toward the camp. Before long, they could see the outline of barracks and huts rising in the twilight in front of them. The men and women were separated, and each group was ordered into one of the barracks, where they were instructed to sit on wooden benches. Immediately some men pounced upon them and shaved their heads. The procedure was quick, rough, and left most scalps with bleeding cuts and scratches.

Following this initiation, they were ordered to undress and run into some showers. Most held their breath again; all were apprehensive, shivering with fear and the cold of the night. When the faucets began to drip water, at times hot and then ice cold, they felt like they'd struck gold.

The shower over with, the screaming guards and their assisting inmates commanded the new arrivals into the adjacent room, where other inmates, also clad in striped uniforms, tattooed numbers on their forearms. They were dexterous and worked rapidly, immersed in total silence. They never paused or erred, etching the tattooed numbers on the newly arrived at record speed. Then they were sent to another hall where other inmates threw dirty, mostly striped, torn pants and tops at them. No underwear was issued, and as for footwear, they were given wooden clogs, with no regard to size.

Then another order echoed through the night, "Run to the nearby barracks and stay inside till ordered otherwise."

They received no food or water, but in the course of this night, few cared for food. They knew that they stood at the threshold of leaving this world. Bobby was in a state of shock, numb. He could not feel hunger, thirst or revulsion at his present state. He felt nothing, no pity or concern for his parents who, he thought, were suffering a similar or worse fate. He was drained, empty, functioned like an automaton, responding to orders and hoping to remain unnoticed.

Soon they fell asleep, but in spite of their exhaustion, the night was a restless one. A few squabbles broke out between the tightly crammed men, for when one man moved the rest had to turn as well. However, they were so tired that these skirmishes quickly fizzled, and all fell silent again. Bobby, who never mastered the art of learning in school, proved to be an outstanding student of survival and of the rules of this one particular vicious jungle, where only the fastest and most ruthless stood a chance. The Nazi mandated rules demanded that every man be for himself, be resourceful and imaginative, using any means for survival.

The barracks were locked up for the night and again, the men had only one pail to relieve themselves. A man trying to wend his way to the pail had to step over crowded men lying helter-skelter, in deep sleep. If he stepped on someone, and it was likely that he would, it triggered a furious response. Sleep was the most cherished time in any camp, not only because it offered rest and replenished energies but, most importantly, it released the inmate temporarily from the pain of starvation, illness, awareness, and the ever-present threat of death. It numbed all fears, sometimes even bringing a pleasant dream. Anyone who interrupted the only state of bliss the inmates knew was loathed and hated, though it was understood to be an irrational emotion. They all knew that the one trying to make it to the pail had run out of options, but if the man woke up another or added to the foul odor, fights could flare up quickly.

However, none of these altercations got out of hand. The inmates knew only too well that they must remain quiet, for if they were to wake up the Kapo, whose cozy little abode was adjacent, all hell would break loose. The Kapo shared his little room with his boy-lover, a pampered brat who loved to egg on his master to kill some of those disturbing the night. If the Kapo became upset, he would rush at the men and club several to death.

The night seemed young when the shrill sound of a whistle woke up the tired men. In spite of their fatigue, they became instantly alert, listening to the curt, sharply barked orders. They were to step out in orderly columns to their first roll call. The Kapo and his assistants counted the lined-up men, adding to it the number of those who had died during the night and those too ill to move and remaining on the floor of the barracks.

Once the number of inmates correlated, the men were permitted to return inside. Most attempted to reach the few faucets dripping cold water, to wash the sleep and grime off their tired faces. Access to water was accompanied by squabbles, shouts, and blows liberally dispensed by the Kapo, who seemed in a filthy mood. Talking was forbidden for the entire day, and during roll call absolute silence was mandatory. Failure to comply was punishable by such a severe beating that the offender was not likely to rise again.

After roll call, the inmates received some tepid water called "tea," and the working commandos began to fall into formations and march off through the darkness to their daily twelve-hour shift. They marched in smart columns in the direction of the gates, closely supervised and often brutalized by the Kapos and their stooges.

Near the gates was a platform from which the camp's orchestra accompanied the marching units with pleasing tunes, popular songs and smart marches. The belted out sounds struck Bobby as bizarre, out of place in Auschwitz, where harmony and music were in sharp, jarring clash with all around. The stench, the knee-deep mud, the shouted orders, the exhausted inmates, the lack of food: This was the real camp in which melodious sounds were out of place. In Auschwitz's ugly pandemonium, nice music was almost offensive

Bobby, along with those others who had arrived the previous night, remained behind, waiting for their work assignments. Meanwhile they were ordered to spotlessly scrub the floors and clean the barracks. This assignment completed, they were sent to clean the latrines, which were always in a horrid state.

Bobby was convinced that this duty would certainly kill him. To his surprise, he noticed that the old-timers, the camp-wise veterans, did not seem to object to this revolting task. To the contrary, they appeared willing to go.

Before long, Bobby understood their reasons for this surprising cooperation. The members of the cleaning commando were issued their work tools, buckets, brushes and rags, and off they marched to the most disgusting dumps imaginable. Most of the inmates suffered with severe cases of diarrhea caused by cholera, salmonella and other pathogens, hardly ever reaching the outhouse in time, leaving the toilets unbelievably soiled. Nevertheless, this place had one priceless advantage. Because of the nauseating stench, the inmates remained generally unsupervised, able to talk openly without fear of punishment by the Kapos; few of them had strong enough stomachs and zeal to approach the repugnant latrines. It was here, and here alone, where the inmates exchanged information, bartered if they had anything, or shared pertinent news about their and other inmates' fates.

Bobby burned with curiosity about Auschwitz. Soon he found an old-timer who was included in the cleaning commando just for this one day. He was too ill to join his own work group, but at the same time could not risk staying behind in the barracks. Those who remained were quickly dispatched to the infirmary, where they received a slug of phenol injected directly into their hearts. The *Blockaelteste*, an old acquaintance of the sick man, wanted to help, and transferred him temporarily to an inside commando.

The man was a veritable treasure trove of information. Bobby immediately wanted to know what happened to those selected to the right side. To say that the reply startled Bobby is an understatement. The man first looked searchingly into Bobby's eyes, finding out if Bobby was a "greener" or if he might be a troublemaker. Soon he guessed that Bobby was a beginner and therefore needed to be clued in. He turned his eyes skyward and whispered, "They are all up there, with God."

Bobby thought he was dealing with a lunatic. The man had to be stark, raving mad; how could anyone murder thousands of people within a few hours? Was there perhaps another camp in the vicinity, where those no longer able to work were taken? The man continued to stare into Bobby's eyes and motioned with his chin in the direction of the tall chimneys. He whispered furtively, "There, see, they all went through the chimney." Bobby listened, shocked and defeated, unable to make sense of this information.

Unconvinced, he asked another old-timer, who was busy exchanging a cigarette for a piece of bread. Bobby waited in the wings till the clinching of the deal, and then he put the same question to the other man, just to receive the same answer, only in very cut and dried words. All those deemed unfit for work were killed in gas chambers on the night of their arrival. The lethal agent used was Cyclon B, a well-known insecticide. Once dead, the bodies were burned in the adjacent crematories. The man pointed toward the black, bellowing rings of smoke, rising to the skies, forming dark clouds and saturating the entire compound with the smell of burning flesh.

This sight and stench seared the truth into Bobby's mind. Suddenly it was clear; it dawned on him that both his parents lost their lives the very first night upon arrival in Auschwitz. All in him rose in anguish against this terrible injustice, but he remained silent, gnashed his teeth and fought back tears, anger, and fury. For a moment all became blurred, he did not feel his hunger or his parching thirst, and was oblivious to the disgust of the outhouse. In that moment, all he could think of were his parents, who, as the slang in Auschwitz had it, "went through the chimney."

He stood there like the biblical pillar of salt, when the veteran inmate noticed and took pity on the shocked youngster. The man watched Bobby, while pretending to ferociously shovel the piles of human waste. He maneuvered himself near Bobby and ordered him to pull himself together immediately, unless he wanted to follow his parents right now.

For good measure, he offered another piece of important advice. Bobby should comply willingly with all orders, as quickly as possible, for the Germans and the Kapos had a time fetish. Nothing was ever done well or fast enough, regardless of how much the inmates tried to please their tormentors.

The man continued to show Bobby the best techniques to avoid or minimize the savage blows meted out by the barrack's Kapo. All Kapos, the man said, had to exhibit brutality. That was expected and ordered by the Nazis, but some exceeded the call of duty, bringing brutality to new heights, sadistically torturing the inmates and enjoying the savagery of inflicting pain and murder at will. Most of them were career criminals, who had spent many years behind bars. They were murderers on the loose, licensed to kill, placed in positions of authority to practice their trade. They were loose cannons that were praised by and scored points with the Nazis for their brutality.

Bobby was warned about the Kapos who competed not only in the number of Jews murdered, but also by perfecting their techniques. According to the older inmate, one of the cruel Kapos prided himself on being able to slay a man with a single blow.

If all this was not bad enough, the man warned Bobby about the periodic selections, usually taking place during roll call or inside the barracks. These aimed to weed out the weak and ill, no longer useful for labor, and therefore to be expedited through "the chimneys." As the man paused to catch his breath, Bobby, now somewhat recovered, managed to ask a question: "Who are the men in the striped uniforms, so busy running on the platform?" His mentor answered that these men were members of the commando responsible for clearing and processing the newly arrived. They were forbidden to utter as much as a word to the novices of Auschwitz about the fate awaiting them. If caught whispering, they would be taken behind the train, out of eyesight of the newly arrived and executed with a single bullet to the base of the skull.

Suddenly, Bobby realized that the man, a complete stranger, who had whispered the answers best to give to the SS officer, had risked his life for him. In the bedlam of the crazed crowd, he never saw his face; he never would be able to thank him for his life-saving words. Bobby, the quick study on survival, understood the value of the latrine commando.

The last piece of advice came in the form of an urgent admonition: "If you get a chance to volunteer for an assignment in another labor camp, by all means do so. Leave this death pit, if you can! The next camp may not be much better, but no place on earth spells greater danger than Auschwitz."

Bobby discreetly began to search for a way out. He heard of work with the Buna commando, where the inmates toiled on a construction project. However, Buna was a satellite of Auschwitz, and rumors were that Buna was even worse. Bobby knew very well that a wise inmate must listen closely to the grapevine. In Buna, the backbreaking drudgery was accompanied by brutal beatings and frequent killings by a particularly cruel group of Kapos. The starvation diet did not differ from the one in Theresienstadt or Auschwitz and, in addition, cholera contaminated the water in Buna. Many thirsty inmates drank the infested waters and died a quick, spasm-filled, painful death. Bobby's source stated that the average time a prisoner survived in any of the Buna commandos was one to two weeks at the outside.

Another dubious option was re-assignment to Auschwitz's industrial complex of "Monowitz," where the prisoners toiled for the giant military factories of "Krupp,", "I/G Farben," "Siemens" or "Herman Goering" industries. Even if the prospects there seemed slightly more opportune, no one was recruiting at the time and according to hearsay, conditions there were not much better. Workers were kept on a starvation diet and were quickly dropping off, like flies, due to illnesses caused by malnutrition. They were subject to frequent screening and if any physical defect was discovered, they were marked for a phenol injection. This was another shock for Bobby, but he no longer dismissed anything as unbelievable; no scenario was too outlandish to come to pass in Auschwitz.

With the information about the injections, Bobby received another warning: Never go to sickbay—the *"Revier."* Never report to be ill, for the Kapo would note his number and send him to the *Revier.* The only real purpose of this facility was to kill patients with a slug of phenol. Before long Bobby noticed that immediately after roll call, numbers were read and responders were marched off to sick bay, where "Dr. Klehr" injected phenol into their hearts, killing them instantly.

Dr. Klehr was not a physician. He was a habitual criminal, who donned a white coat to assume a physician's appearance. Inmates assigned to help in the sick bay recounted terrible stories of people fighting against the procedure, all to no avail. Dr. Klehr always had numerous men around to lend a hand and subdue the poor devil, locked in a mortal struggle for his already lost life. No one ever received an exemption from the phenol shot. The phenol execution was fast and efficient, reduced to a clinical procedure, sending thousands to their final rest by the experienced hands of "Dr. Klehr."

Bobby absorbed all the lessons carefully. He learned fast, and he learned well. He mastered not only the art of sensing and anticipation, but also to deftly avoid danger, to elude the nets trapping those less vigilant. Always stubborn and recalcitrant, Bobby committed his mind to outlive and escape the Nazi talons, to see the day of liberation. That this was the least probable event did not bother him.

He kept his wits about him, carefully listening to the whispered news, trying to sift the plausible from the tall tales, products of anxious, crazed minds cracking under the anguish few could bear. He did not leave anything to chance; he scouted and surveyed the area, concluding that no escape was possible. For the time being, he lay low, gathering more information and learning.

Nevertheless, Bobby was fortunate; his chance came after all. It happened about two weeks later, right after roll call. As customary, those inmates working outside the camp marched off, accompanied by pleasing tunes belted out by the camp orchestra. Those left behind were ordered to stay put. It was a general command, affecting all men working within the camp. Bobby and the others immediately guessed what this command implied. A selection would follow, either for able-bodied men for another assignment or to weed out the sick and weak. Bobby, stiff with fear, like the rest, stood at attention, waiting for the axe to fall.

Several inmates with green triangles on their tunics stepped to the forefront. This was an ominous sign. Bobby feared the greens. He witnessed a few vicious beatings of Jewish prisoners who for some reason displeased a green or perhaps for no reason at all, only being the wrong man in the wrong place at the wrong time. These sadists vented their malice and indulged their perversities, all to the praise of their German masters. The greens competed for greater violence, akin to a sports event, seeing who could kill more and faster.

Bobby knew well enough the significance of the various colored triangles attached to the upper left side of an inmate's tunic. They indicated the reason for the incarceration. The red color triangle revealed a political prisoner (mostly Communists and their sympathizers), green were the criminals, purple was reserved for Jehovah's Witnesses, black pointed to shiftless elements (frequently Gypsies), pink was the color for homosexuals, and at the bottom of all, deemed the scum on earth, were those marked with yellow triangles: the Jews. If it happened that the Jew also qualified simultaneously for another group as well (e.g., political prisoner), his yellow triangle would be combined with red, indicating the double jeopardy of the man.

In Auschwitz's hierarchy, a green triangle disclosed that its bearer was incarcerated for murder, usually multiple murders. Most were sadists as well, who enjoyed brutalizing, particularly the free-for-all Jews, just for the fun of it.

Bobby had learned to avoid the "greens" on the second day into his stay at Auschwitz. A young boy like him was especially endangered. Many of the greens were homosexuals with a predilection for pedophilia. They would readily pick up a young inmate to take him as a lover, who would then be removed from the rank and file and live in the cubicle with the Kapo. These boys were well fed, but in turn, they had to comply with every sexual perversity their powerful protectors wished. Most of the Kapos were greens, and Bobby abhorred them with a gut-level animosity, holding them in deeper disdain than the Nazis. While the SS routinely killed or selected inmates for death by gas, the greens tortured people for their perverted gratification. Once seized by a green to be a pleasure boy, Bobby thought that death would be a welcomed release.

Hearsay had it that when the Germans prepared a large scale selection, which would result in a high number of prisoners to be gassed, the greens formed the first line, backed by armed SS, just in case of unrest or rioting. Bobby waited, barely breathing, upright and angry beyond belief. How could another man take it upon himself to send others arbitrarily to death, on a whim?

However, Bobby was fortunate on this June morning. The SS singled out some 50 inmates, including Bobby and ordered them to run to the nearby barracks. There, already assembled, were other men, all relatively healthy looking. This was a good omen, hinting that selection was targeting men for hard labor, not for their final curtain call. Bobby was enormously relieved.

The next order sent them to the showers, and they received different prisoners' garb, less torn and dirty, but still no underwear or shoes. They had to do with the wooden clogs, which scraped their skin off, but with no other options, Bobby did the next best thing and bandaged his bleeding, scratched feet, full of bloody blisters with rags and marched off quickly, so as not to miss the distribution of bread allotted for the journey. That proved that they were being transferred to another camp, for inmates destined for gas never received food; the practical Germans did not waste good food on nearly dead Jews. Such frivolity was unacceptable.

Rumors circulated that they were assigned to munitions factories somewhere northwest of Auschwitz. While on the road, they exchanged furtive glances, and, as always, talking was forbidden. Most were glad to leave Auschwitz, nursing cautious hopes that the new camp might be better, providing some chance for survival. Perhaps the fact that the inmates hardly ever had time to pause and think was a blessing.

The Nazis deliberately kept the inmates in a state of frenzy at work, with roll calls, assorted tasks including queuing for food and, as if that were not enough, they would issue an order to exercise, doing push ups until many dropped off dead.

Most of these frantic orders were meant to exhaust the inmates. Nothing made sense, only the lunatic, spastic mad run around had to be maintained. After all, inmates always teetering on the verge of collapse could hardly plot a riot or organize a rebellion.

Just before loading onto the trains, the inmates were ordered to pick up bread, and this time they received a small piece of salami as well. At first, they stared in disbelief at the delicacy, but within seconds, they all gobbled it up. What followed was the routine dispatching of a transport. The Kapos and the SS herded them to the waiting freight cars with the customary shouting and beating. The Kapos and the SS always seemed to run amok, particularly when a transport was either approaching or leaving the compound. Never was an inmate fast or agile enough. Finally, all aboard, the train set into motion.

Bobby was almost happy, as much as any inmate could be; he knew in his heart of hearts that nowhere could conditions be worse than in Auschwitz. Once they all were jammed into the cars, they could take advantage of the slackened supervision and began to whisper. The SS stood guard outside the packed cars, so the perennial ban on talking could not be enforced.

All the inmates shared the dream of escaping the Nazi terror. Only a handful ever succeeded to elude the guards, the highly charged wires, the dogs trained to attack and tear the inmates apart. Few were able to climb over fences and other obstacles to abscond from the world of the doomed. The Germans took impressive time-tested measures to prevent any attempt to escape.

This time the journey was relatively short. Within a night, the train came to a halt, and orders were roared to get out of the wagons on the double. Once outside they formed, almost by reflex, neat columns of five and were commanded to march to some huts, not clearly discernible in the twilight of the fading night. Soon they entered a gate, resembling the one they left behind in Auschwitz, only this one did not carry the ironic logo,

"*Arbeit macht frei*" (work sets you free). They were sent into an empty barracks, equipped with three-tier bunks. Each bed was made up, blankets neatly tucked. The barracks looked much cleaner and neater than those in Auschwitz or Theresienstadt and the air was cleaner; no stench blanketed the place.

In due course, the shrill whistle summoned them for roll call, where a tall, hefty man stepped forward and opened with a speech in a high raspy voice. He told them he was their new Kapo. One look at his neatly pressed tunic disclosed that indeed he was a habitual felon, sporting a green triangle. He told them that they just arrived at the concentration camp Sachsenhousen where, for the time being, they would remain. They would be expected to work for long hours to redeem themselves.

A fleeting thought crossed Bobby's mind: "Toil till death," that was the only redemption the Nazis had in store for Jews. Their new boss droned on and on. They were expected to keep their bunks neat and clean, failure to do so would result in severe punishment of twenty lashes with a cat-o'-nine-tails, commonly used to flog prisoners for any type of infraction.

The presence of the Kapo was intimidating. He certainly did not look like a man one would like to lock horns with. His menacing appearance and tone suggested that he could slay, and perhaps might even enjoy slaying, a man with his bare, mammoth hands.

The briefing continued: They would receive about half a liter of tea every morning, lunch would be brought to their workplace and consist of soup, and in the evening they would receive more tea and some bread. The Kapo told them to set aside half of their daily bread ration for the morning, otherwise they might not be able to get through the day's hard labor. They would need solid food.

He continued his harangue, warning them to keep their bodies clean, dereliction would bring about infestation with lice, which spread typhus, nearly always fatal in the camps. The men were familiar with all of that, but had to stand at attention and listen carefully.

Sachsenhousen had one comforting feature; there were no gas chambers. Death might come by illness, hunger, beating and perhaps, if lucky, by an SS man aiming his gun well. If none of these materialized, there was always the threat of being sent back to Auschwitz, where the gas chambers worked around the clock, always ready to devour the bodies of those who spent their final gasping breaths working for the brutal German war machine.

The Kapo's menacing, blustering tirade seemed endless. He stood ramrod straight with legs wide apart, like some modern-day Caesar, deriving malicious joy at the sight of the cowed and frightened inmates.

At the closing of his speech, delivered in a crude and vulgar German, the Kapo issued another warning. He restated the strictly enforced rule for all inmates. Anyone who stole anything edible from a fellow inmate would be executed on the spot. If not by the violated inmate, who might be too weak, then by the others or the Kapo himself. This was the basic rule in all the camps: Anyone who took food from another was guilty of murder, since no one could survive without their meager daily ration. The execution of the thief would be immediate and fully approved by the Kapo.

Bobby knew the law, since the inmates had put it into place, attempting to bring some order to their jungle life. In spite of this firmly enforced rule, some man would try to steal from the man next to him, particularly if the owner was near death. If caught, other inmates would beat the offender to death. If the inmates could not for some reason kill the culprit without noise or quickly enough, the Kapo would proudly step in, demonstrating his honed expertise in dispatching a human being.

The introductory speech was concluded, and the inmates were sent back to the barracks with the last admonitions to keep their bunks clean and to never talk while at work.

A young chap, a veteran of Sachsenhousen, whispered to Bobby that the camp was near Berlin and by far not the worst of places. Bobby's new acquaintance busied himself removing some invisible speck of dust from under the bunk and in a stifled voice, continued briefing Bobby. He muttered that not far away, in Ravensbrueck, near Mecklenburg, existed another concentration camp, where SS physicians performed medical experiments on Jewish inmates, which were very painful and upon completion, all the victims were killed. The new informant heard it from a

Blockaelteste (an inmate appointed by the Nazis to oversee and supervise an entire group of prisoners' barracks), surely a well-informed man. Sachsenhousen was strictly a slave-labor camp, no medical experimentation or gas installations were operational.

Bobby listened, somewhat reassured, repeating to himself that he must still be on the lookout for an escape hatch, from this "better camp."

Next morning they were ordered to march to the construction site, but the Kapo had no work for them. He ordered them to carry sacks full of stones from a large pile to a far-removed corner at double time. They drudged; hauling the heavy rocks on their backs, sweat running down their faces in shiny rivulets, the soreness building. The blows of the Kapo prodded them to an ever-faster speed, trying to avoid additional pain.

Then, bored by the monotony of the day, he ordered the inmates to form a gauntlet, pick up some branches and beat those having to run between them. After a while, the Kapo ordered a switch. Those who did the beatings had to change places with those who ran. The Kapo seemed amused by his own ingenuity, of how to diversify his day and relieve the boredom.

A shrill sound of a whistle interrupted this circus; it was time for lunch. On cue, the inmates formed an orderly line, each waiting his turn for a ladle of soup. Though all were famished, no one pushed or seemed keen to get ahead. Even a novice in the camp knew that it was best to get one's portion from the bottom of the barrel, where the occasional potato peel or a piece of turnip could be found. The surface layers hardly had any solids; it was mostly tepid liquid. They all were aware that this was the main meal of the day, and a great deal depended on the intake of some nutrients.

Then they were allowed an hour's rest, which to them always seemed much too short. All were convinced that only minutes had elapsed when the high-pitched shriek of the whistle summoned their return.

The afternoon's work consisted of much of the same. Only this time they dragged the stones to the same place from where they had picked them up in the morning. It was clear on that day, and many other later days, that there was no actual work; they had to run and work to please the supervising SS men, who in turn invented something to do to justify their cushy, lucrative and safe jobs.

The SS men cultivated and appreciated the supervisory assignment in concentration camps; such work stood in great contrast to the much-dreaded Russian front, where the Germans were locked in deadly and ferocious combat. (On the Russian Steppes, frozen in the vast, snow-covered plains of the merciless Russian winter, the Germans suffered enormous bloodletting. Just the thought of the Russian front terrified the SS men, whose lives in the camps were like vacations while pretending to be in battlefield conditions. The SS men and their protégés, the Kapos, knew they had to justify their safe and often enriching time in the camps, for their avoidance of the Russian front and hence survival, depended upon it.)

An average working shift in any camp lasted twelve hours, and Sachsenhausen was no exception. Finally, the first day ended, announced by a shrieking sound of the whistle. The inmates fell quickly into formation, ready to return to the camp. In the beginning, most commandos returned complete, only the occasional inmate fell ill and had to be carried back. Later more fainted or died and these, too, were brought back for evening roll call.

When an inmate fell at work, the Kapo would rush to the spot, where the unfortunate lay, and start raining blows till he either succumbed or came to. If the inmate did not get up or die quickly enough, the SS man might choose to get involved. The SS man would motion the Kapo to step back, and the Nazi would shoot the victim at short range.

Bobby concluded that his best chance was not to attract any attention, be inconspicuous and if possible, invisible. Though he never stopped his search for escape, so far he had found no loopholes in the vigilance of the guards. The entire compound was fenced off; the watchtowers were brightly lit and manned by SS men aiming their machine guns at the interior of the camp. The inmates were closely guarded during the day and locked up at night. Still Bobby was not willing to give up; he searched for the chink in the German armor.

Some weeks passed and Bobby had a sudden, lucky break. He was chosen to join the commando that worked in the munitions factory. This was sheer coincidence, almost like a win in a lottery. The reassignment marked a great improvement in his day-to-day life. The work was under one roof, and part of military production. The actual work resembled the drudgery of construction; here, too, they had to carry heavy crates and hoist them onto large lorries. Nevertheless, the drudging inmates were protected from the harsh winter cold and received somewhat improved food rations.

The mid-day soup was thick, full of potatoes and carrots and, on occasion, there was a small piece of meat floating in it. Some of it was rotten, but the ravenous men devoured it all. The evening meal was also augmented. The commandos who worked for the military received a larger chunk of bread, occasionally supplemented with a blob of margarine or jam. These were doled out with a spoon, and most inmates swallowed it the moment they received it. On a rare occasion, they obtained a small scrap of sausage. All of this tasted divinely better than any delicacies in their past lives.

The winter arrived early and seemed particularly severe, adding to the many hardships. The temperatures dropped, the mercury falling far below zero. The barracks were freezing cold. The only source of warmth was a fire in the central stove; stoked with wood the inmates had to find and carry in from a nearby forest.

Most of the inmates were weak, victims of chronic malnutrition. Most had frequent diarrhea, oozing sores, and bouts of fever, declining vision and quickly fading strength. Still they were the targets of envy by many who toiled in outdoor commandos, exposed to the harsh elements, the storms, blustery winds and snowfall, clothed in tattered rags, their bodies at the end of their tethers.

However, Bobby was young and wanted nothing more than to live. His resolve turned into a grim obsession. He forced himself never to indulge in sadness or memories of the past. He only concentrated on the present moment, where to find the next morsel of food or a way to cover for his weakening body. With the passage of time he worked on disguise and self-effacement, needing to hide his failing physique from the keen piercing glances of the Kapos and the SS.

However, Bobby's luck still had not run out. As chance would have it, one of the meanest Kapos took a fancy to Bobby. This scared our young man out of his wits, for most Kapos chose young boys for their sexual gratification, forcing them to perform outlandish perversities for which they in return received ample food and other commodities. However, the Kapo did not make a move to rape or molest Bobby. Perhaps he felt pity for the fifteen-year-old boy, whose youthful looks, blue eyes and blond hair mimicked the German description of the classical Aryan look.

Be it as it may, something stirred in this rough, unapproachable, ordinary criminal, who boasted that he even killed many in normal times. While Bobby's self-appointed protector brutalized others, whose work he deemed slow or slovenly, he would leave Bobby alone. Even when his output slacked, the Kapo hardly ever beat him or even shouted. Why was he so self-effacing to Bobby while he never tempered his hatred and violence towards the other men?

Indeed, he treated Bobby exceptionally well. At work, he studiously ignored Bobby's slipshod and deplorable work performance. He even went so far as to augment Bobby's bread rations and looked away when Bobby found some leftover food on the way to work or in the factory itself. In all likelihood, it was this inexplicable leniency by a professional killer that saved Bobby's life during this bitter winter of 1944 and spring of 1945, when his health and strength began to sap and decline.

One great event launched the beginning of the end of the war, at least for the inmates of Sachsenhousen. The Allied forces conducted massive air raids, bombarding the industrial and munitions plants in the vicinity of the camp. The inmates not only heard the explosions and the heavy thunder of impacting bombs – they waited, hoped and prayed for these attacks that promised to level the Nazi war machine. Now more than ever, they wished to live, for finally they had tangible proof that the end was near.

In addition, for those who no longer had the stamina to go on, the knowledge of an imminent German defeat brought comfort to their final hours. They relied on the victorious Allies for vindication, now that they were about to push the forces of darkness back to their Valhalla, the mythological place of souls of German heroes.

Night after night, Bobby would listen with his eyes wide open, peering into the darkness, waiting for the sirens announcing an air raid. He strained his ears for the roar of the Allied airplanes as they approached to inflict punishing blows on the German countryside. The inmates were moved to tears, grateful for the heavy thunderbolts and shock waves accompanying the many hits. All listened into the night's darkness, encouraged and emboldened by the evidence that the days of infamy were ending. Moreover, they wanted to live, to be there when the hour of reckoning came upon Germany.

The inmates noticed another sign of German distress. They observed with relish the darkened, worried expressions of their oppressors, now concerned with the likely retribution coming their way. The inmates would on occasion overhear a word or two of a conversation by regular workers and, putting one and one together, they concluded that the Russian armies were advancing in a deep thrust from the East, and could not be too far away. Some inmates claimed to hear the sounds of Russian artillery howling nearby.

All pointed to an early end, and Bobby wished urgently to be there. The many civilians working in the factory became less cautious. They exchanged news about the fluid situation on the battlefields, and when the inmates pooled the tidbits they overheard, it became clear that the Russian army had succeeded in throwing the Germans back, deep into Polish territory. A group of guys who trusted each other met daily in the one safe spot, the latrines, where the conversation buzzed with upbeat hope. This news was music to Bobby's ears; he could hardly wait.

One March morning the inmates were roused even earlier than usual. It was pitch dark; snow covered the ground. Inside the barracks were frosty and the air chilly. The inmates waited anxiously for orders. Soon the irate and angry voices of the Kapos declared that the camp was under evacuation orders. All had to pick up their meager belongings. The Germans had decided to move the inmates to the west or southwest, far away from the Russians, who were quickly closing in on Berlin. The Germans wanted to disassemble the camp and conceal any evidence of crimes perpetrated there.

The nervous Kapos yelled for the prisoners to form columns and, as usual, nothing went as fast as they wished. Disgruntled, they began to beat the inmates using their cudgels, killing a few. In the distance, several SS men dawdled, their guns poised, waiting to give the order to move. Before leaving the camp, each inmate received a piece of bread, slightly more than one days' ration. Then off they went.

For a moment Bobby tried to decide whether to gulp down the bread or, in light of the special circumstances, try to keep a morsel for later. Soon he made up his mind not to save anything, and he relished devouring it all. He repeated to himself that this was the only safe way, to keep it meant taking a chance of losing it to another stronger inmate who might steal it from him, in this volatile, less rigidly supervised setting.

They trudged for several hours. The sun was already well above their heads when the SS men decided to break for a short rest. Bobby was hungry, thirsty and tired. He decided to use the time for a discreet search for food and more importantly, to test the intent of the Germans in foiling a potential escape. No count was taken and the numbers of inmates decreased, some falling by the wayside, too weak to continue and were either beaten to death by the Kapo or shot by the accompanying SS men. The corpses were left on the side of the road; no one had an accurate count. Perhaps the once much-valued census no longer mattered, for the Germans had other problems to contend with.

The entire group followed the order to sit for the break. They rested, using the break to nurse the sores on their feet, covered with bleeding blisters, ripped open by the long hours of marching in their pathetic footwear. Most wore clogs, but Bobby was exceptionally lucky. He owned a pair of fitted boots given him some time ago by the Kapo, Bobby's self -styled benefactor, at the time when Bobby's frostbitten toes had begun to show signs of gangrene. The gift proved to be a lifesaver.

The long hours of marching on the frozen grounds of Europe killed all who had inadequate footwear. These trudging columns of the one-time concentration camp inmates were visible on most of the roads and highways of Europe in 1945, the last year of war. The staggering shadows, most near death, tried to keep going, to at last see the day of liberation.

This phenomenon became known as the Death Marches, another macabre invention of the Nazis. Like most other inmates, Bobby stilled his thirst with a mouthful of snow, still covering the ground on that chilly March of 1945. Not far away, within reach, Bobby found a few frozen beets. He gulped them down carefully, mindful not to attract the attention of some angry Kapo, or worse, an SS man.

Slowly in his mind a plan began to crystallize. He would gradually fall behind till he found himself in the last row of marchers. He began by inconspicuously trudging along, somehow moving slowly, gradually falling a few rows behind. He took care to remain in the center of the not-so-perfect rows of five. At this stage of the march, the lines were not very orderly, many dropping off, others barely keeping up.

When Bobby began to work on his scheme, he encountered few difficulties. Nobody seemed unduly alarmed where he marched, as long as he remained upright, on his feet and within formation. It took Bobby a full day, intermingled with three rest breaks to get himself to the strategic spot, whence he could try to escape. The breaks were the important times; the SS men ate some food during those occasions, and afterwards they vanished into the forest to relieve themselves. The inmates had none of these luxuries.

There was no food distribution and when the call of nature came, they had to remain within the procession. Long ago, they had been stripped of their sensitivities; no longer were they abashed by what once was considered crude behavior. In the camps, most of the inmates loathed their bodies, which subjected them to so many aches, needs and problems. Their systems craved food they could not have; their intestines were tormented with cramps caused by their eating rotten, decaying scraps. Indeed their bodies tortured them by demands for the very basics, which they could not satisfy.

When night descended, the group was forced into a barn, where the Germans locked them up and posted a guard outside.

Bobby decided that the night was a write-off; no attempt to escape could succeed under such closely guarded conditions. However, as his eyes were closing shut he made up his mind that the very next day he would secure from the very beginning a position at the very end of the column.

At the crack of dawn orders were shouted to get up, quickly fall into line and start marching. The SS men appeared tired, less polished, their crumpled uniforms no longer up to the image of the dapper officers of late. Their creases were gone; their entire demeanor much diminished and wilted. The fact that they were not immune to consequences exacted by rough times and less comfort would have been pleasing to the inmates, if not coupled with the rising fury of the SS men. They responded to their reduced state by inflicting greater suffering on their hapless charges.

Usually, the SS relegated the physical abuse to the Kapos, stepping in only to deliver the coup de grace, in the form of a gunshot. However, on this morning the SS behaved like rabid dogs. They beat the inmates with the butts of their guns or with whatever was handy. The morning was a bitterly cold one; even the weather conspired against the marching Jews. None of these details was lost on Bobby, who observed it all with hawk-eyed determination.

In the morning, while lining up, he grabbed two fistfuls of snow, washed his face with one, and the second was a breakfast substitute, since nothing edible was forthcoming. The cold snow refreshed him somewhat, though his insides writhed with hunger. As usual, his spirits were high; he was on the lookout for a lucky break. There was a chance that they might cross a field where he could pick up a frozen potato or other vegetables.

However, at this moment his priorities lay elsewhere, for he had targeted this day for his escape. He felt that his strength was sapped, and he was sufficiently realistic to realize that he would not last much longer before he joined the many left behind, lying on the frozen snow with a bullet in their brain.

The sorry procession moved slowly, and Bobby remained faithful to his decision and stayed near the rear. They marched about an hour or so when Bobby began to feel unwell. He knew that his time was running out and that he had to attempt his escape.

By his plan, he would drop out of formation when the last row turned a corner, close to some trees, brushes or a forest. He would be out of sight, quickly hidden among the trees.

For the last time, he touched the knife he had concealed on his body, for which he bartered. Some time ago while still in the camp, he exchanged it for several rations of bread. The knife had a sharp pointed cutting blade. To Bobby, it was his only insurance of not being taken alive by the Nazis. In addition, on a more pragmatic note, the knife could be used to kill a rabbit or anything he could catch in the forest to still his hunger.

The carefully planned opportunity presented itself soon enough. The long column took a rather sharp turn, leaving the end of the formation out of sight for those in front. Most of the SS men were gathered at the head of the group, one marched in the middle and only one man at the tail.

As the marchers were turning the corner, Bobby decided that this was as good an opportunity as ever could lend itself. It had to be now, for he felt that he could not last much longer, and only God knew how long it might take before the Nazis would concede defeat. They might eventually do just that, but first they would try to murder every Jew in their power.

Moreover, as if prodded by fate, the SS man marching in the rear was nowhere in sight. Bobby surmised that the man went to the front for his periodic chat or perhaps to share a bite with his buddies. He would not engage in further speculations of his whereabouts; he was pleased not to have to concern himself with the dangerous presence of the armed man. When the last man turned the corner, Bobby dropped down. The men around him barely noticed; all were too spent to care.

Within seconds, Bobby was alone. He quickly crawled into the nearby bushes, his immediate hiding place. Once he reached the underbrush, moving on his belly as quickly as he could, he slunk across a small clearing to reach the first trees of the forest. Being in full sight, he made his best speed and breathed a sigh of relief when he reached the cover of the tall trees.

He straightened up and was about to run, when to his horror he noticed the figure of the SS man, standing with his back to him. The man was urinating in the privacy of the forest, feeling quite safe. It was the missing rear-guard SS officer. Bobby, now on high alert, was certain only of one reality. Only one of them could survive this unexpected confrontation.

Bobby owed it to his silent crawling that the SS man was not aware of his presence, but now every second of this bizarre impasse counted. Fate had locked them in an incredible circumstance from which only one would emerge alive. If the SS man were to turn around, he would immediately know that he faced an escaped inmate; after all, Bobby still wore the remnants of the striped uniform. If the Nazi were allowed to act, he would shoot Bobby without batting an eye. Within a split second, Bobby knew that he had to jump the man first.

Instantly Bobby swung into action. He pulled his knife from his boot and attacked from behind. The supreme danger, the sudden mortal threat to his life charged him with the adrenaline rush he needed to generate this strength. His mind worked with a clarity and speed he no longer thought he was capable of. As he landed on the man with all his power and very limited weight, the surprise gave him the much-needed edge. The impact toppled the man over, he fell face down, which somewhat muffled his screams.

Bobby plunged his blade into the neck of his mortal adversary, while pressing his face into the moss, hushing whatever sounds the injured man was letting off. Then he turned him over and stabbed him again and again in the belly, heart, arms and back. Bobby was suddenly possessed by a silent, cold fury spewing from a powerful hatred.

When the body no longer moved, Bobby let go. The man's eyes were wide open, and he looked at Bobby with a glassy, lifeless expression. Bobby was not sure if the SS man was dead, but he kept stabbing the listless body repeatedly.

Later he could not remember how many times he thrust the blade into the body of the man who to him came to represent all the evil and crimes perpetrated by the Nazis. Finally, he had to stop. He was out of breath and exhausted. He looked at the corpse, void of pity or any emotion. On the spur of the moment, he decided to strip the man of his uniform, take his gun and flee deeper into the woods. As rapidly as he could, he undressed the man; picked up the now torn uniform and gun, always aware that time was at a premium. Before long, the man would be missed and a search party would be dispatched. Bobby hoped to put as much distance as possible between himself and the lifeless body. After completing this macabre task of stripping the corpse, he resumed his hasty retreat, much hindered by the thick underbrush.

He did not know how long he ran. He slowed down only when the first shadows of late afternoon hinted at the end of the most incredible day of his life, the day he killed another human being and won his life and freedom!

The March days were still quite short and cold in this part of northern Europe. Bobby was tired; he stumbled, tripped and got up again, trying not to slow down, terrified that the SS man was missed and his body would be found. The thought that some SS men were in hot pursuit of the murderer of their colleague was enough to launch his flight again.

Perhaps they would set their dogs on him. Two of the SS men had taken dogs along for the death march. He didn't know if the dogs could sniff him out and, if so, what distance did he need, to get out of their range? He heard that the only effective way to mislead the well-trained animals was the scent of a Russian tobacco, "Machorka," soaked in petrol, dried, and scattered in the path. Bobby had nothing so sophisticated and had no doubt that, if caught by the dogs, he would be torn to pieces by their teeth and, if seized by the SS, he would be shot on sight.

When darkness fell, Bobby began to repair his future outfit, the uniform of his victim. First, he had to wash it with snow to remove as much blood as possible. He was sorry that he had damaged it so badly. He spent much time washing the tunic with snow until the last traces of blood absorbed into the material were no longer particularly conspicuous by its reddish-brown color. He then put the uniform over his torn, striped rags, hoping to elude German patrols, at least from a distance.

He hoped and convinced himself that the search for him would not be renewed the next day. The other SS men were wrapped up in their own concerns, frightened by the coming day of reckoning and the ensuing punishments. Most were plotting their own escape and beginning to build a web of lies for elaborate alibis of their wartime activities.

Bobby put on the uniform, but he was hardly pleased. It hung loosely around his bony frame, though its rightful owner was a slim man. Bobby was emaciated, his bones covered with yellowish, sickly skin. Luckily, the dead man wore a belt, which Bobby used to hold up his pants. Bobby hoped not be seen by many in this bizarre outfit. It was meant only to camouflage and deflect attention should he run into people. As he buttoned the jacket, he noticed with disdain the many tears inflicted by his blade, but little could be done.

The rest of his odyssey was nearly an anti-climax. Not that all was smooth sailing; he had a few close calls when he ran into some peasants and later met some other civilians, who gaped at his outlandish presence. But in the closing days of the war, there were many strange figures on the roads, impostors of many shades, all trying to elude dangers reigning in the interregnum when the Nazis were done for and no new order was yet established. Europe was turned inside out; the times were so anomalous that little seemed extraordinary during the dying days of the Third Reich.

It did not take long for Bobby to reach the Czech border. The weather improved slowly, but the nights were still quite frosty. Bobby still preferred to march during the night and sleep in the day, well hidden by the many coniferous trees. Then came May, the month poets sing and write about. In May 1945, the entire world had reason to be jubilant, not only those in love. The world got a new lease on life, for the madness and the bloodshed of the Nazis came to an end.

Once well within Czech territory, Bobby decided to shed the SS uniform, lest some Czechs take his disguise in earnest and beat him to death, believing him to be a genuine Nazi. In those days, one could find death faster than the time to explain oneself. He took off the dirty, crumpled uniform, now layered with caked dirt from his having lived in it day and night for his few weeks on the run. Once he had changed back into his prisoner's garb, he felt safer. He was well aware that the Czechs had countless grievances and unsettled accounts with the brutal occupiers, who for some six years had inflicted great suffering on them.

Many years passed. Bobby learned the trade of carpentry, married, divorced, re-married a few more times and tried to make friends, all with limited success. For the most part, he remained aloof. He did not find many peers who could understand the strangely silent and often bitter young man. Few were sensitive enough or even curious about his war experiences, or wished to befriend this strange, taciturn man. On a rare occasion, and only among a chosen few, he would reminisce about the death march, which exacted so many of the lives of his peers.

He once told me that on many a night he was revisited by his nightmares, and he would wake up, covered in sweat. One more time he would feel the sensation of the knife burrowing into human flesh, and the rage when he first thrust the knife into the abdomen of his archenemy. Though rationally he knew he had no other options, he wished he could have been spared the ghoulish necessity of plunging a blade into another man's body. His worst hours came to him at night, when he could not differentiate from self-defense and a deliberate act of murder.

He relived many times the haunting experience of extinguishing the life of another human being. He could not rid himself of the memory of the vacant gaze of the man whose name Bobby never knew. The entire sequence of events lived on in Bobby's nightmares: the first look of incredulity, then fear, and only later the emptiness as life faded from the dying body. Bobby was often angry at his own inability to rid himself of the haunting memories, blaming himself for being a weakling unable to stomach the fact that he needed to execute an enemy with whom he was locked in a life or death struggle.

None of Bobby's relatives survived the Holocaust. In his mature years, he removed himself from his roots, attempting genuinely to become a Czech national. The Communist government, ruling from 1948 till 1989, placed a ban on all religions, considering them, as Karl Marx stated, the "opiate of the masses." Bobby had no quarrel with atheism. The flicker of his faith was extinguished in the pyres on which six million of his co-religionists were burned to ashes. Many, probably most, were firm believers in a kind, omnipotent, just Almighty.

Hanus: Partisan

Partisans fighting the Nazis in the Lithuanian forests.
Theirs was a largely unknown struggle against terrific odds. Yet
their story inspired hope among the inmates of the camps, who
heard rumors of resistance to the Nazis and longed to escape and
join the partisans in their struggle.

The only individual who stood a fraction of a chance for survival in a concentration camp had to be endowed with the dauntless desire to avoid his date with the executioner. The brave, almost foolhardy individual would scheme against the towering odds. The fainthearted despaired, as did the realists, once they understood all they were up against. Most longed to live just a little longer; few hoped to survive the years of unrelenting misery, persecution and bone-crushing cruelty. It took a unique sort of individual with the heart to tangle with the insurmountable odds, to focus on the infinitesimal possibility of prevailing.

The only certainty was death, which lurked everywhere, at all times of the day and night, from the early morning roll call, often followed by selection, where many were found wanting, sending the weak or ill inmates to the gas chambers. Even if this hurdle were surmounted, other hazards abounded. Inmates fell prey to sadistic Kapos or irate SS men who frequently beat prisoners to death, often to satisfy their sadistic urges. Kapos were powerful supervisors charged by the SS to assure compliance and enforce the work performance of the inmates, by any and all means. The word "Kapo" is an acronym for *Kameradschaft's Polizei* euphemistically meaning "police by peers." These men and women were anything but comrades; they were appointed by the camp commandants and were chosen from the ranks of violent criminals who were often habitual felons with a history of brutality and sadism. They were expected to abuse the inmates, with a full license to kill, brutalize and torment as many as they wanted, at their will.

In the Nazi camps death came with many faces: illness, starvation and violence by the guards, even in one's own sinking spirits, by accepting defeat and surrendering. The frequent consequence of this despair was the run for the electric fence, perhaps the least painful and most freely accessible way to end one's life. To choose death on the highly charged wires was the only decision an inmate could take of his own free will, to assert his autonomy.

Most of the younger men and women initially refused to believe that all Jews were summarily sentenced to death. Once they truly grasped and understood this insane ruling, most became furious. The seething anger over the absurd "Final Solution," the execution of an entire nation whose only guilt was the coincidence of their birth, rose to new heights.

These tidal waves of rage were subdued by the fear of retaliation that the Nazis would inflict at any sign of noncompliance. The main discouraging trepidation was the routine inclusion of many uninvolved, for the Nazis always reacted by eliminating entire families, people living on nearby streets, neighborhoods or whole villages as a deterrent for those who might plan future acts of rebellion.

The irrevocable death sentence for all Jews could not be appealed, rescinded or openly fought. It was this affront and consequent outrage, the uneven odds, and the injustice of classifying Jews as a lesser race, which provoked in many a Jew the wish for vengeance. It would be easier to die taking at least one of the Nazis with oneself to the Netherworld.

The intrepid ones searched for a loophole in the seemingly impenetrable chain of fences and security walls placed to foil defiance and escape. Many hoped to join roving bands of partisans, but only a few succeeded. The SS guards or their cohorts shot most of those who tried to flee, and the rest perished before they reached the dispersed, rambling units of the freedom fighters. The guards, most of whom were local collaborators volunteering to help the Nazis, constantly monitored the camps.

Any unauthorized movement was met with a barrage of bullets, fired from the watchtowers or guard stations. No questions were asked. Any plan to flee had to be methodically worked out, taking every detail and potential adversity into consideration. For example, the escapee had to run with agility and be unencumbered, but matches, a knife, bread and warm clothing were essential if he were to last in some cold forest hideout. It goes without saying that he had to be young, in good shape and in sturdy health.

Even so, luck was integral to the equation. It was the single determinant of even a single day's survival in a camp or on the run. Evidently, all Jews, regardless of which camp they found themselves in, had to hope for good luck. But they also had to plan carefully, indeed to the last humanly possible elusive variable. Good fortune could run out quickly on an inmate, particularly if he let his guard down.

The story of Hanus exhibits such courage and dauntless determination. It could appear at times to be the acts of a daredevil magician. Had he not risked flight from the death camp of Maly Trostenec, he would not only have joined the rest of the inmates in death, but would also have deprived the world of the testimony of the sole surviving witness of this nefarious concentration camp. But for Hanus, mankind would have never known what transpired there.

The saga of Hanus supports the theory that to outlast the state-sponsored mass murder of Jews, the individual had to possess certain personality traits. Among them, a cunning swift resolve, fearlessness, and an ability to improvise, quickly change or adapt one's plans to a fluid, rapidly changing scene. However, all those qualities would not have been enough, if not for the most important component, already mentioned: luck.

Hanus was born around the outbreak of the First World War to a middle class family, which early on sustained a tragic loss. His father died when Hanus was merely an infant of seven months. His father, then a young man, contracted pneumonia, which in the pre-antibiotic era often proved fatal.

The Meyer family, left fatherless early, faced many tough times. The young widow was abruptly confronted with the necessity of providing by herself for her two sons, a six-year-old and the baby Hanus. This was a tall order, for most women of that generation were neither prepared nor sufficiently educated to earn a decent living. Mrs. Meyer was a diligent and talented woman, but her family's future was bleak.

At first, the young widow tried and partially succeeded in scratching out a living by painting on silk. In those days, it was fashionable to decorate custom-designed lampshades with hand painted patterns by gifted artisans.

Just when Mrs. Meyer thought she found a niche, which
would allow her to raise her sons in some measure of comfort, fate
struck again. Her eyesight began to weaken, fading quickly. That
was a hard and bitter blow, nearly driving the young woman over
the edge. It was impossible to engage in her delicate work with
impaired vision. Her only other choice was to find a different
source of income.

She was at a loss where to turn and, as was customary in
those days, the family was convened to help resolve her dilemma.
Her family was small. The relatives of Hanus' parents had passed
away early, the only source for advice left was the widow's
brother, Hugo. Both boys were required to have a legal guardian
and this duty was thrust upon uncle Hugo as well. Between him
and another sister, Helen, they pooled their resources and came to
the rescue of the threatened, fatherless family. They could not
raise an impressive amount, but it was sufficient for the purchase
of a small perfumery, which in those days also sold other bric-a-
brac. The store was conveniently located in Prague's center, but it
did not attract an affluent clientele. It barely kept the family afloat;
no frills or extras were affordable, and the boys grew up
accustomed to making do with the bare necessities.

The boys were serious, conscientious and mature beyond
their years. They studied well, with the older son graduating in due
course with a degree in law. The family rejoiced, hoping the future
would be easier, but again fate threw in a monkey wrench. Hanus
was still in high school, when all could see that the quickly
deteriorating political situation would soon affect their lives.

After much deliberation, the family decided that Hanus
should give up his academic aspirations and instead enter
vocational training, and so secure an early means to independence.
Though disappointed, he was not disheartened, for he believed that
better days would eventually restore his prerogative to study. For
the time being, he entered a training program for dental
technicians and graduated in 1937. The diploma guaranteed
modest financial self-reliance.

Before he could take advantage of this marketable skill, he
was drafted into the Czech army for the two-year compulsory
service. Hanus was still on active duty when in 1938 Austria was

annexed, closely followed by the Nazis' menacing turn against the
Czechoslovak republic. The attacks were initially restricted to
border skirmishes provoked by the local followers of the Nazi
movement, but the perpetrators manipulated and schemed so that
the guilt was placed on the Czechs. Loud, shrieking propaganda
exhorted the ethnic Germans living in Czechoslovakia to join the
local Nazi party and attempt to dismantle the republic. The local
Germans gladly complied. Although they had no legitimate
grievance, they clamored for unification with Germany, now under
the leadership of the charismatic demagogue, Adolf Hitler.

The western democracies, ill prepared for military
confrontation, opted for unprincipled cowardice and sacrificed the
tiny state in the heart of Europe. All eyes focused on Munich,
where a conference was convened, attempting to find a solution to
the problem and there, without Czechoslovak representation, the
state was torn to pieces. Not only did the Western democracies
order the Czechs to vacate the disputed "Sudeten" (the northern
part of Bohemia where most of the ethnic Germans lived)
territories, they gave an ultimatum to the Czechs, threatening that
if the region was not vacated, the one-time Allies would join the
Germans to secure the withdrawal of the Czech army.

There was no alternative or recourse for the Czechs. They
were forced to surrender without a shot, giving up their massive
fortifications built into the mountain ridges designed to fend off an
attack from the north. No sane observer doubted that the mutilated,
indefensible remnant of the republic would follow suit in the not-
too-distant future. Indeed, within several months, in March 1939,
Hitler overran the remainder of Czechoslovakia. The two western
provinces, Bohemia and Moravia, were placed under direct
German rule in the form of a "Protectorate," and the more eastern
part of Slovakia was given independence "Nazi style." A fascist
party took reins of the Slovakia government, faithfully following
all the German bidding with the pretense of an autonomous state.

The Czechoslovak army was dissolved and the dispirited
soldiers returned home. Among the demobilized was Hanus, who
returned to Prague to his mother, who by then lived alone. The
older son had married a Gentile girl, who disliked his family and
under the Nazi rule soon found justification to sever all contact
with her husband's Jewish relatives. Even that was not good

enough, for soon she decided to take advantage of the German recommendation to mixed couples and divorced her Jewish spouse. This was by no means an exception, for the Nuremberg racial laws opened the flood gates of divorce, offering the Gentile partner all the marital assets, if he or she ousted the Jewish partner from their shared abode.

As the Germans hoped, few resisted the proposal. Most succumbed to fear, anxiety and the awareness that the Jewish spouse was an enormous liability. He or she could drag the rest of the family into an abyss of poverty, restriction and persecution. If the couple had children, the non-Jewish wife was advised to declare them sired by a Gentile lover. Thus, all expected rights would be conferred upon them, for they would then be considered to be of pure Aryan blood. In those days, few showed the moral fiber, fortitude and love for their spouse to withstand the pressure of these enticements.

Hanus' brother was one of the many who found themselves on the street, thrown out by his "loving" Aryan wife. Though he had been only infrequently in touch with his family of origin during his marriage (for they always seemed to be a thorn in his wife's side), he now rejoined his mother, who gladly took him in, and for a brief time the three lived together once again. They were soon separated, as each was deported to a different place of infamy, euphemistically called "resettlement," that the Germans prepared for the Jews.

Hanus was an enthusiastic young man with an upbeat temperament even under the worst conditions. He was handsome, a go-getter, popular with men and women, a man who knew, or thought he knew, where he wanted to go and what to achieve. Life for him carried a promise of wonderful experiences and, in spite of dimming hopes, he decided not to torment himself with acrimony, but to place his personal ambitions on the back burner, pending the return of normal times.

Although Hanus was intelligent and smart, studied with ease and had a healthy common sense, he underestimated, like almost all, the peril of his new overlords. In his naïve judgment he was in good company, for most central Europeans minimized the looming danger. They laughed contemptuously at the hateful, pestilent rancor and considered the spewed hallucinatory hatred of the Nazis a product of an insane mind. Meanwhile the Nazis tightened their domination over Europe and prepared their armies for the war to come.

Like the majority of Europe's educated youth, Hanus' peers were undecided if Hitler's crazed political credo were a bad joke or an insignificant, ephemeral aberration. Maybe it was an outgrowth of the depression of the1930's or the fulminating outburst of some lingering malaise. Perhaps the many unemployed, lining in long queues in front of soup kitchens for their only meal of the day, had to find an outlet for their anger. Those thrust for the first time in their lives into poverty and unable to cope with the rampant inflation were probably more susceptible to the phantasm of a lunatic. All these evaluations were, of course, wrong and terribly naïve, but they lulled many into the belief that the Nazis were but a fleeting scourge.

The German invasion found Hanus in Prague. Following his discharge from the army, he had resumed his work as a dental technician. He contemplated escape, and there were some opportunities for him to join a clandestine group that smuggled people across the Slovak border into neighboring Hungary. However, Hanus wavered. It was not the hardships or risks; rather, he felt uneasy leaving his elderly mother alone. His brother also searched for an exit gate, preferably for the three together. This indecision ultimately led to their undoing, as the Germans set out to end all Jewish attempts to flee and then sprang the trap shut.

Hanus by and large moved through Prague freely, almost like in the old days. His Gentile friends helped him shop, so that he was not dependent on the few hours Jews were allowed for their purchases. His buddies also ran many of his errands, which were risky or outright impossible for a Jew to complete.

Hanus, on occasion, dared even to remove his yellow star from his clothing, as Jews were subject to a rigorously enforced curfew that fettered and burdened him. This was risky and Hanus, when tardy, preferred to stay overnight at friends' homes, just to avoid the risk of a dragnet, targeting Jews failing to comply. Even the inadequate food rations allotted to Jews did not bother Hanus. His friends purchased food on the black market, and he still had enough money to pay the exorbitant prices. One laughs easily when one is young, strong and confident. Only when the deportations to the camps began in earnest did Hanus understand that he, too, was in peril.

The Nazis called for mass expulsions and resettlement of all Jews. It was in the fall of 1941 when the first Jews of Prague were called, allowed to take 50 kilograms (120 pounds) of personal belongings for resettlement in the East. They were stripped of the rest of their belongings, severed from the rest of society, imprisoned in ghettos and camps specifically designed for cruel extermination. The Germans publicly declared: "The Jews will be taught to become productive members of society."

The first thousands left Prague for the destination of Litzmanstadt (Lodz), where they were packed into the already overcrowded ghetto and lived a wretched life in abysmal and abject poverty, until the ghetto's liquidation. In early 1942 conditions deteriorated to the point that the outbreak of epidemics was imminent. To alleviate the ghetto's unimaginable congestion, the Nazis applied a remedy to their design. They siphoned off the excess Jews by murdering as many as possible in the shortest time. They gathered the Jews of Lodz and deported them to the nearby extermination camps of Belzec, Sobibor, and Treblinka, where they were asphyxiated with carbon monoxide. Many avoided this fate, falling prey to hunger and illness, aggravated by crowding and wretched conditions long before the gas robbed them of their last, painful breath.

In the fall of 1941 the deportation roster called for the removal of whole families, and Hanus, being single, was left alone. His good luck was not to last much longer. Rumors circulated that a new camp was to be established and even a name cropped up: Theresienstadt, well within the boundaries of the Czech Protectorate. Most Czech Jews considered it a godsend; they wished to stay in their country, not be removed to the far and inhospitable East. The first signs confirming the rumor appeared in the fall of 1941 as a contingent of young men was called up to adapt Theresienstadt from a garrison town into a concentration camp.

Barracks were needed for the many thousands of men, women and children to be confined there. Two groups of able-bodied men were called up, AK1 and AK2 (*Aufbau Kommando*) to build Theresienstadt into a transit camp for Jews. Hanus, then a man of thirty-one, was included in the first group, which reached the drab little town in the late fall of 1941. Construction was barely under way when the first thousands of Jewish inmates began arriving. The preparations were unsuitable, the military barracks in place required significant adjustment, and only the foundation of the new wooden barracks was being set. Thousands of people were crammed into an area barely suitable for a few hundred.

But the precarious conditions prevailing in Theresienstadt were hardly a concern to the Nazis; to them the camp was a holding place, a sluice through which Jews had to pass to reach their final and intended destination: Death. It was not their intent to improve the conditions for their victims. For themselves, the German command was allocated a nice building outside the camp. Their living quarters were spacious and comfortably far away from the captives inside the fenced-off town.

In fact, for the Nazis the camps presented a once-in-a-lifetime opportunity. To begin with, they sat safe and replete, far from the dangerous combat zones, ruling like suzerains, deciding issues of life and death over countless defenseless captives. Additionally, many of them engaged, albeit in great secrecy, in black market activities, lining their pockets with a substantial nest egg for the days to come. They spent their days in offices filing stacks of papers, relishing the many statistics, manipulated and manicured to please higher officials in Berlin. The Germans had a penchant for long columns of numbers, real or invented, presented in immaculate, esthetic penmanship and, most importantly, the bottom line had to add up. So life was good in Theresienstadt and as far as the SS men stationed there were concerned, the activities could have lasted till doomsday. They shuffled people back and forth, often needlessly, only to create a real and, at times, pseudo-agenda.

The Germans found new assignments for Hanus' group. The Nazis decided to make money by leasing some inmates to outside companies. Hanus, with some others, was ordered to Kladno, a mining town, where countless miners toiled deep underground for coal, the staple of most industries and main fuel for home heating. While miners were traditionally rather well paid, the Jews from Theresienstadt toiled long hours for food rations.

In spite of the drudgery, Hanus felt that they were better off than in Theresienstadt, being less restricted and much better fed. Though the Jews were billeted separately from other miners and forbidden contact, they developed a lively connection with them. Hanus and his friends were fiercely interested in the vagaries and developments of the war, waged against the modern day's Genghis Khan. While the world was locked in a ferocious battle between an evolving democratic civilization and a cruel dictatorship bent on sinking the world into the dark ages of a brutal police state, the Jews stood alone on the precipice of extinction. Although the theories of the Aryan supremacy seemed taken from the philosophies of those dark ages, they were enforced and even believed by many. The insults and names hurled at the Jews defied all logic. They demonized the Jew; proclaimed him the root of all Germany's problems and called him parasitic vermin. Jews were described as the bloodsuckers that lived off and exploited the sweat and toil of all Germans.

Every single Jew was sentenced to death by a government in control of one of the world's most powerful nations with a mighty military machine. Time was running out for the Jewish presence in Europe, and Jewish survival depended entirely on the outcome of this war, which gradually engulfed the entire world. With every passing day, the Nazis reported new victories, adding more Jews to the roster of the doomed. Entire Jewish communities vanished from the face of the earth, washed away by tidal waves of hate.

Early on, the miners from Theresienstadt established a routine, which allowed them to gather information. Soon the other colliers learned of this special Jewish unit, the one always kept apart, isolated and incommunicado. The Jews were also assigned the most dangerous tasks. Many men felt sympathy for the commando unit kept as slaves and to show their feelings they whispered news as they passed each other or were out of sight of their supervisors. They inconspicuously passed along some cigarettes to their Jewish co-workers, a deed much appreciated, as the smokers among them did not receive any cigarettes at all.

Then, one day in early June of 1942, the mood in the mines changed abruptly. Even before descending to the pits, the men sensed heightened tension and excitement. The apprehension was somewhat exacerbated by the heavier presence of guards and security personnel, scurrying to and fro. The Theresienstadt commando unit observed and waited patiently to go down the shafts where they could discover the reason for all this strange commotion.

Soon enough they caught bits and pieces of conversation from which they extrapolated the happenings of the outside world. The shocking and surprising news was the almost fatal assassination attempt on the life of the Nazi's highest representative in the Protectorate, Reinhard Heydrich, who deservedly earned his sobriquet: "the butcher of Prague." On hearing this unconfirmed report, most of the Theresienstadt commando had mixed feelings. Some rejoiced; perhaps Heydrich would meet his maker and receive eternal justice, but the other more sober consideration elicited momentous anxiety.

Heydrich was a rising star in the "Waffen SS," with a reputation for exceptional cruelty. Even by his peers he was neither liked nor trusted and was known for his boundless ambition. Most importantly, he was one of Himmler's favorites and even the Fuehrer Adolf Hitler prized his ruthless brutality, prodigious energy and fanatical devotion to the Nazi cause. Heydrich, in his function as the Reich's Protector of Bohemia and Moravia, drenched the country in the blood of thousands of Czechs. He suppressed any sign of discontent with pitiless brutality, intimidating the nation with threats and coercion. At the first sign of restiveness, he ordered dragnets and immediate executions, at times for trivial infractions. He implemented sadistic methods for interrogations and took care to let the Czechs know exactly how the Nazis treated those who dared oppose them.

The Theresienstadt group pondered the news. How was it possible for an assassin to access Heydrich, a very closely guarded SS officer, and who, when, where? They could find no additional details. The red alert, the mad scramble by the police and the presence of so many undercover agents, pointed to a major emergency. The large encompassing investigation, engaging so many security forces would not have been set for lesser fry.

That very night, Hanus and three of his peers were seized and thrown into Kladno's jail. They were kept in isolation for the next month, but as elsewhere, there is no jail without an active grapevine. Our foursome tried to key into the inmate information system to hear the reason for their detention and what was going on the outside. They were not disappointed.

Soon they heard the tapping of Morse code and they caught on. They were shocked to discover that they were among the suspects being investigated for aiding Heydrich's assassins. True enough, bad times followed. They were subject to many interrogations, brutal beatings, and kept without food or water. They were separated in isolation cells, but all to no avail. They could not confess to a crime of which they had no knowledge.

Each day they waited impatiently for the musical taps from the neighboring cell bringing news. They heard that thousands were in the same boat, languishing in jails, and daily many more were taken into custody, picked up by the never-ending dragnets. From early on after the occupation, the Germans declared the right to apprehend anyone without a warrant and after Heydrich's assassination attempt scores were incarcerated on a flimsy pretext or none at all. One of the most frequent excuses for arrest was a missing identity card, want of which was discovered during one of the many spot checks on the street or frequently even in ones home. In addition, the Nazis declared martial law, sanctioning apprehensions, limitless detentions and executions of those deemed suspect.

No involvement with the two assassins could be traced to our foursome; their guilt consisted of being born Jewish and having been at one time members of a left-leaning political youth organization. Anything to the left of center was an anathema to the Nazis.

Eventually they learned that the two men responsible for the attempt, ordered and sanctioned by the London-based exiled Czechoslovak government, were parachuted into the Czech heartland only hours before the assassination. Their story provides an important backdrop to the conditions in the Protectorate.

In England, many young patriotic Czechs who fled the Nazi invasion were all too keen to offer their services in the uneven struggle. Out of many able volunteers, two parachutists were chosen, carefully trained and dropped in the dead of night into the Czech territory. They were to wait at a street corner in Prague for Heydrich's chauffeur-driven limousine. He went to work every day using the same well-known route. At this corner, his limousine had to make a sharp turn and, in doing so, slowed almost to a stop. Kubis, who was a crack shot, was to stand on the near corner, take aim and shoot his target as he floated by. The back up man, Gabcik, ambling across the street, was to toss a grenade at the Protector, but only in the eventuality that Kubis ran into trouble and could not terminate his target. To avoid any glitches, the two men were to monitor the street closely, never losing sight of each other.

The two executioners had the advantage. Heydrich, though a young man was set in his ways, never deviating from his route into Prague from his residence in the castle of Panenske Brezany. He always followed the same schedule, confident of his safety. Perhaps living in the isolated castle, perched on a hill in a little township, surrounded by sycophants, he never heard how much he was loathed and hated by the Czechs.

On the appointed day, the two men strolled about casually. They easily mingled with other pedestrians of the morning rush hour in Prague, where many waited for streetcars, while others walked to work. They remained inconspicuous, dressed in everyday, rather shabby clothes. However, Kubis carried a raincoat, thrown casually over his arm, the pocket concealing a revolver.

The limousine approached on schedule. The car began to slow down. Kubis stood casually as if waiting for a streetcar, his raincoat nonchalantly flung over his forearm. Across the road, Gabcik slowly paced back and forth, a man with nothing on his mind but a morning stroll.

Then Kubis rapidly swung into action. He stepped forward, aimed almost at point blank range at his enemy's chest, and pulled the trigger. To his utter dismay, the gun jammed. In despair, he squeezed the trigger again and again without any result.

As Kubis stood repeatedly firing without effect, Heydrich regained his composure. He stared in disbelief at the young man aiming an ineffective revolver at him. Although a murderer, Heydrich was no fool, quickly realizing that he was out of immediate danger. Self confident, trusting in his ability to control the situation, he took charge and committed what proved to be his fatal mistake.

Enraged, Heydrich overruled common sense and sound judgment and ordered the driver to stop the car. He rose from his seat, pulled out his own gun and aimed at Kubis, who was still struggling with his gun.

As the two mortal enemies squared off, facing each other, Gabcik, positioned on the opposite side of the road, realized that Kubis was in serious trouble and decided the time had arrived for his move. Now he aimed carefully and hurled his hand grenade at Heydrich's car. It landed on the back seat, exploded, and badly shook the standing Heydrich, who reeled and staggered, dropping his gun while clutching both hands to his abdomen. The explosion tore the horsehair stuffing out of the car seats and the shrapnel drove some of the horsehair deep into Heydrich's abdominal cavity. Again, the driver pressed for a speedy retreat, but once more Heydrich refused. He commanded his chauffeur to chase on foot and apprehend the man who tossed the grenade while he, Heydrich, would take on Kubis, who had abandoned the struggle with his gun and taken to flight.

His own attempts to run after Kubis never got off the ground; he collapsed as he alighted from the car, falling on the dirty pavement of Prague writhing in agonizing pain, helpless, bleeding profusely onto the cobblestones of the city he ruled with an iron fist. Meanwhile his driver gave up the futile chase of Gabcik, who easily eluded his pursuer. For the moment both men, the avengers of much Czech suffering, were lucky, reached a safe house and were, for the moment, out of harm's way.

Not so Heydrich, who lay in pool of his own blood, furtively observed by passersby, who kept their distance. Within minutes, a policeman arrived, recognized the injured man and commandeered a passing van. No one wanted to help, for fear of future consequences. Finally the police, assisted by Heydrich's driver, placed the gravely wounded Protector into the van and sped him to the nearest hospital.

The physicians on duty in "Bulovka," the nearest hospital, were shocked to find themselves attending to the Reich's Protector himself. Following a brief examination it was obvious that surgery was imperative; shrapnel from the grenade had nicked the patient's spleen, causing hemorrhage. The hospital notified immediately the local German high command, which turned to Berlin for directives. Rumors circulated that Hitler flew into one of his rages, fuming and screaming hysterically, threatening to kill all involved with the attempted assassination of one of his favorites, indeed his possible successor.

Hitler authorized immediate and wide-ranging reprisals, while simultaneously forbidding surgery by the Czech physicians. They were to stabilize the patient and provide emergency treatment until Hitler's personal physicians arrived to take charge. Meanwhile, Berlin's top surgeon and his team were assembled and in record time flown to Prague. Immediately upon arrival they operated and removed the punctured spleen. Following the splenectomy, Heydrich began to recover. Most breathed sigh of relief; the physicians thought there was reason for optimism. Just when the medical team thought the worst was over, Heydrich's condition began to deteriorate, his symptoms pointing unmistakably to massive sepsis.

The names of the physicians taking turns to consult reads like a roster of medical excellence, the "Who's Who" for Europe's medical stars, for Hitler dispatched to Prague the best medical minds from the lands he occupied. All agreed that the horsehair wedged in Heydrich's abdomen was the seed of infection, and in the pre-antibiotic era, little could be done to reverse this fatal course.

As Heydrich lay dying in his hospital bed, squirming in agonizing pain, he asked for the continuous presence and support of a priest. The priest knelt at his bedside trying to comfort and assuage the deeply religious Heydrich. Though he was afraid, mortified of the after life, he did not confess to any crime and remained convinced that he carried out God's bidding while on this earth. The clergyman gave him his last rites, but Heydrich never found peace or acceptance in his demise. He was a very angry man till the bitter end. Heydrich's remains were flown to Berlin, where he was buried following a pompous state funeral.

The angry oratory of the illustrious Nazi mourners did not bode well for the twosome who sent him to the beyond.

His death unleashed a fury of unparalleled proportions, engulfing the entire Protectorate. The Germans declared martial law; thousands were apprehended and thrown into jail. Many were shot on sight and two villages without Jews, Lidice and Lezaky, were literally laid to waste. The inhabitants of both localities were accused of abetting the two assassins, and all the men from both villages were shot to death. The women were sent to concentration camps, and the children were seized and brought to Germany for adoption and German acculturation. The livestock was slaughtered, the homesteads were set ablaze, and the villages were razed to the ground.

Relentless dragnets swept the country; every city and village was combed for clues, accomplices, anything to lead to the identity of the two elusive assassins. Under martial law, the courts sentenced thousands to death, charged with treason for failing to confess or being uncooperative. The condemned were put to death immediately; no appeals were granted. Most of the executed were oblivious to the events that led to the liquidation of Heydrich and which had triggered the violent German explosion. Thousands of Jews were also dispatched to death in illogical retribution; none had the foggiest idea who ordered and organized the execution of Heydrich.

Initially Kubis and Gabcik, the two men who rid the world of the bloodiest murderer, Reinhard Heydrich, did well. They hid, changing safe houses as pre-arranged by their handlers. A decision was reached to hide them in the basement of a small church, right in the heart of Prague. Few would suspect that the two most wanted men would find shelter in the catacombs of a place of worship.

The passing days did little to moderate the pressure to capture Heydrich's executioners. Quite the opposite, the threats became more shrill and vengeful. The massive manhunt intensified, the search parties worked relentlessly, combing the city for the two elusive men day and night. Then someone rediscovered the idea of monetary incentives. The Germans posted a substantial financial reward for a clue to the whereabouts of the two most-wanted men. This was a timely lure.

One of the men from the conspirator's inner circle betrayed their location to the German authorities. Later he claimed that he got cold feet; his wife had just delivered a baby, and he was seized with panic that his young family would be murdered. He made sure he collected the cool one million crowns, then a small fortune for a man like Mr. Curda.

Now the Germans tightened their grip on the two conspirators. They surrounded the little church and opened fire. The two men returned fire effectively, giving no indication that they were even thinking of surrender. In the beginning, the Germans wanted both men alive, but on encountering stubborn opposition, they decided to flood the cellar and drown them inside. Gushing, cold water was pumped incessantly into the underground cellar, but Kubis and Gabcik did not intend to be captured alive.

As the Germans closed in, shooting and simultaneously pumping water higher and higher, they returned the fusillades till the penultimate bullet. When each man had only one bullet left in the barrel of his gun and the water rose up to their mouths, both men knew they had fought a good fight, and the time had come to call it quits. Determined not to be taken alive, nor to drown, they embraced and simultaneously fired their last bullet into one another. Thus, they died in the flooded cellar, denying the Nazis the pleasure of torture or forcing them to talk. They controlled their last moments and the timing of their end.

Long after the Germans were certain the two men were dead, they entered the basement of the church. They pulled out the two bodies and left them on display, lying on the sidewalk, the corpses to serve as warning to the nation, demonstrating the fate of those who dared oppose the Third Reich.

Yes, the fate of the informer, Mr. Curda: The tragedy completed a full circle. The traitor collected his blood money and remained safe, albeit only till the end of the war. He had the dubious distinction of being the first man indicted and tried for high treason in the newly liberated Czechoslovak republic. The trial took place in 1945; the tribunal found him guilty and sentenced him to death on the gallows. He was executed forthwith.

Meanwhile, Hanus languished in a jail in Kladno, imprisoned without charges, for the entire duration of the frenzied search for Heydrich's assassins. He was repeatedly questioned, beaten savagely and denied food, while his interrogators tried to squeeze out a confession about his involvement in the attack.

Eventually his tormentors had to conclude that he had nothing to do with the crime and about one month after their apprehension the men were deported back to Theresienstadt. This time they were to remain there only overnight.

On the day after their return, they were herded into another transport, marked BC 14, leaving Theresienstadt for an unknown destination. To their surprise, they were put on a passenger train, in itself a very odd event since freight and cattle cars were used to transport Jews. They were crammed tightly into the closed car while their luggage was tossed onto open wagons. The deportees would have preferred it switched around, for it was a sweltering July day. They were hot and thirsty, although they wore few clothes. Many fainted and some died in the packed wagons, holding 70 to 80 people in such proximity that all they could do was stand upright. Many were overcome with hunger and weakness; no food or drink was distributed. Every time the train slowed down or came to a halt, the caged Jews begged onlookers for water, holding their dishes through small cracks in the walls of the old train. But they were out of luck, for either the bystanders were intimidated by the shouting SS men, who continuously warned everyone to stay clear of the train, or they had no pity on the poor trapped wretches.

Somewhere in Poland, the train suddenly ground to a halt. All were ordered quickly out and transferred onto another train equipped with freight cars only. Inside these boxcars more died, overcome by heat and thirst. The dead remained propped upward for lack of space. They were tormented by the lack of sanitation. Each tightly jammed car was provided with only one pail for human waste. It overflowed and filled the car with unbearable, repugnant stench. The unrelenting agony drove many over the edge and, eventually, some to madness. The nightmare lasted for two days when, finally, to every one's relief, the train came to an abrupt halt, and the wagons were torn open, two at a time.

The car door in front of Hanus suddenly flung wide open and he squinted, with burning eyes unaccustomed to the light, at a soldier of the *Sicherheitsdienst* (Security force) and some SS men. These men shouted shrill orders for all to get quickly out and follow orders immediately. No matter how much the weakened and exhausted inmates tried to comply, nothing was fast enough. The Germans prodded the unnerved group with shouts, blows and intimidated them with poised guns held by SS men accompanied by snarling dogs. The Germans hit the staggering Jews with clubs and with the butts of their guns with such ferocity that many fell to the ground, to be shot to death when they failed to stand up fast enough.

Hanus glanced quickly around, hoping to discern in which part of Poland they found themselves. The view in front did not offer any hints; they had come to a halt on a dead-end sidetrack, which ended in a crude terminal in the middle of a large meadow partially surrounded by forest. The lush woodland was inviting; perhaps it would provide shelter and a hideaway if only he could make a run for it. It took him slightly longer than a second to return to sanity and realize that an escape was but a pipedream, the entire cluster of newcomers was tightly encircled by SS men, some locals, and their dogs. The paramilitaries, mostly volunteers from the Baltic states, wore uniforms resembling the gray green of the Germans. They obviously were trying to impress the Nazis by exceeding the brutality of their German masters. Hanus suddenly felt a sharp pain in his side; an SS man shoved his gun into his ribcage, prodding him to march faster while screaming ugly obscenities and threats. He motioned Hanus in the direction of a large table, placed on the far end of the clearing.

At the table stood a young SS officer questioning the men about their professions; separating craftsmen from professionals with higher education. With some forewarning, most denied being university graduates, knowing the Nazis loathed Jewish intellectuals and prioritized them for immediate annihilation. As the queue advanced Hanus found himself standing in front of the SS man who was to decide his fate. The two men who went before him claimed to be miners. Hanus had misgivings about such a spurious choice and when his turn came, he blurted out, more on an impulse than on reflection, that he was a locksmith. Behind

Hanus stood his good friend of many years, who almost automatically repeated that he, too, was an expert in the repair of locks and keys. The SS man approved of Hanus' trade and motioned both men, the self-declared artisans, to join the tiny group set somewhat apart from the rest of the large, hapless crowd.

It was then that Hanus saw a shocking sight. On the ground, near the center of the meadow and close to the large table, lay the carelessly tossed body of a young, beautiful woman. She was dead, executed by a single bullet to the nape of the neck. A fine trickle of blood was slowly congealing on her white, long neck gathering into a small pool of partially coagulated blood, ever so unhurriedly extending around her neck. The dry soil soaked up thirstily the essence of her life. Right above her lifeless body straddled an SS officer, his legs far apart, clutching his still smoking gun in his right hand.

Standing over the dead woman, he began to shout, screaming at the top of his voice at the bewildered and petrified crowd to take a good look at the executed girl. They all stared transfixed at the tragic sight, unable to fully grasp this horrific scene. Most who stood on the grassy meadow gradually regained some composure and began to concentrate on the incoherent speech of the uniformed SS man. They understood that the wrathful officer admonished them to take warning. The young woman was guilty of attempting to smuggle some of her jewelry into the camp's barracks. She was brazen enough, he said, to try to violate the clear German decrees. The only appropriate penalty was instant execution.

The ranting went on, as he tried to envelop his murder in legalistic lingo. He informed them that they had crossed the border into Belarus and were subject to different laws. All the regulations would be enforced with utmost vigor and strictness; none would receive mercy or leniency.

The SS man rambled on, in his never-ending blustering tirade: They were to turn in all the valuables they had brought and any treasures hidden on their bodies. Those who complied would be shown mercy, and permitted to enter the camp, but those who did not co-operate, well... He paused and pointed a meaningful finger at the lifeless body of the beautiful woman. Then, after a moment of silence to drive home the point, he exhorted them to hand over all their valuables: money, jewelry, fountain pens, watches, wedding bands. All was to be placed in the open large suitcase prepared for the contraband. It did not take more than one glance at the nude corpse to persuade the terrified mass into compliance. They turned in much that they hoped to conceal on their bodies in hopes of placating the SS man. In record time, the huge trunk was filled to capacity.

Over the next few days, Hanus learned that this was nothing but a hackneyed trick, quite successful in moving people to give up their last prized possessions. To intimidate the newly arrived and produce a powerful shock, the SS chose one member of the arriving transport, preferably a young and pretty woman, shot her at close range, execution style, and left the corpse on display to emphasize the dread of things to come. The dead body was such a mighty deterrent that none would risk a similar fate even for the most prized of possessions. The Germans, who were well aware that most would be dead within the hour, saved themselves the work of body cavity searches, which they would have to do otherwise.

As the small group of "artisans," perhaps six or seven men, awaited further instructions, one SS man approached and asked if any had family members among the assembled large crowd on the other side of the meadow. None would claim a relative, for fear of being sent with the doomed masses.

Then all hell broke loose. The guards commanded the entire large group into the waiting trucks as speedily as possible. Only now Hanus noticed three large trucks parked on one side of the meadow. The bedlam that ensued their unloading from the train was so overwhelming that most did not notice the awaiting large lorries. Amidst ear shattering noise created by screaming SS men, the frightened people scrambled into the trucks to avoid more vicious beatings. Piercing orders drowned their cries and moans and only a few eluded the lashing whips and blows.

One SS man with a bullhorn informed the group that all newly arrived would be driven presently to the camp itself, where they would find shelter and receive work assignments. A few of the inmates dragged their feet, anxious about their future destination and the ride in the closed rear of a truck. Though the frowning expressions did not bode well, one of the SS men responded to the unrest with surprising calm, reassuring that all would be transported to the same place and enjoy the same treatment: Not to worry! That was the only truth the SS man uttered during his long oration.

All Hanus could see were the three large lorries waiting, not enough to transport all the people, even squeezed body-to-body. Then the back doors of the lorries slammed shut and the vehicles drove off. Once the motorcade was out of sight, the SS ordered the unloading of two more wagons of the train and the entire sinister procedure began all over again. People, luggage, speeches: The script was reproduced verbatim.

It came as a surprise to Hanus to see the three lorries returning in a relatively short time. Although by then none of the inmates had a watch, Hanus guessed that it took less than a half hour for the vehicles to roar back to the meadow. He concluded that the main camp was a short distance away. The same routine was followed until all the wagons were emptied, with only one exception; the first boxcar remained sealed.

Nearing the end of the unloading, the SS ordered a search of all the evacuated boxcars and the removal of any dead and dying. Most of those still inside were dead, and their lifeless bodies were thrown unceremoniously into the open field. Among them a few were still alive, if only barely so. Unable to move, too weak to respond, dirty, smeared with excrement, they were well on their way out of their earthly misery. The stiff corpses mingled with those still alive, the mass quivered sporadically, the scene in sharp contrast with the lovely meadow filled with bewitching flowers.

With every passing minute, the SS men became even more irate, losing all self-control. They beat down on those evacuating the last of the wretched and degraded cargo, bloodying many, who staggered and reeled, rushing away to work faster yet or at least appear to do so. The SS men whipped and clubbed anyone within reach, indiscriminately, clearly rushing to finish what they considered a busy and hard day's work. Finally, it was over. The meadow was littered with the dead and dying; another transport of Czech Jews had been processed.

At last, the SS men barked orders to unlock the first wagon. Into sight poured a pile of dead bodies, all revealing clear signs of execution with a single bullet to the back of the neck. The wagon was cleared; the bodies tossed on the growing pile of dead and dying. Although Hanus toiled with the commando unit, all putting out their best effort, the SS men continued to shout and curse that all Jews were lazy swine, slow and stinky. To punctuate their damnation, they dealt vicious blows to the right and left with the butts of their guns and their truncheons.

The violent fury fed on itself, soon reaching its apex. At that moment an SS man noticed a young Jew, hesitating, not knowing where to place the body of a young girl, still alive and talking to him, repeatedly begging for water. The infuriated SS man rushed behind and smashed the barrel of his rifle onto the head of the young man with such ferocity that he killed him instantly. As if oblivious to the fact that his victim could no longer comply, he screamed at the top of his lungs: "Throw the f... Jewess on top of the others. It is all the same. They go to the same place, you bloody, idiotic Jew!"

Every prisoner worked at a feverish speed, hurling all onto the truck, the dead, sick and weak, till only one body remained: The young woman who served as a warning and deterrent to the others. Her body was pitched on top. What exactly followed once the doors were slammed shut was only speculation. None who lived through this hour of terror lived to tell of their last minutes. It is likely that all the trucks had the same destination. They drove with their cargo, unloaded in the nearby forest and returned for more of the same.

The small working group left behind fell silent, numb, waiting for orders. The initial order sent them scurrying to load the luggage of the entire transport onto the returning trucks. Three civilians, who spoke German and who seemed friendlier than the rest, accompanied these large loading trucks. Two of the newly arrived Jews plucked up their courage and whispered a question to the three civilians: "Where are we now, and where did the rest of our group go?" The furtive answer seemed totally unbelievable. The man replied softly: "They all went to heaven."

That response sounded preposterous, insane, beyond belief. The transport was comprised of 978 people, most still alive a few short hours ago. Hanus did not have a watch, but he had an excellent sense of time, and he would have vouched that only two or three hours had passed at the most since they stopped here on those dead-end tracks. How was it possible to murder that many people in such a short time?

Hanus, even after all his experiences, was still a novice, a beginner in understanding the Nazi mastery of murder. Later he would learn how the Germans established and controlled the most cruel and efficient murder-machine in man's bloody and infamous history. What seemed so incomprehensible to Hanus, specifically the slaughter of nearly a thousand men, women and children in such a brief time, was in reality a very unrefined, if ruthlessly effective process, honed to extreme efficiency. All those who were "to be motored to the camp" were in reality loaded into the lorries to take them to their death. When the doors were slammed shut, the driver sped away in the direction of a nearby forest. The exhaust pipe was redirected, carrying the carbon monoxide into the cabin now jammed with the newly arrived. Usually the engine needed to run for fifteen minutes to fill the air with fumes that snuffed out the lives of the imprisoned men, women and children. Then the lorries came to a halt, close to a huge, freshly dug pit.

The supervising SS men made sure that the time required elapsed and only then commanded the waiting Russian prisoners of war to unload the bodies into the large hole. Then they hosed down the cabin and sent it back for the next load. Therefore it went on and on till the last of those destined to die joined the many corpses in the deep pit. As the end of the day drew near, members of the Lithuanian SS unit that was attached to, but subordinate to, the Germans in rank (often exceeding their masters in savagery), executed the Russian prisoners of war. The Lithuanians were volunteers who joined ranks with the Germans and were used as auxiliaries for the dirtiest jobs, which the Nazis loathed to do.

Before they executed the Russian prisoners of war, the Lithuanians inspected the area to make sure that all was clear and no trace of the massacre was left behind. Then they would mow down the Russians with machine gun fire and only after making sure that there were no living witnesses to the mass murder, the day's job done, they left for home for a hearty supper with their wives and children. After all, many were ordinary, devoted family men, loving husbands and fathers.

Once Hanus understood the dynamics of mass murder as practiced in Maly Trostenec, he swore that he would flee to avoid this fate, no matter the risk. He would not wait for the noxious fumes to snuff out his breath; he would find a way to cheat death, survive the atrocities, and bear witness to the unbelievable barbarity perpetrated in the forests of Belarus. He was despondent, all right, but he was also raging, "How could they, these sons of b..., perpetrate these crimes every day and hope to get away with it?"

Hanus was lucky when he almost intuitively declared himself to be a locksmith and, although he knew very little about locks and keys, he was a fast learner and able to figure out many technical problems simply by thinking through the right approach.

Maly Trostenec was a strange place, desolate, forsaken by God and man. It was located some 16 km away from Minsk, a large city in Belarus, which before the Nazi onslaught was an integral part of the Soviet Union. Previously Maly Trostenec was a *sovchoz*, an agricultural community formed following the forcible collectivization of all farming estates under the iron rule of Stalin. Maly Trostenec of 1942 bore many reminders of its original calling. There were large barns, a few wooden buildings and little else. A fence made of powerful barbed wire, closely watched by armed SS guards in watchtowers, encircled the compound.

Maly Trostenec was peculiar in another way. All the SS men guarding the camp were Lithuanians, enthusiastic henchmen of the Nazis. However, the Germans, who had a rule for almost every eventuality, implemented a regulation forbidding the Lithuanians from entering the camp itself. Their task was to guard the camp from the outside, without establishing any contact with the inmates. Probably the Nazis realized that a black market would develop, and they wished to remain the sole ones to plunder and steal. Maly Trostenec was under the jurisdiction of the SS command in Minsk. The Germans called the camp *"Gut"* which translated into English means "possession or estate or property."

As in many camps, the day by day interior administrative duties rested with the office of the Elder of the Jews, assisted by his appointed Council. The authority and accountability of the Council was answerable to the SS command post in Minsk. All the council members were Jews from Austria and most were corrupt, selfish and living in frenzied fear of their own inevitable and all-too-near demise.

About 450 inmates formed the nucleus and infrastructure of the camp. The transports arrived every two weeks or so from the four corners of Europe. Most arrivals were judged superfluous or sickly and therefore loaded on the trucks with the reversible exhaust pipes. Even those granted a temporary reprieve remained in permanent danger from illness or the displeasure of some SS man. Maly Trostenec was renowned for one distinction; it was designated as the processing center for rich Jews and their families marked for liquidation. The Germans tried to keep the number of prisoners steady at around the 450 mark; to this end, they staged bi-weekly selections, weeding out the sick and replacing them from the newly arrived.

The inmates had to try to keep in good shape, for they had to work very hard. Their days made medieval slavery appear a pleasant fate by comparison. Some worked as artisans in the camp's workshops, while others were employed as tailors altering clothes brought in by the arriving Jews. These craftsmen worked strictly for the Germans, receiving all requirements and specifications from them. Some men worked on maintenance of the camp, which was dilapidated and in constant need of repair.

Another odd trait of Maly Trostenec was that the inmates were relatively well dressed, often much better than their counterparts in other camps. Although they slept on the bare floor of the barns, they were allowed to use warm blankets—thick, woolen ones. Hanus cautiously inquired and received intriguing answers. It was relatively simple to appropriate material from the heavily packed main storage barn, which held the many suitcases and trunks (of the murdered Jews) now awaiting removal to the mainland German depots.

The warm and high quality attire stood in marked contrast to the dire starvation rampant in Maly Trostenec. The food rations were kept at such an inadequate levels that death due to malnutrition was projected after only a few weeks' stay. The hard labor, combined with famine, took a heavy toll on the inmates, who perished at a rapid clip. But that was exactly the aim; the Nazis did not want to feed or shelter their slaves, for they could substitute any number of them with newly arriving fresh blood from the vast European reservoir of Jewish communities. Most of newly arrived died on the same day, and the handful who were assigned to duties in the camp had at best a few weeks' reprieve. Even the hardy ones were soon transformed into a specific phenomenon of the German camps: the shadowy, ghost-like apparitions, the Mussulmen.

Consider the daily food rations: The morning meal consisted only of a small amount of tea. Lunch was a small amount of mixed potatoes and rotting turnips, and the evening meal was again the same tea supplemented with a thin slice of bread. The bread was mostly covered with mold, baked from a mixture of sawdust-like flour. The bread and for that matter all the food tasted sour and rotten. However, the inmates were so starved, beyond caring whether the food was edible or not. Their only all-overriding desire was to still their tormenting, ever-present hunger pangs.

Faithful to their philosophy of dealing with inferior races, the SS kept aloof, keeping their distance from the camp proper. They preferred to remain a remote threat, like an angry deity, dispensing punishment and death from a considerable distance. The Nazis, where possible, relegated the physical savagery to their underlings, their Ukrainian or Lithuanian sidekicks. Where these all-too-willing helpers were unavailable, the Germans recruited other categories of inmates to brutalize the Jews. Some concentration camps had non-Jewish inmates, often hardened criminals, and these frequently volunteered for and were then promoted to in-charge positions and as supervisors; in the camps' parlance they were labeled "the Kapos."

Maly Trostenec was a camp strictly reserved for Jews, guarded locally by Lithuanian SS units under the command of the Gestapo headquarters in Minsk. The SS preferred to stay in Minsk and issue orders from there. Their main objective, after completing their prime directive, the physical annihilation of the Jews, was the maximal exploitation of the Jewish resources under their jurisdiction. The Nazis decided that it sufficed to keep only two SS men on location, while the rest remained in Minsk. The SS man who watched with a keen eye for the proper implementation of all regulations was an *Oberschar-Fuehrer*, the equivalent of a sergeant major, by the name of Heinrich Eiche. A colleague named Tosch aided him.

It was sometime in the summer of 1942 that the Germans decided that the lodgings in the barns were much too good for Jews and ordered the construction of very primitive barracks. These were to be equipped with three-tier bunks, squeezing the inmates into a much smaller area.

One of the most important assignments in Maly Trostenec went to the female prisoners. They worked in a large barn where the many trunks and suitcases confiscated on arrival were stored. The women chosen for this all-important task sat in long rows, working assiduously at top speed, without breaks or interruptions.

The first chore was to break the lock on the suitcase or bag, for no one had the keys to the purloined luggage. The next step called for the separation of articles into their diverse categories; men's clothing set into one pile, female textiles gathered in another. The same went for toiletries, food, shoes, leather goods and all the odds and ends which people brought, hoping to improve their woeful lot. All these items were carefully catalogued and stored, pending their eventual transfer to Germany.

However, these objects were but minor sidelines, mere byproducts of the main objective. The real target and quest for the SS was gold and jewelry, precious stones and hard currency, things small in size but great in value. The Germans knew and experience taught them that their victims tried to hide their worthiest, most cherished possessions in what they hoped were the least obvious hiding places, where few would search.

Unfortunately, there were precious few options, for they could bring so few of the basics that even the greatest ingenuity was of little help. They could bring only one piece of luggage and a blanket, and to make sure that nothing escaped the watchful Nazis, most arriving Jews were subject to thorough body searches.

Still, some were unwilling to give up and tried to use their body's cavities, a method that usually failed because they were frisked with relentless efficiency and rough brutality. Those better informed chose the walls of their trunks or the inside partitions for their stockpile. Some stashed their most prized possessions into the hems of their skirts or the cuffs of their pants while others favored shoulder pads and the tubes of their toothpaste, shoe soles and other more or less inconspicuous places, but even the best of brains generally failed to salvage their valuables for which they risked so much.

In Maly Trostenec, the commando of women worked in a conveyor belt fashion, in silence, doggedly and in a great hurry. They were issued exact directives in carrying out their tasks. They were ordered to cut to shreds suitcases, shoulder pads, tear open all hems and cuffs, no place was left intact if it could possibly have been used as a hiding place. They were very successful; hardly a day passed that did not flush out all kinds of prized valuables.

All that was found was delivered to the camp's infirmary, where the nurse in charge, a Viennese Jewess named Nora Petzelke, for unfathomable reasons was charged with safeguarding the inestimable collection. At least once a week, a van, dispatched by the SS in Minsk, was entrusted with the task of collecting the much-prized booty.

The rest of the plundered objects were of little interest to the German command. Large mounds of clothing, medicines, glasses, shoes, toiletries, matches, saccharine, and scores of other trivia remained virtually untouched. Far from home, the Nazis had little use for the routine, everyday objects, deemed hardly worth the trouble to send to Germany. All they cared about was to put their hands on as many high-priced, easily exchangeable items as possible, easily converted to fluid cash. The rest was of no interest, except to forbid the Jews their use.

During 1942, none of the storage barns were emptied, though filled to capacity, bursting with more and more of the victims' possessions. The valuables stored in the infirmary, on the other hand, were regularly, almost religiously collected and transported to Minsk.

The almost incredible truth is that the punctual weekly pick-ups consisted of several large crates filled to the brim with priceless riches, representing veritable treasure troves. Within lay the hopes, savings and wealth of generations of hard working Jews. The deportee viewed them as a lifeline, a potential means to prolong the owner's life. The expectations were unrealistic; the assets lined the pockets of the Gestapo. Officially, the confiscated valuables were to be safely stored and at a convenient time transferred to Germany. Credible sources claimed that the Minsk SS officers split the loot amongst themselves, sending a small part to the coffers of the Third Reich.

The temptation to exploit this once-in-a-lifetime opportunity, to enrich themselves, spread to the smaller fry who longed for a cut of the spoils. Members of the Lithuanian SS units and the men employed to transport the crates, watched over the plunder. Last, but not least, some of the more privileged inmates in the camp itself watched with envy the growing wealth of the SS men in Minsk. Before long a conspiratorial ring formed that began to pinch from the plunder, siphoning off some prized items. Initially it was a trickle, but soon the culprits became brazen and the thin stream widened to a substantial flow.

As often happens, the situation came to a head through an unlikely happenstance and as the French say: *"Cherchez la femme"* (look for the woman as the cause of the problem). The treasure's faithful watchdog, the reliable and time-tested nurse charged with storing the wealth, Nora Petzelke, fell in love with one of the lower ranking German SS man. Whether he reciprocated her feelings or succumbed to avarice, we will never know, but he was the mastermind of the grand conspiracy.

Nora had to be in love with him, because as a Jewess she could not use the treasures; she knew her days were numbered and had a snowflake's chance in hell of living to see the end of the war. She was all too aware of the risks, but love is known to turn the best of heads and lead people to high-risk behavior even in dangerous times. Through Nora, her lover accessed the collection of priceless loot and diverted much of it into his pockets. Be that as it may, rumors of this "insolent crime" eventually reached the ears of the SS commandant in Minsk.

As could have been expected, he became irate, indeed furious. To the arrogant Teutonic overlords it seemed an unbelievable, incongruent affront to think that anyone could be so impudent as to dare rob the only authorized thieves: the SS officers of Minsk. It was even worse. Amongst the ranks of the SS elite unit was a man who committed "Rassenschande": the crime Nazis considered the most abominable in their legal code. This one crime was loathed with utmost revulsion, viewed as polluting the pure Aryan race. A German who sunk so low as to have, horror of horrors, a sexual relationship with a Jewess, would be cast off. No other felony was rated as ghastly as the particular offense of an Aryan and a Jew engaged in sexual intercourse.

The SS command of Minsk decided that the punishment would be commensurate to the crime. To drive their point fully home they would teach the brazen and recalcitrant Jews a lesson. In the process they will show the lower ranks of the SS unit the consequences of violating the laws and warn the ungrateful Lithuanians to mend their ways—or else!

Initially they charged the previously much-trusted nurse, Nora, with theft and treachery. As far as Nora's accomplice, the SS man was concerned, his superiors decided not to publicly concede his participation in the embezzlement and to keep secret his affair with Nora. They summoned the offender to Minsk, confronted him with the charges, and executed him secretly and without fanfare, thus avoiding the embarrassing publicity of a Nazi betraying their laws and faith.

Nora, in turn, was handled in an entirely different manner. She was to serve as a deterrent to further intimidate the inmates, who teetered on the brink of unpredictable panic. Nora, the fallen trusted confidant and faithful watchdog, would pay dearly for her infatuation with a racially pure German. They quickly took her into captivity; put her through indescribable torment, trying to force her to name her co-conspirators. They also wanted a detailed description of the stolen objects and all the information she could provide about the extent of the conspiracy.

The interrogations went for days and nights. When they felt satisfied that she had divulged all she knew and was near death anyway, they staged her public execution. The order was issued for all inmates to report to the yard and form a circle around the gallows, and wait. All stood at attention, their fear concealed, uncertain if Nora's hanging would be followed by their summary execution.

The action was long in coming; they stood there for several hours before Nora was dragged to the gallows. No one could recognize the rather attractive Nora. Her face was a distorted mass of dried blood caked onto her skin, her nose broken, and her eyes swollen shut. She had no hair on her scalp; it was ripped out, leaving her skull covered with crusted blood. Her hands were mangled, the nails torn from their beds. Nora no longer seemed human as she drifted in and out of consciousness. As they hauled her suffering body, the fractured bones caused her legs and arms to flap around like a broken, lifeless puppet.

An anguished sigh passed through the ranks of spectators, carried by a gust of wind. They all knew the energetic, pretty and sturdy Nora, and seeing what was left of her revealed that she had been put to the rack, tortured, and murdered in small installments. She could not ascend the gallows, and the hangman had to pull and hold her body up, to place the noose around her neck. Most believed that he hung Nora's corpse. All had to watch in silence and witness how the SS punished a disobedient Jewess.

For good measure, to maximize the terrifying effect, the SS men picked, at random, several prisoners, and then included a few men from the Lithuanian contingent. They ordered them to stand near the fence and then shot them as examples of instant dispensation of Nazi justice. The macabre performance most certainly had the desired effect on the dumbstruck inmates and guards alike. It deeply shocked Hanus and his camp buddy Laco.

As it was, both men were constantly on the look out for the opportunity to escape. They made different plans, but most did not stand up to scrutiny and had to be abandoned. An escape was a tall order, for the camp was well guarded; both men knew next to nothing about the surrounding topography. The close proximity of dense forests was a great advantage, as was the supposed presence of roving bands of partisans. However, Hanus lacked any reliable information about making contact with the freedom fighters. Although both men worked as locksmiths and therefore enjoyed greater mobility than the average inmate, they could not reconnoiter the area outside the electrified fence.

In no small measure, they were intimidated by the many previous escape attempts, all of which failed. Most were shot during the attempt – and these were the lucky ones. Others who had the grave misfortune of being caught alive, were marched ceremoniously back to the camp where they were interrogated, publicly flogged, tortured and ultimately hanged in the full view of the camp's entire population. Hanus and Laco were keenly aware of the mortal danger of a flawed escape and determined not to be brought back to Maly Trostenec alive.

Hanus lived with an unflinching, single-minded resolve not to have his life end as Nora's had. This was not to be his final hour; he would make certain of that. If they were apprehended, they would end their own lives. To this end, he approached one of the girls who worked in the sorting barn and purchased a razor blade, which he stitched into the fold of his pants. Hanus, however, was more ambitious; he was determined to take a few Nazis with him. He was consumed by the wish to avenge, even if only symbolically, the Jewish suffering created by the Nazis.

They had to find a way to get their hands on a firearm. This initially sounded outlandish, but upon scrutiny became a real possibility. Cautiously and discreetly, he broached the subject with some Lithuanians, who had known him for a long time and had reason to trust him. He worked with them, was always polite, reliable and taciturn, and they respected his ability to get out of harm's ways. Hanus in turn was aware that the Lithuanian SS volunteers were a greedy bunch; some deeply involved in the siphoning of the absconded jewelry.

From the day the bubble burst, when Nora was captured and she disclosed the involvement of the Lithuanians, the Germans took a dim view of their hired henchmen and showed them the cold shoulder. The Lithuanians, who wished to continue the lucrative business, were on the lookout for a smart insider. Hanus seemed to be a promising candidate. Someone like Hanus or Nora was needed, because the members of the Lithuanian SS were not allowed to enter the camp itself; they were posted on the outside perimeter. These were the strictly enforced orders of the SS commandant from Minsk.

In little less than a month, Hanus and the guard worked out a deal, and what seemed inconceivable was slowly becoming a reality. The deal obliged the Lithuanians to smuggle into the camp, piece by piece, two guns for Hanus and Laco, and Hanus in turn would pay them with gold and hard currency. The guard was so avaricious, his demands so exorbitant, that Hanus doubted his ability to collect so much loot, but in the end he succeeded. The girls who had the opportunity were mostly fond of Hanus, and so bit-by-bit he gathered the extortionate price.

The rest was not at all complicated. It happened frequently and was rather simple for the Lithuanians to summon the camp's locksmiths for a repair right at the camp's fence. The demand to fix a broken lock never aroused suspicion and the conspirators remained safe. The Lithuanians delivered the guns in piecemeal fashion as Hanus handed over their high priced reward, which anyone could translate into comfortable, lifelong financial security.

Hanus and Laco realized that proper planning of such a risky escape demanded much deliberation and the gathering of extensive information. Many uncertainties had to be addressed: the best timing, the least conspicuous hideaways for items they had to carry, the acquisition of the warmest possible clothes, but above all they had to gather data about the layout of the surrounding thickets. They had to cross them to reach the dense forest, where, according to hearsay, they could find and join roving bands of partisans.

Hanus and Laco paid attention to every minute detail, planning for every possible contingency, till they believed that they were ready. As it was, their time seemed to be running out, for they had reason to believe that they might soon become victims of an upcoming selection.

Although they belonged to the group of needed artisans, they could not fail to notice that they nearly fell on two previous selections. One full year in a nightmare like Maly Trostenec was equivalent to decades of rough life elsewhere, and their appearance clearly showed the brunt of it. Their faces became deeply lined; with thinning hair and bulk, they had the appearance of much older men. Their muscles began to vanish and though they managed to supplement their diet with bartered food from the guards, they showed signs of protracted malnutrition.

The only people who hardly ever starved in Maly Trostenec were the women assigned to open and sort out the contents of the luggage. Almost all trunks contained some food, often delicacies, rare in the best of times, let alone in a concentration camp. It goes without saying that in spite of all the close supervision, they managed to gulp down as much as was safe, and smuggle some out. Though they were frisked daily and, if found stealing, were immediately executed, they continued their efforts to alleviate the scourge of hunger. Some girls had a loved one to whom they would pass the food, or they would exchange it for items they needed. Hanus befriended a few women engaged in this hazardous work, who passed some morsels to the friendly locksmith. Usually he bartered with the Lithuanians, who in spite of the risks were always willing to deal for gold and precious stones. Hanus could put his hands on some exquisite jewelry, for often he was summoned to the barn where the bags were sorted, and there he would furtively and dexterously pick up several pieces at a time.

It was Hanus' good luck that the Lithuanians had to trust a Jew, for whom in turn all the gold in the world was of little use. While the goods were in the hands of the Jewish girls, who took enormous risks to smuggle some out, the rapacious Lithuanians waited, salivating for the deal.

The rules were much the same in all the Nazi camps. The main differences were the nationalities and personalities of the guards. The Jews were doomed, but fought to delay their deaths, and the sentries differed only in their predatory insolence. In every camp it was the task of the inmates to sort out unimaginable wealth, which if smuggled out could help the inmate buy another day with a few less hunger pangs. In spite of the enormous risks, the inmates continued their efforts, for they knew that they were lost anyway and it was no more inviting to die of starvation than by gassing, beating, the gallows, or a bullet.

Hanus and Laco decided on a time and date for their escape. The plan centered on the change of guards, which took place every three months. The novices were not as trigger happy, to shoot at every indistinct shadow moving in the darkness. Though most were no less vigilant, they were still a little more reluctant to extinguish human life.

Our two friends decided that the optimal time to flee was during early dusk. They calculated that they would benefit from the cover of darkness and they would have a significant lead; their disappearance would be noticed only many hours later. Their head start would make all the difference in the world, for during the first 12 hours they could run without fearing pursuit close on their heels. By the time the alarm was sounded, they would be a considerable distance from the camp.

They made many inquiries about the lay of the land from the guards, who were willing to sell this information. Hanus learned that the closest brigade of partisans was operating in close proximity to Minsk.

Fortunately, they could traverse the entire distance through forests and some of the local villagers might be helpful. Most of Belarus' population hated the German invaders, who wrought much suffering and devastation on their land. In any case, they would be a lesser threat, in the eventuality of going astray and stumbling onto a hamlet or a man in the forest. If the worst came to the worst, each had a gun and, in an unwanted encounter, it would be either their lives or the enemy's life.

Having prepared themselves with most scrupulous care, they set the date for their escape for August 1943.

On the designated day, they arranged for a task near the fence, not unusual considering the nature of their work. They often repaired locks and other patchwork for the SS in the vicinity of the camp's enclosure. They had surreptitiously buried some civilian clothing on the outside of the fence a few days before. After some hesitation, they rejected the notion of taking food, for fear of being weighed down. They took the most important items: the gun, razor blade, matches and a knife. These, too, they buried outside a day before decamping. Their preparations complete, they waited anxiously for dusk.

As the twilight descended, each man gathered his courage and went separately to the fence to work as planned on a broken, external lock. Once there they pretended to be hard at work, but when certain they were unobserved they quickly dug up their hidden escape provisions and quickly, each man on his own, ran for the nearest cover, where they lay low, breathlessly listening into the dark, moonless night. All was quiet and pitch black. They did not dare utter a word or even a sigh. Silently they changed, shedding the prisoner's rags for peasant's clothes. Reassured by the silence around them, they began their flight in earnest.

Their escape was an arduous and dangerous one. They faced many dangers, including wild animals, rain, cold nights and fear, fear of any shadow which loomed in the dark, thick forest. They became hungry and thirsty, sustaining themselves on some berries and leaves. They stilled their thirst with the early morning dew and rain when available. All of which was insufficient for two young men, whose strength was already sapped by the ordeal in Maly Trostenec. Any time they noticed, even at a great distance, people moving, they froze, mortified by fear of detection and capture.

Luckily, they never had a close encounter with another human being in the forest. They kept their guns loaded and ready to fire, even as they crawled in the heavy underbrush. The forest was thick with tall and powerful trees, while the ground was covered with soft, green moss, like so many forests of Europe. The mushrooms they found were devoured with the appetite of starving wolves. They avoided all open spaces and clearings and slept, during the day, somewhere in a dark corner of the forest. One man would sleep while the other kept vigil for potential dangers. They ran for many nights, at times losing their way, fumbling around, frequently moving in circles. Finally, they began to identify the territory rumored to be in the hands of the partisans.

It was their inordinate good fortune that neither the Germans nor the Lithuanians were particularly keen on pursuit in the wild forests, where the danger of facing the muzzle of a gun aimed at them by an escapee or a partisan was all too real. It was the most unusual of combination of unique courage, ingenuity, excellent planning and very good luck, which finally brought them to the unit of local freedom fighters. To say that they were overjoyed is an understatement, for it was their burning wish to join in the fight against the Nazis.

They presented themselves to the commander of the partisan unit, who to their surprise did not spread out the welcome mat. He had many doubts, for Belarus in 1943 was crawling with spies, defectors, Quislings and other unsavory and shadowy characters. Both men were subject to long and grueling interrogations. They had to answer trick questions to prove their truthfulness and genuineness. The hours of questioning were exacting and tiresome, but neither man resented it, for they knew the caution of the commander was not only justified but imperative. It was the commander's responsibility to prevent infiltration of his unit by spies, who would lead his fighters to disaster.

Following many days of testing, the upper echelon reached the conclusion that both men were genuine and sincere, and could become members. They were then trained in guerilla warfare. Although both men had served in the Czechoslovak army, the tactics of a successful partisan campaign differed markedly from regular military training. The partisans had a type of submachine gun; our twosome had never operated one before. As matters stood, the freedom fighters had a limited number of firearms, and the supply of explosives and bullets was erratic.

Only the best of the best were entrusted with these weapons. Undoubtedly all the men were highly motivated, but not all were equally gifted in this type of warfare, fighting in a hit-and-run fashion, mainly at night and hiding during the day, striking the enemy with surprise at his most vulnerable points. Often a specific action required they blend with the local populace, and to this end they had to master the art of camouflage. No dilettantism was permitted; they had to act like superbly trained professionals.

Neither Hanus nor Laco had a quarrel with such a thorough and precise protocol. The freedom fighters could hardly afford to lose men or equipment; the odds were against them, outnumbered many times over and armed with only light weapons. Every sortie was planned in light of the peculiar nature of their battle. To a man, the squad swore not to be taken alive. They would be horribly tortured, and the squad commander knew only too well that every man had his breaking point. Subject to long hours of torture, anyone would break and disclose classified information.

Hanus and Laco were fast and eager students, burning with desire to qualify and join the active assault units. To their satisfaction, both men were considered fit for action in short order, and they began attacking German columns and installations near Minsk. Hanus described his thoughts and feelings when engaged in his very first sortie. Later his military activity became routine, but his first, so long-anticipated, took him by surprise. Initially he had a little self-doubt: Perhaps he would be overcome by fear, lose his cool, perform less than perfectly?

To his delight, none of his misgivings materialized; just the opposite happened. Even during the most dangerous moments, he never lost focus; in fact, his mind seemed sharper than ever. He felt satisfaction and delight that he was on the attack, and perhaps in some small measure, if it was even possible, exacted retribution for all the suffering the Nazis inflicted. There in the wide expanses of Belarus, Hanus noticed with little compassion how the "German Supermen" whined and cried when hurt or dying. Their grandstanding faltered quickly when they bled and suffered just like other human beings.

Hanus relished in the sensations of no longer being a victim—the humiliated, beaten, dispensable Jew. As he stood tall and proud with his gun in hand, he felt that he somehow regained his dignity and pride. He could not remember exactly when and where it was that he began to feel like a lesser human being. Now he felt that he was reborn as a defender in the fight for justice. This sufficed to reawaken a feeling of worthiness and, to his surprise, old memories, long suppressed in Maly Trostenec. It came to him as a revelation that he could now remember his loved ones, his family, the girl he dated, which all had seemed far away, as if existing on another planet. Perhaps while he teetered on the razor's edge of life and death, he chose to repress his memories, to make his own existence less painful. Now as he again walked tall, he was flooded with all the sweet reflections of the past.

Not all went smoothly from that moment on; fate was not yet done with Hanus. More challenges and pains lay in the wings. As the war progressed and the Russian army gained ground, many partisan units were absorbed into the Soviet army, transforming Hanus into a Russian soldier. During one fierce battle in Belarus,

Hanus' friend, companion and accomplice Laco Kraus was killed. A grenade exploded right next to Laco, killing him instantly.

Hanus was shocked. How was it possible that Laco cheated death for so long, just to fall into her clutches, on the eve of Germany's defeat? Like most young soldiers, he was aware of the possibility, even the probability of injury or death, but in his mind, it was always the next guy, not Laco or himself. Together they had surmounted so many dangers, escaped looming threats; certainly it seemed that destiny willed them to return home together, safe and sound.

Hanus mourned Laco with all his heart; something he would have never done had Laco died in the camp. Death in the camp would have been considered a release from bondage, but the death of his best friend when peace and freedom were within reach was a bitter, grievous tragedy. How much more of life could they have shared?

Laco was more than a friend, or even a brother; he was a faithful companion, ingenious and loyal. Theirs was a unique relationship forged in the fires of hell and steeled by a shared determination. For the first time since the war began, Hanus cried; disconsolate tears ran down his face as he experienced his irreplaceable loss.

The partisans buried Laco with the full glory of a fallen comrade, accompanied by a gun salute and military honors. Hanus, not a pious man, said a prayer, thanking the Almighty for having granted Laco the privilege of dying in battle, saving him from a humiliating death at the hands of the Nazis in their infamous slaughterhouses for the Jews.

The Russian armies fought valiantly, advancing quickly in hot pursuit of the German armies. The once much-touted German military machine, believed to be invincible, retreated in panic, their brigades falling apart in monumental disarray. Hanus' unit pursued the Germans to the Czechoslovak border. Upon crossing into Czechoslovakia, the Soviets granted permission to the Czech soldiers to join the Czechoslovak brigade and liberate their homeland in glory, marching under their own colors, bearing their country's flag and arrayed in their own formations.

Had Hanus and Laco not escaped, they would have been part of the bitter end of the grievous place named Maly Trostenec. It has remained a cursed spot, soaked in blood, tears, misery and death. In June 1944, the retreating German forces led the SS command to review their course of action. The new plan was to conceal all traces of the crimes perpetrated there and in other camps and to eliminate any remaining witnesses. The idea of accountability for crimes against humanity before the global courts was now being taken seriously.

In the case of Maly Trostenec, they well-nigh succeeded. Just prior to the German final retreat, there were 169 Jews still alive in the camp. The faithful henchmen of the Nazis, the Lithuanians, rounded up all the inmates into one of the large barns and when every last Jew was inside, they sprayed them with machine gun fire. When all were dead, the Nazis set the barn ablaze, attempting to blot out all traces of their crimes.

There was an unsubstantiated rumor that some eight inmates, members of the Council of Elders, got wind of the impending execution and fled. When the barn was ablaze the guards left, with the escapees supposedly hiding in a nearby field, overgrown with tall crops of grain. This part of the story could never be verified; none of these eight was ever heard of, nor are their memories recorded. Perhaps the fable of the eight was a figment of someone's imagination, or they met with ill luck later in their flight and perished after all. The Lithuanians reported the final moments of Maly Trostenec's grand pyres, after the war, ensuring its historic accuracy. Historians estimate that well over 250,000 unfortunate Jews perished in Maly Trostenec.

Since none of the eight hypothetical survivors could be found, it is therefore fair to assume that Hanus is the only eyewitness to Maly Trostenec. In this camp thousands upon of thousands of Jews perished, almost unnoticed, disappearing from the pages of history. Were it not for Hanus, nobody would have known of the infamous death camp, Maly Trostenec. Why did Hanus not come forward sooner with this story? This, too, is another sad page of history.

After the war, Hanus and many others spent their best years under iron-fisted Communist rule, which left no room for dissent.

For reasons of their own, it was the unflinching Soviet policy to deny the uniqueness of the Jewish tragedy. The Soviets rewrote history by including the Jewish fate in the nations with which they dwelled, so that the six million murdered Jews became a statistic of their specific domiciles. The Soviets had no tolerance for differing opinions from the official party line.

Hanus by then had a young family and could ill afford to fall out of grace with the dogmatic ruling party. Therefore, the truth had to wait until I received a letter, written in the trembling hand of an old man. In his lengthy epistle, he explained that he never was a man of many words and still found it difficult to describe what happened in Maly Trostenec.

With the war's end, Hanus had only one burning wish: to return home, search for his family and begin a new life. His intention was temporarily delayed by the Soviets, who requested his services as interpreter. His dossier disclosed his command of several languages: Czech, Polish, German, Russian. His skills were much in demand.

On his final discharge, he embarked on a search for his relatives and was occupied with this frantic quest for the entire year of 1946. As he pieced the truth together, he was overwhelmed and shattered by the bad news.

While he languished in jail, after Heydrich's assassination attempt, the Germans appointed a Gentile manager for his mother's store, who in short order brought the business into bankruptcy, ruining all that Mrs. Meyer so painstakingly had built up. Before too long, she and her older son were conscripted into a transport for "resettlement." The transport was destined for Treblinka, one of the infamous death camps in Poland, where both perished. They did not go to death together; the Germans separated men from women, murdering people in gender-segregated groups. Hanus' aunt Helena was sent to Auschwitz, where she failed to pass selection.

He searched for his uncle Hugo, Hanus's guardian and father figure who in the pre-war years held a teaching position in the commerce academy in Carlsbad, his field of expertise being business administration. This city, renowned for its beautiful spas, is located in the region of Czechoslovakia known as the Sudeten.

With a large German populace, it was the location where the first Nazi followers organized into hostile groups to undermine the fabric of democratic Czechoslovakia. Under the leadership of Konrad Henlein and ordered by Berlin, they provoked confrontations, which escalated into brawls and skirmishes. These were exaggerated by the Nazis and used as an excuse for Hitler's demand for reunification of the Sudeten.

Uncle Hugo's business class was attended by one such zealous young man, who daily insisted on greeting the class with the then-prohibited Nazi salute of a raised right arm accompanied by the loud exclamation of "Heil Hitler." The principal of the school tried to end this violation, but his admonitions fell on deaf ears and the enthusiastic buffoon continued in his provocative behavior. Unfortunately, his inciting behavior upset uncle Hugo so much that one day, when the young bigot repeated his salute to Hitler, uncle Hugo lost his temper and slapped the ruffian's face.

An immediate investigation followed and since any corporal punishment was strictly forbidden, Hugo was found guilty by the Czech authorities and transferred to another, similar teaching institution in Prague. His saving grace, the investigating commission acknowledged, was that the young roughneck provoked this retaliation by his repeated actions.

However, the Nazis of Carlsbad did not forget or accept the ruling. When in 1939 Hitler's armies occupied the whole of Czechoslovakia, the Nazis of Carlsbad recalled the humiliation of one of their youths and in vengeance arranged for Hugo's immediate arrest. He was sent to Dachau and in a little over a month his wife was notified of his death. The succinct note ordered her to deposit a certain amount of money for the right and privilege of collecting her husband ashes. The poor, heartbroken widow did as told and received a small box with ashes and in the due course she, too, was deported to Auschwitz, where the white-gloved "Angel of Death," Dr. Mengele, deemed her too old for the right to live.

Fate was unmerciful to the Meyer family. Even the one man who succeeded in fleeing to England, cousin Walter, did not live to see the German defeat. He joined the RAF, became a pilot and flew many missions over Germany. He was an ace, indefatigable in his quest to punish Germany for its many infamies. He volunteered for many hazardous and difficult missions. Tragically, in April 1945, only a few weeks before the end of the war, during an air raid over Berlin his plane was hit, and he died in the crash.

When Hanus returned to Prague, in the late summer of 1945, following an honorable discharge from the army, he did not find a single relative alive. Even the building in which they lived was not spared. It was one of the few structures demolished during the Czech uprising in early May of 1945. Only a handful of houses were damaged in Prague, and it seemed a symbolic end for the home of the nearly wiped out family.

Hanus had to summon all his inner strength and energy not to despair. For a while, he felt that he might not be able to carry on and build on the ashes of all that he loved. Fortunately, his friends rallied around him, helping him lift some of the dark clouds of depression and despondency, whenever they threatened to completely vanquish his shaky equilibrium.

Upon his return from the Soviet Union to Prague, Hanus found and married his pre-war sweetheart, a Gentile girl with whom he had three children. All brought him a great deal of much deserved joy and happiness; all studied well and became high achievers in their chosen fields. His later years were spent, if not in happiness, then in some measure of peaceful tranquility in the midst of his harmonious family.

I feel privileged to have had the opportunity to have been, even if only briefly, in touch with Hanus, who shared with me this story of his life, intertwined with the fate of Maly Trostenec, where so many of my own relatives perished.

A chimney at Majdanek.
The ever-present flow of fire and smoke from the crematories
covered the skies above the death camps and filled the air with the
unique odor of burning hair and flesh.
(Photo courtesy of the author.)

Jossl: Zionist

Treblinka: A memorial marking mass graves
at this notorious death camp.

J ossl stood for Joseph, and some of us, at times, would call him Jossele, not because the sound of this endearment suggested a childish streak in the man, but simply because he was a dear and wonderful friend. He was a rare breed; a man, who to know was a privilege and to become a friend with was exceptional luck.

Jossl differed greatly from most young Czech Jews, among whom he worked, functioned, socialized and eventually became incarcerated. He was not born in the western part of Czechoslovakia, where the Jewish minority was by and large entrenched in a solid middle class.

Most of the Jews from that part of the republic enjoyed the comforts of a secure home and a solid education, enriched with many extracurricular activities. It was almost the rule to offer lessons to the younger generation. Lessons in music and sports, an integral part of any upbringing, and foreign languages were an absolute must. Most of us were tutored, at great parental expense, just to provide us with the best available cognizance.

In the two western provinces, the period between 1918 and1938, a brief twenty years, opened new vistas to the Jewish minority, as equal rights were bestowed on the Jewish population. It goes without saying that the Jews eagerly seized this opportunity, denied them for so long. The middle class, to which most Bohemian and Moravian Jews belonged, was relatively well off and doted on their offspring, valuing above all else education and intellect.

The two eastern provinces differed markedly in every conceivable aspect. In Slovakia and Ruthenia, conditions reflected the greater animosity and anti-Semitism of the rather unsophisticated, rural population towards their Jewish minority. The farther east one went, the more intense the prevailing plight of the Jews.

The local population was rather gullible, sparsely educated and easily brought under the domination of the local clergy. The official line of ecclesiastic teachings continued to foment the centuries-old prejudices against Jews, accusing them of deicide, treason and exploitation of simple folk. The two eastern provinces were out of sync with the rest of the country in advancing every human endeavor. At times, it seemed these two parts did not form one and the same state.

The Slovaks and the Ruthenians were governed for centuries by their more powerful neighbor, Hungary, who willfully neglected the economically and culturally deprived peoples under their domination. They remained impoverished, and their paths evolved along entirely different lines than that of the Czechs. By far the most marked difference was the dominant influence of the local clergy, which kept the population steeped in dark and rabid anti-Semitism, exacerbated by envy and jealousy of the slightly less destitute Jews. This toxic potion often bubbled over and created dangerous and lethal conditions, bringing Jewish lives and livelihood into jeopardy.

Although (or perhaps because) the Jews never felt safe or comfortable among the Slovaks and the Ruthenians, they remained the more faithful to and observant of their ancestral faith, diligent in religious studies and Jewish traditions. They followed dutifully the ancient teachings, trying to educate their children as best they could. The families were usually large, and many barely scraped out a basic living. Most remained dirt poor and at best could provide religious teachings for the boys. To educate daughters was not deemed imperative; the right place for the woman was in her home, where she was mandated to keep the religious commands.

Life was led along strict rabbinic rules, which commanded the brightest of men to engage in lifelong study of the Torah. Because few could afford to join the Yeshiva (a center dedicated to religious studies), most fulfilled their obligation after work. To eke out a livelihood meant, for the most part, backbreaking drudgery extending for many long hours of the day. Thus, most women were left on their own to tend the family hearth and create a tradition-filled home.

Slovakia boasted many famous Yeshivas, among which was the world-renowned "Pressburger Yeshiva," widely recognized and respected, visited by many important religious scholars and consulted by many illustrious sages. However, most Slovak Jews could not attend the respected center, and as far as their secular education was concerned, they lagged behind the West. They were also no match in terms of material and worldly success. Their lifestyle was by and large unchanged.

Jossl called his home a small village in Eastern Ruthenia, at the poorest and most desolate tip of the poverty stricken province. Several other families settled in the hamlet, all indigents, living from hand to mouth.

Some of the men made a living as peddlers. Each would shove his pushcart, filled with household goods and assorted odds and ends, hoping to barter with peasants in surrounding villages. The more affluent peddlers dealt in furs or engaged in the horse trade, which consisted mainly of smuggling the animals to the neighboring Hungarian border villages, which had the same desolate appearance and lifestyle. There they would haggle fiercely over every penny, hoping to squeeze a small profit out of the sale.

Most of the men folk left home at the crack of dawn on Monday, to rejoin the family Friday afternoon, just in time to welcome the Sabbath, the highlight in the life of every Jew. All this drudgery barely brought in enough for the basics, supplemented by eggs and poultry from the hen houses in the backyard of every shack.

Still, Sabbath was the most festive day of the week, and almost every family would spend the extra money to purchase the luxury of a fish traditionally served to mark the crowning glory of the "Sabbath." Thus, the toil of the pious Jew culminated in a pinnacle of religious deference in the circle of his family. The numerous children of the family were raised to help the overburdened mother, who hardly knew any leisure, luxuries or interests except the well-being of her family.

Compounding these privations was the implacable and unrelenting hostility of the Gentile population. The irrational hatred never changed, threatening the Jews as much as in the days of their forced segregation in walled ghettos. Though the federal government of Czechoslovakia outlawed anti-Semitism and prosecuted pogroms against Jews, tolerance, let alone acceptance, was far from the hearts of the local population. Many believed the Jew to be the Christ killer, absorbing the sermons from the pulpits; others based their hatred on the vicious charge that Jews were loan sharks, exploiting the ignorance of illiterate peasants. Jews were portrayed as crafty, cunning schemers, who somehow outwitted the simple indigenous population.

In many ways, the eastern Jew had the much harder life, with fewer opportunities and less affluence than his western brother, but unlike him, he derived more spiritual comfort from his faith and close-knit community. Even as the Bohemian and Moravian Jews began to assimilate and integrate into a more liberal society, the eastern Jews had neither the opportunity nor inclination to mingle and seek acceptance.

In some ways, this was a blessing in disguise, for this enforced self-sufficiency spared the eastern Jew the many insecurities, anxieties and uneasiness complicating the lives of those Jews longing for admission into the mainstream. At the crossroads, many western Jews questioned their religious beliefs, bringing their entire existence into question. The shaky balancing act gave ample reason for introspection. The ardent attempts to adapt, change and conform to Gentile norms often eroded what was left of the Jewish foundation of life.

Many an assimilated Jew became more troubled, searching within himself for the ugly stereotypes justifying anti-Semitism, till he convinced himself that, yes, there was something inherent, perhaps a congenital deformity to the Jewish character which evoked and fueled all the hatred hurled at Jews for the last two pain-filled millennia.

The continuation of this trend brought the assimilant to religious conversion, frequently inspired by professional advancement and social acceptance. While some of those who accepted Christianity improved their careers, most failed in their social integration. Moreover, this attempt was aggravated by the personal discomfort of the apostate, who longed to submerge within Gentile society, just to find out that his baptism notwithstanding, he was still perceived as a Jew.

To make matters worse, in spite of all the valiant efforts the new Christian found out that his own reactions and responses differed from the genuine McCoy. It goes without saying that the harder he tried to sound genuine, the thicker he put on his act, and the less credible were his desultory attempts, which harvested only suspicion as to his real motives.

It was a no-win situation and all knew it, except for the poor assimilant, who blamed the imperfection of his act for his failings. The tragic neophyte was unwilling to accept that Jews were indeed different. Though they were no Christ killers, loan sharks or devils incarnate and did not aim to rule the world as the "Protocols of the Elders of Zion" insisted, they still thought along somewhat different lines than most Gentiles.

The roots of the dissimilitude were the results of contrasting conditions, over two millennia spent in a hostile Diaspora. This history and experience etched into the Jew's personality the priorities and imperatives for survival, factors not shared by the national majority. The eastern Jew, whose opportunities were markedly circumscribed, often envied his better-integrated brothers, overlooking the toll exacted by adaptation and frequent isolation.

Jossl's father made a precarious living, forever teetering on the brink of absolute penury. He was one of the many pushcart peddlers selling household items and a hodgepodge of merchandise, pushing his meager goods from village to village. On his cart he carried some dresses, scarves, soaps, towels, dishes, multicolored threads, needles, some small tools: all that he hoped the villagers might find useful.

On occasion, he had to sell on credit to a peasant who promised to pay next time, but who often reneged, and Jossl's dad would lose. In spite of all these adversities he would leave, without fail, every Monday, walking alongside his horse and cart, for yet another week of rounds among the villagers, hoping this one time for better luck.

He would, like clockwork, return home on Fridays for the one day even the poorest Jew feels like a king, welcoming with his family the advent of the holy Sabbath. That was the one evening when the family table was covered with a white tablecloth, and wine would be poured for the traditional Kiddush. Mother would light and make a blessing over the candles, and to the youngsters suddenly the humble dwelling became a princely dining hall.

These were some of the memories Jossl took from his home and cherished through his all-too-short life. Years later he would relate his delight watching the flickering sheen of candles mounted on tall silver candlesticks reflecting on the snow-white tablecloth. These few precious items represented a family heirloom, the only dowry his mother brought as a young bride into her new home.

All traditional benediction and prayers were faithfully followed, even though the father showed signs of fatigue etched into his face by the hardships of the past week. Often he looked haggard, drawn and aged beyond his years. There was a smoldering anger under the surface, suppressed only in deference to the holy Sabbath.

Many times, when the father returned home, the children sensed his bottled up anger and did their best to avoid him. The four boys and two girls knew that he had a short fuse, which ignited at the slightest vexation. In easier times, he was a kind man, who cared for his wife and children, and he was bothered by the fact that he could provide only marginally. Jossl remembered him usually being frustrated, burdened by the grinding poverty, unpredictable and temperamental.

Jossl, the oldest of his sons, was often on the receiving end of his father's blows, usually with his belt. Jossl felt that he was chosen as the lighting rod for his father's frustrations. In those moments, he hated his father, judging him to be cruel, unjust and a brute. After a while, his anger would subside, and he'd feel pity for the old man, realizing that he was only the scapegoat for his misery.

It did not take long for Jossl to tacitly forgive his father, and with the arrival of the Sabbath he would willingly accompany him to the small shul, where they joined the rest of the congregation, praying devotedly in gratitude for the arrival of the sacred day granted to the Jews.

Jossl's pious eagerness was a show; he decided long ago that he would build his life differently. He would not spend his years in unprofitable drudgery. Jossl read all he could put his hands on. He not only learned more about the world outside the perimeter of his village, but also of the many new ideas conceived to improve man's lot.

Jossl could read only in the absence of his father, who would consider reading anything but a prayer book a total waste of time and a luxury his son could ill afford. It was Jossl's much adored mother, herself eager to learn and awed by study, who understood and supported his curiosity.

Whenever Jossl spoke of his mom his voice softened, filled with warmth, at times quivering with emotion. She was his heroine, who encouraged and inspired him to learn and aim high. She was indulgent and outright proud of her eldest, who showed much promise and a scholastic aptitude.

Sometimes during the early decades of the twentieth century, the Ruthenian Jews became more intimately acquainted with Zionist ideology. Many idealists made it their life goal to travel and spread the Messianic message to all four corners of world, bringing new hope to the ill-treated and abused Jews. The ideology found wide appeal among those who had little to look forward to in their host countries. Quickly, like a wild fire, it found many supporters who longed for new vistas, hoping to cast off the shackles of second-class citizenship.

For long many centuries, the pogromized, robbed Jew was discriminated against, kept at bay on the margins of society, never allowed to enter without the passport of conversion. A new dream promised a rebirth of an old nation, a return to Zion, where Jews could live freely, fulfilling their destinies and following their traditions. What a glorious mirage, transcending all expectations! Some thought it was but a chimera, but Jossl took it to his heart; to him this was a vision worth living and working for.

It was sometime around his Bar Mitzvah when Jossl joined the ranks of the Zionist youth movement. His enthusiasm grew by leaps and bounds; he loved the theoretical study, combined with physical training readying the cadets for military duties as well as work in the fields, which would be needed to reclaim the neglected land of Palestine.

The movement provided abundant reading material about Jewish history and Jossl, always a voracious reader, immersed himself in the study of Zionist ideology, socialism, history and a host of other related topics. Jossl developed an enthusiasm for the ideas of an egalitarian, non-materialistic society as the first, remedial step in healing the fractured and warped Diaspora Jew.

The early Zionists foresaw an interim period of healing and adaptation to the conditions prevailing in Palestine, a barren, much longed for, old-new home. Jews were alienated from agriculture, for in the Diaspora they were forbidden to own farms. They remained relegated to small commercial ventures or crafts, money lending, peddling, running pawnshops, and other minor economic activities.

Jossl became an ardent member of the left-leaning faction of the Zionist movement, the Hashomer Hatzair (the young pioneers). He would not miss a meeting or a lecture; he attended all as if his life depended on it. His newly found ideals gave him direction and filled the void with purpose. However, a vexing sensation caused him to vacillate between Communism and Jewish nationalism.

The dire poverty and being the sole supporter of nine beings, forced Jossl's father to deny his eldest the opportunities of higher education. In fact, times were so tough that Jossl and his four brothers shared two pair of shoes amongst them, often resulting in some having to skip classes if the other brothers wore their footwear.

The little hut they called home consisted of two small rooms and a kitchen. The parents had one, the four boys shared the other and the girls slept in the kitchen. None had a bed and they slept in two- or threesomes. The blankets, though stuffed with eiderdown, were old and worn and, like everything else, were too few for the large family.

Jossl's father placed him in an apprenticeship with the local cobbler. Jossl left school heartbroken, hating to leave and immediately loathing the calling of a shoemaker.

The father would not have thought of consulting his wife or the young man whose future he decided. He completely disregarded Jossl's predilections and in doing so inflicted a major injury on his son. Jossl was contemptuous of the craft of a cobbler and believed it to be a dull, uninspired and unprofitable trade. He longed to read books. He was not eager to join the ranks of artisans; his ambition was to become a scholar. However, he knew better than to remonstrate with his despotic father.

Even his supportive mother could not put in a word; she was well aware of the precarious situation of the family. Education was a privilege to be dreamed of, not simply embarked upon, at least not in eastern Ruthenia, by the son of a pushcart peddler. Jossl noticed a few furtive tears that she could not conceal and decided to put on an air of acquiescence. He would not pour salt into her open wounds.

Surprisingly, the members of his Zionist cell were delighted with his training; it fitted well with Zionist ideology. The modern day Jew, decreed the Zionist philosophy, had to return to manual labor. Either he would work the land to dry out the many swamps and irrigate the parched fields or he would become a craftsman, contributing with his labor to the self-sufficiency of the Jewish nation.

The Zionists viewed Judaism's overrepresentation in the intellectual fields as anomalous, an anachronism, and a burdensome hangover from the cursed days of the Diaspora. The long dispersion from Israel alienated the Jew from his soil and productive manual labor. It would be this labor, alone, which would redeem and normalize Jewish life. Only then would Jews be equal with the rest of the family of nations.

As always, for Jossl the Zionist teachings could not be wrong. He was determined to break his ties with Europe and build his future in the Promised Land. Jossl spent all his free time working for the movement, which found a following among the impoverished youth of Ruthenia. He immersed himself in planning for an early departure from Ruthenia to Palestine, from the dismal conditions of an unwanted, barely endured minority.

This mindset allowed a tolerance of his apprenticeship with the local cobbler, which he learned to view as a stepping-stone to his Aliyah ("return": more accurately, "ascent" to Palestine). Additionally, he was able to continue to study, within the movement, history and politics from the Zionist perspective.

He became even more alienated from his lukewarm religious piety. The Zionists preached another devotion to Judaism, not based on religion, but rather on political and national identification. The aspiring pioneers had their brand of religious interpretation, dismissing orthodoxy, which they thought kept visible and invisible walls around the persecuted nation.

The Zionist revision of religious practice based observance on the Decalogue and the affirmation of the Covenant by marking the high holidays. All else was considered redundant, indeed wasteful, and therefore objectionable, for it prevented men and women from fulfilling the sacred goals of Zionism: to work the land, rebuild the old-new homeland and gather in the returnees.

The Zionist ideology was rooted in the foundation of secular redemption. The long hours of prayers practiced by the orthodoxy were deemed inefficient, if not a waste of time, and were therefore done away with. It was felt that the pious lagged in secular progress, and the reliance on divine redemption turned the Jew to passive acceptance of the inequities and his suffering. Many rabbinical rulings came under scrutiny; indeed many values, if not completely rejected, were seriously questioned.

The main emphasis was on the establishment of a Jewish homeland. Was it not high time to recognize the errors and usher in a new era before another even worse tragedy befell the Jews? With hindsight, the Zionist philosophy sounded like a cry of warning from the Biblical prophets, not heeded in the past and grasped by few in the twentieth century.

To Jossl the Zionist platform was based on irrefutable and historically sound arguments. He absorbed it with the passion of a teen, filling the void of commitment and direction of his life. Jossl was not only an ardent disciple of his new faith; he aspired to become one of its apostles and spread the word of the nationalistic ambitions of the Zionists. He became so absorbed, he spent all his free time and energies advancing the cause. The movement became his guiding star.

Soon fate brought more substantiation to the Zionist struggle. In Germany, a new political party usurped power: the "Nazis." Their basic tenet called for vitriolic anti-Semitism, stressing the need to excoriate all Jews from German society, indeed to create a Germany without Jews. (*Judenrein Deutschland*). Their rabid, violent anti-Semitism was by no means original; many before had spouted a similar absurdity that often resulted in much harm to the defenseless Jews. The only unique feature the Nazis could lay claim to was the hallucinatory demonization of Jews and the pathological ambition to destroy Jews the world over.

Most nations did not identify with the depraved, hateful plan that not only projected deracination of Jews, but plotted their eradication. However, some still offered tacit approval, while others admired the bold project though doubting the feasibility of its implementation.

Closer to Jossl's home, in Hungary, matters were not as extreme. Though Hungary had a long, painful history of Jew baiting, and the fascist party there was inimical to Jews, matters were more restrained, mainly due to Marshall Horthy's reluctance to follow the German example. Since his son was married to a Jewess, matters hit closer to home, forcing some moderation. Hungary, along with the rest of Europe, was not yet conditioned for the Nazi-invented new industry of mass murder. The Hungarian fascists were a brutal bunch, but their main goal was to rob and only as a by-product inflict bodily harm.

Most Jews watched and listened attentively to the deteriorating conditions, but few recognized the enormity of the peril quickly engulfing them. Most believed their own wishful thinking that the Nazis were bluffing, courting the scum, the roughnecks, and the assorted riffraff of society. However, the Nazis rejected even those Jews who accepted Christianity with baptism; the ruling of the Nuremberg racial laws stipulated that anyone with one Jewish grandparent was a Jew. Many an anti-Semite found himself suddenly on the receiving end of this hateful, discriminatory practice.

It was in the late thirties when Jossl successfully completed his years as an apprentice shoemaker and enrolled in a trade school for the concluding compulsory year of certification. For that reason he had to move to a town, where these courses were offered, to fulfill the requirements stipulated by the guild. Only a candidate who successfully passed the practical as well as the final theoretical stage was eligible for certification as a fully skilled artisan. Jossl moved to a Slovak town, from where he hoped to immigrate to Palestine immediately upon receiving his diploma.

Jossl passed his exams but was asked to delay his departure by his peers in the Zionist cell. He was advised to take a job with a local cobbler and await future directives. Such was the discipline of the young "Hashomer Hatzair" members that he did not even question or protest an order which went much against his grain.

The reason he was kept back was justified. The Zionist leadership anticipated that a flood of émigrés would want to escape Europe illegally, and these groups needed young, intelligent and courageous leaders. The illegal refugees would have to cross several frontiers, all hostile and well guarded. In addition, at the end of the road British forces closely watched the shores of Palestine. Britain, the mandatory power, prohibited Jews from entering Palestine, caving in to the pressure of the greatly alarmed Arabs. Thus, only special individuals might succeed, and Jossl was considered ideally suited. He was not only intelligent, but also brave and quick to improvise –a rare but needed set of attributes.

Additionally, the leaders of this clandestine operation had to be hardened individuals, of a daredevil attitude, who had proved their mettle. Hazards for the illegal refugees loomed at every step; all were illegal, and none had a valid passport or entry permit to Palestine. Jossl appreciated the trust and placed the cause above his own personal desires.

He was drilled in the techniques of handling the many types of situations and emergencies which could complicate the journey, such as various contingencies at border crossings; life-saving procedures were practiced. The sea voyage was often perilous, frequently undertaken in old, overcrowded vessels no longer seaworthy. At the end of the road, when they reached the well-patrolled shores of Palestine, the last stretch of water often had to be swum or waded through under cover of darkness. The illegal émigrés had to make the attempt on a moonless night with reduced visibility, for if the British spotted the illegal immigrants, they forced them back on the ship, turned them around, and sent them back into the darkness of Europe.

It follows that the men chosen to lead the illegal refugees had to possess many talents; they were men who could make rapid decisions, improvise with limited resources, and endure the physically strenuous journey, yet leave enough in reserve to assist the exhausted immigrants who often had to be carried ashore.

Jossl passed the training program with flying colors, mastering quickly the skills and knowledge needed for this clandestine operation.

He was initiated by leading a small unit over the border to Hungary, and from there to Yugoslavia, where they boarded a boat retained by the "Sochnut" agency responsible for assisting immigrants to the planned Jewish homeland. The site of embarkation and the flag were changed often and many port officials' palms were greased with substantial bribes to help them overlook the strange, unauthorized vessels heavily laden with human cargo, departing in the dead of night.

If all went as planned, the refugees would reach the shores of Palestine on a moonless night, where they would be met by dedicated kibutzniks, who speedily whisked them away. The success of the operation hinged on swiftness, decisiveness and attention to minutiae.

Jossl did well in his new role. He even enjoyed the high tension, the adrenaline rush, and the thrill of the cloak and dagger atmosphere. The men who handpicked him watched his performance with growing interest. They were more than pleased with his performance, keen intellect, organizational skills and presence of mind under seemingly insoluble conditions. No challenge seemed insurmountable. His superiors decided that a man capable of such commanding leadership could fill a riskier post, and they transferred him to the Protectorate (occupied Bohemia and Moravia), where he had to operate right under the noses of the ruling Nazis.

Jossl was less than happy about the special task thrust upon him. However, primed by the many years of training, he quickly subordinated his personal feelings to the demands of the urgent rescue mission. The greater hazards of the new assignment bothered him less than the additional delay of his own plans to settle in Palestine and start a new life. Such was the self-discipline of a young Chalutz (Pioneer), and again, he did not complain.

He followed his instructions carefully, doing his homework with great care. He had to study new techniques, maps and different subterfuges, learning to spirit people out of a country closely guarded by the Nazis. He received a new alias, identifying him as a Gentile construction worker employed by a private firm. All was fictitious and would not stand thorough scrutiny, but for a casual check, it was credible enough. He was asked to wear shabby overalls and hobnailed top boots. As always, the organization was strapped for money and provided a shoestring budget, just enough to subsist on, but that was the last thing to bother him. Never used to luxuries, he would have considered it unethical to spend more than a bare minimum from the meager kitty of the organization.

Since his documents were not quite convincing, Jossl would rarely sleep two nights in a row at the same place and was always on the move, sharing rooms with other members of the Youth movement.

In his capacity, he would meet those he was to smuggle to safety, rehearse their new identities with them, tell them what to anticipate, and brief them about the rigors of the journey. He told them they could bring only a small carry-on with their essentials. Each person was to bring one change of clothes, a knife, matches, money and little else. Much depended on swift and unencumbered mobility.

The group met in Moravia, each member traveling independently. From there, they planned to cross into Slovakia, where they would hide in a forest near the Hungarian border. There they would wait for darkness and then cross into Hungary, escorted by a bribed local guide. They had to reach the Hungarian side in the wee hours of the night. The few members of the border police who were bought off were present only on certain days and in the early hours of the new day.

The target days were Tuesdays and, if all went according to plan, the next day would be spent in the deep forest. They would rest, leaving one on guard, taking turns for their much-needed sleep.

Once in Hungary, they would split into two groups, sleeping in pre-arranged places, and journeying in horse-drawn wagons of peasants who carried their goods into the towns. When night descended, some would walk and others hide, tucked under straw in the back of the wagons. The entire crossing of Hungary demanded utmost operational discretion because some Hungarian fascists were overzealous and potentially very dangerous.

When all the splinter groups reached the border of Yugoslavia, they considered themselves almost out of the worst danger. In 1941, Yugoslavia was an independent country, hostile to the Nazis; there was no threat that the refugees would be turned back and forced to return to the Nazi inferno.

In Yugoslavia, the reunited group would reach a port and in the dead of night would board small boats, waiting for them near the harbor. They would then meet their ship, procured by the Jewish Agency. Usually these vessels sailed without official permits, and while the Jews paid a small fortune for their use, most were nearly shipwrecked old scrap heaps destined for the junkyard. However, the Jews had few options left and therefore settled for use of these rickety craft, some of which capsized on the high seas, drowning many an illegal immigrant.

Once near the shores of Palestine, the ship would anchor some distance from shore, and the refugees would either swim or wade in, depending on the individual circumstance at the site of disembarkation. Those who could not muster the strength had to be carried to shore by the group leader. All this frantic activity had to unfold in silence and complete darkness. The British coast guard and police patrolled the beaches intensely for illegal immigrants, who, if caught, were returned to Hitler's Europe without mercy.

The code name of this clandestine operation was "Black Rose," once the name of a Prague coffee house where some of the conspirators met. This name came to stand for the clandestine smuggling of Jews from Prague. Although "Black Rose" faced many obstacles, several with tragic outcomes, the fact was that many reached the safety of Palestine who otherwise would have ended up in Hitler's ovens.

Jossl led many such expeditions, while hoping to see his own departure day from the accursed continent. Meanwhile, he sent many messages to Ruthenia encouraging his family to leave at any cost and join him in Palestine. He never received a reply to his many letters, but that in itself was no sign of misfortune. He

therefore did not worry when he lost contact with his family; he
only hoped that they were heedful of his warnings and were
already on their way to Palestine.

At this junction of his hectic life, he met Jacob Edelstein, one
of the top functionaries of Prague's Zionist movement. Edelstein
had just returned from his own mission to Palestine and promised
Jossl that the next group he took out would be his last. Jossl was to
make final arrangements for his own emigration and join those
whom he would smuggle out in the next few days. Jossl was
genuinely happy; he thanked Edelstein from the bottom of his
heart and began joyously his preparation for his final journey as an
emissary for the "Black Rose."

From the very onset, little went smoothly. As if jinxed,
problems began to accumulate. The group was comprised of seven
people, out of whom five arrived in Slovakia on their own and
joined Jossl, to await the arrival of the last two men. However, the
two were nowhere in sight, though the time set had come and
gone. Both men were important officials of the Zionist
organization, who had to leave, for their arrests were imminent.

Under different circumstances Jossl would have given the
order to proceed without them, for they could ill afford to delay
their departure; all the connections were precisely timed and
success hinged on a well-orchestrated and synchronized plan.
Nevertheless, this one time Jossl hesitated, weighing the situation,
which perhaps warranted exceptional consideration. Perhaps there
was an explanation for the tardiness of the two men; they might
have been detained in Prague or suffered some mishap on the way.
Jossl wavered and finally decided to wait. This proved to be a
grave mistake that brought about calamity for all of them.

Jossl ordered an overnight stay in one of the hideouts in the
forest. At the appointed time the Slovak guide showed up, ready to
lead them over the border to Hungary. Jossl used some hapless
excuse to put off the crossing for another night and asked the
Slovak to return then. The group continued their vigil.

It was a frosty February night. High snow banks covered the
frozen ground, and that winter the snowstorms were exceptionally
powerful. The sparkling white glare was glistening and radiant. In

spite of the peaceful and serene sight, all the men were nervous and apprehensive.

Jossl, well-versed in improvisation, suggested preparations for the cold night. They would collect branches to construct a shelter, where they would huddle for comfort and warmth. Two men would stand guard and be relieved every two hours. In this way, all would get some rest in preparation for the continuation of their expedition, and the night would not be a total write-off. Though each man wore a parka over layers of warm sweaters, they were soon chilled to the bone. To warm up, they melted snow and heated it for tea on a tiny, square cooker, using a small cubed spirit (alcohol-based fuel), part of their emergency back-up gear.

The hot tea helped for a short time, but the numbing frost persisted. The night was exceptionally cold, the temperatures dipping way below the freezing mark. There was little else to do but wait, and Jossl suggested that two men begin their patrol and the rest get some sleep. If they would huddle close, they might retain some warmth and get some much-needed rest.

Before commencing the night's vigil, one of the men pulled out of his pocket a mickey of vodka, originally intended as a bribe at the difficult crossing. The unexpected ordeal of the icy night convinced all that never was a bottle of liquor put to better use than to dip into the spirit for some warmth. The bottle was passed hand to hand, all imbibed heartily, and soon the bottle was empty. It made some improvement in their mood, and they crawled under the small enclosure built from fir branches, sat on their knapsacks and drew near for warmth.

Soon they slumbered. Even Jossl, the ever-vigilant, cautious and alert fellow, let his guard down. The swig of vodka, rarely tasted, relaxed him, and he gave way to his fatigue. He closed his eyes, lulled into a false sense of security and drifted off for a brief moment.

He awoke up with a jolt, disoriented, quickly realizing he was staring into the muzzle of a gun pointing right between his eyes. Instantly alert, he knew something was terribly wrong. Holding the gun was a frowning, menacingly angry policeman. Jossl made out his uniform; it belonged to the members of the "Hlinka" guard, the militia of fascist Slovakia. These paramilitary units fashioned themselves after the Nazi elite units and were mainly comprised of volunteers. All were rabid anti-Semites, out to kill any Jew, not in the position to offer a hefty bribe for his life.

Jossl understood that unless he could scrape together a large amount of money quickly, they were lost. To make matters even worse, two others, none too friendly, accompanied the policeman. Jossl knew that all three had to be bought off, lest the policeman kill them all on the spot or, in the best possible scenario, throw them into the local jail.

One of the patrolmen demanded their papers. When presented the forged documents, he stared at them with the eyes of a barely literate man, who could not distinguish a legitimate document from a forgery. However, what he failed in literacy he made up for in cunning. Men with nothing to hide do not spend the night in the deep freeze of a winter's night in the depths of a Slovak forest.

The patrolman continued for a long while perusing the documents and finally lifted his eyes and brought them to rest on the knapsacks scattered around. His buddy pointed his flashlight straight into the eyes of the fugitives, briefly blinding them. Jossl knew this precarious situation demanded a diplomatic approach, so he proceeded to open a dialogue, testing for their willingness to deal and the amount they might demand.

Jossl produced a warm smile and suggested, while tellingly rummaging in his pockets, that perhaps the gentleman and his friends could reach a mutually convenient agreement with the group. He, Jossl, would certainly make it worth their while, if only they would be patient and put up with their limitations.

These words worked like a magic wand. The three sentries waited, with barely concealed greed, for the sum pulled out of Jossl's pockets. Jossl knew that he had to start slowly, they would bargain mercilessly for more, irrespective of his opening bid. He had to impress them; these gendarmes did not look like men to lock horns with or take lightly. They would encounter no ill consequences if they killed the entire group and stole everything.

It was therefore mandatory to offer the bait with the promise of more money to follow. Thus, it would be unproductive for the gendarmes to murder them this very night, for the captives could be viewed as the hen who might continue laying golden eggs, if kept alive.

After a moment's search, Jossl produced an impressive amount of cash, all in Czech currency. It was a powerful inducement indeed, and the senior man grabbed it hungrily, stuffing it into his pockets. Jossl shifted his gaze to the other men and in a conciliatory voice offered them an even larger sum in a few days. If they let them continue on their way, they would pay within a week or so the same amount, or perhaps more.

It seemed that an agreement was a foregone conclusion, when suddenly the guard decided that they could not stay overnight in the forest, where they could come to some harm. He would arrange for them to spend the night in the local pub. Jossl tried to talk him out of it, but the guard had the power on his side: a cocked gun, aimed at Jossl's head. The group trudged through the snowdrifts, cursing under their breaths, pinning their hope on the morrow, which might find a more obliging patrolman and, with some luck, even find the two tardy men.

Unfortunately, none of their fervent hopes came to pass. Instead, events took another, even nastier turn. The "Hlinka" guards marched the men to the village, but instead of a night's stay in the local pub, they locked them up in an empty barn. As they marched through the forest, the captives overheard tidbits of the guards' conversation. It did not take a rocket scientist to piece together their discovery.

Someone had invited the peasant, who was to lead them over the border to Hungary, for a drink in the local pub. The man freely imbibed slivovitz, the strong local liqueur, which soon loosened his tongue. Before long he was bragging about his moonlighting, which yielded a higher income than his day job. He confided that it was a lucrative business to squeeze money from the scurrying Jews needing a guide to cross into Hungary. Another patron indulging in a night of drink, who also happened to be a sergeant in the "Hlinka" detachment, overheard his boasts. The sergeant's appetite for money was whetted by the vision of a windfall from the fleeing Jews.

Two other guards joined the sergeant, and they began to deliberate how best to take advantage of the situation. In a little

over an hour's chatter, they had a plan. It was easy to find the
hideout. All the villagers were familiar with the topography of the
forests and the few potential border crossings. As children, they
would roam the forests and cross the border many times, just in
jest. They decided to sneak up on the men, clearly visible by their
shelter of piled up branches, and take them for all they were worth.
It was as simple as that.

This was bad news for Jossl, who was about to offer them
the hard currency he had stitched in his shoulder pads when the
thought occurred that it was already too late. In reality, all was
lost; the sergeant could not accept an offer now.

As it was, many whispered about the profitable deals with
which the "Hlinka" guards enriched themselves. There was a lot of
jaundiced envy in the hearts of his covetous fellow citizens, so the
sergeant had to watch his steps. If he were to let the men go, it
would be obvious that he had taken a large bribe, and he would
open himself to ridicule or even blackmail. If a bona fide Hlinka
guard lost his trustworthiness, he was in danger of losing his
position in the paramilitary unit. Additionally, he could be charged
and prosecuted for taking advantage of his official position.

Jossl saw the need to change tactics; he had to design a new
strategy for damage control, to minimize the impact of their
capture. The most immediate need was to pass word to his
superiors in Prague to warn the two latecomers, and devise a
stratagem for the rescue of the operation. To this end, Jossl had to
act quickly and in a right manner.

Jossl approached the man in charge of their detention with a
polite inquiry of his future intent for them, his captives. The guard
no longer played the game; he could no longer pretend to release
them for the right ransom. Therefore he answered that he was
about to hand them over to the Slovak authorities, which would
charge them with an attempted illegal border crossing. This was
Jossl's fear, and he wished to avoid it at all costs. The charge
would inflict enormous damage on the entire "Black Rose"
operation. First, it would give rise to much publicity, which in turn
would alarm the villagers whose co-operation with the
surreptitious operation was essential.

The only way out, reasoned Jossl, was to convince the guard that he could, indeed he had to, return the men to from whence they came, the Protectorate. In doing so, he would kill two birds with the same stone. It would confirm him as an honest and faithful officer of the "Hlinka" guard, and he would receive a substantial bribe after all.

If he followed the official path of passing them to the Slovak authorities, he could expect little but official approbation, but if he handed them over to the Protectorate border police, Jossl would award him handsomely. Once the group returned, Jossl could resume contact with Prague, hopefully avert the entrapment of the two men, and salvage the operations of the "Black Rose," keeping the only escape valve from Hitler's hell open. Jossl thought that he could justify the massive bribe he was about to offer, as a last-ditch effort, to their captor.

To make the deal more palatable, indeed irresistible, Jossl promised the payment in foreign currency, not in the valueless local tender. The lure of foreign money was irresistible to most Slovak guards, and the sergeant was no exception. The corruption of the "Hlinka" detachment was legendary; for the right bribe, they would violate any law of the land. Thus, the deal was sealed.

The sergeant had to explain his handling of the affair to his two subordinates, who, ignorant of the laws, accepted his interpretation of the regulations. They had complete trust in his knowledge, viewing him as a well-versed man. The sergeant was a simple man with common sense. He wanted not only their admiration, but also their loyalty for his generosity. He reached deep into his pockets and brought out two fistfuls of money, a part of the bribe Jossl handed him a short while ago. The twosome, clearly happy, pocketed the bills and disappeared into the still night.

Once the sergeant was left alone with his captives, he felt relieved. In those days, every person feared the other, especially in dealings about Jews. Any wrong comment, even unintentional, could spell disaster; helping a Jew was considered a capital crime. The load taken off his shoulders, the sergeant led the men into the barn, where they all spent the rest of the ruinous night uneventfully.

Next morning, before dawn, the guard woke them up and ordered them to march to the Moravian border, where he demanded his pay-off. Jossl, wanting to get the mess over with, asked for a moment in the washroom, where he slit open his shoulders pads and pulled out the currency. The sergeant grabbed the greenbacks and handed them over to the law enforcement staff of the Protectorate.

A report was quickly written up and the Slovak sergeant, evidently ill at ease, disappeared as if the ground under his feet was burning. With his loot in the form of hard currency in his pockets, he wished to be far away. He knew it was manna from the heavens, which had fallen straight into his pockets, and he would not endanger it by dilly-dallying around officials, be they on Czech or Slovak territory.

The man in charge at the Protectorate border crossing was the prototype of a doddering and indecisive official. Jossl, well-trained in assessing the qualities of individuals he had to deal with, understood instantly that he must not even suggest a pay-off. The man on duty would fall into a fit of apoplexy by the sheer fear of engaging in any illegal conduct.

True to his irresolute disposition, he ordered his charges to sit on a bench as he phoned for instructions to headquarters in Prague. There his superiors dissected the Gordian knot for him, authorizing him to send the offenders back to Prague, where the proper authorities would deal with the matter. The essentials thus resolved, Jossl had to convince the timid official that they had the right to a phone call.

The man, for whom the law meant the Gospel truth, accepted Jossl's assurances that each one was legally entitled to a call. Not quite certain he could deny Jossl's cogent plea, he leaned to the side of leniency, allowing one call to Jossl only. That was all that Jossl hoped to achieve. He made contact and, using an insider's cryptic code, he informed Prague of their bad luck and the counter-measures he had taken.

It became the duty of Prague's Jewish community to handle the impasse quickly, discreetly and efficiently. Since the Nazi occupation, the representatives of the Jewish community cultivated, at a substantial cost, a liaison with law enforcement.

This resource was to be tapped only in the case of dire emergency. If there ever was an affair which qualified, it was this one.

Police headquarters obligingly assigned the case to a task force whose top man was aware of the sensitive situation. A decision was reached to resolve the impasse quickly but with consideration of mutual interests and tactful diplomacy. It goes without saying that the Jewish community paid enormously to hush up the affair, but none of the culprits went to jail or were even charged. The transgression was classified as a misdemeanor, a childish prank perpetrated by grown men.

In a secret agreement with the head of the security board, the Jewish community committed itself to remove all parties involved from Prague to silence any future inquiry by the German authorities, should they ever get wind of the affair in the Slovak forests.

All proceeded as planned. Money changed hands, and the five men were included in the next transport of deportees to the concentration camp, Theresienstadt. They left within a week. As a precaution, the organizers scattered their numbers widely apart and, just in case the police became meddlesome, they were interspersed among the one thousand others. All proceeded as planned, and Jossl and his buddies arrived as ordinary inmates unburdened by a police record.

Although Jossl was deeply disappointed with the failure of his escape, just when he thought himself free to leave for Palestine, still he was aware that under the perilous circumstances the community negotiated the best possible deal. In turn, the men in charge of Jewish affairs in Prague felt indebted to Jossl, who did so much for the beleaguered Czech Jews. Additionally, the Council of Elders at Theresienstadt was tactfully instructed to billet Jossl as comfortably as possible, and assist him by any possible means to ensure his survival. The members of the Zionists organization were nothing if not caring in looking after one of their own.

The powers in the camp knew about Jossl and his merits even before he showed up. The Elders sent him to work in the bakery that prepared bread and pastry for the SS.

Theresienstadt boasted two bakeries. One produced bread for the inmates, mixed with some strange flour which tasted like sawdust, somewhat damp and often moldy. Even the starving inmates hardly thought it edible; no one would have considered it fit for human consumption. The other bakery was well-equipped and was assigned to supply the Germans. The bread, rolls, and pastry were of excellent quality, prepared from the best of raw materials and could favorably compare with any sweet shop or bakery, exceeding most even in peacetime.

It was extremely pricey and difficult to obtain a work assignment in the inmates' bakery, for all were hungry, and bread was a valuable currency with which one could barter. Even so, it was incomparably more lucrative to maneuver oneself into the SS special bakery. Not only were the raw materials used of the best quality, but also there was a greater variety in the recipes for the pastries and goods supplied to the commandery. The man in charge was a professional baker, and he paid great care to the excellence and choice of the baked goods. He could ill afford to irritate his Nazi overlords; he knew that the ill-humored commandant would dispatch him to the East without blinking an eye.

There was another fringe benefit to this one-of-a-kind job. By order of the commandant, all food handlers for the Germans were exempt from deportation East. The all-powerful Nazi did not want any changes to affect his culinary delights; those performing to his satisfaction were to remain in Theresienstadt. For as long as they produced his favorite tidbits, they remained under his personal protection. The entire crew from the special bakery lived together in quarters much superior to those of the average inmate. Their consistent health was of importance; no feeble and certainly no sick individual was allowed to touch anything the Nazis would consume. The baker in charge was personally responsible for their clean bill of health.

Jossl began his stint in Theresienstadt as a "prominent." Immediately, he was the target of much envy by most inmates. Anyone installed in the "German bakery" would neither starve, sustain health damage, fear deportation East, nor be housed in the crowded, vermin infested barracks, filled with stench and subject to lethal, contagious diseases.

I met Jossl several weeks after his arrival in Theresienstadt. He came to the sick bay seeking advice from a physician for his chronic ear infection. As a young boy, Jossl suffered recurrent ear infections, which due to his family's poverty remained untreated. The condition bothered him a lot, for the acute flare-ups caused pain and discharge from his ear. His hearing on the affected side was much diminished, and Jossl feared complete deafness.

On that afternoon I was helping in the infirmary with the otolaryngologist, with whom I worked my long shifts. I was triaging the many patients standing in long queues in front of the infirmary. The long, narrow halls of the former military hospital were filthy, noisy and run-down from wear and tear. Although adequate for the military units stationed there earlier, it was totally insufficient for the many packed, maltreated inmates.

Jossl waited patiently for his turn, a rare quality in a place where most pushed and jostled to jump the queue, even if by a single place. A young, sinewy man, who did not use his strength to push ahead of others, he impressed me. He sported a diffident smile, another novelty in a camp, where most who survived for some time were brash and impudent.

When I asked him about the nature of his visit, he introduced himself and explained his ailment. He was concise in telling me of his pain, the fever and the discharge from his ear. He understood that his illness had been neglected, but he was keen to have it treated now and perhaps, he inquired, the physician could have a suggestion for him. It was late afternoon when the specialist finally saw the patiently waiting man. The doctor examined him and finally advised Jossl that there was a treatment, but not in Theresienstadt, where he had no drugs to dispense.

Jossl asked for the name of the medication and hinted that he had channels through which he could organize the needed drugs. The flabbergasted doctor repeated the brand names, which Jossl committed to memory. Actually, Jossl had more than one way to obtain the medicine he needed. He could bribe a sentry, who could buy the drugs in the nearby town of Litomerice, or try to connect with his confidants in Prague, who could arrange for the drugs to be smuggled in.

I do not know which option he chose, but he managed all in record time. The camp's etiquette demanded that questions should not be asked about illicit acquisitions, and we all observed the taboo. Jossl returned many times to the hospital, though his condition markedly improved. Gradually the two of us became friends, and I soon found out that Jossl was exceptionally well-informed about events within and outside the walls of the camp. He would never as much as hint about his sources, but it was an easy guess that he had access to newspapers that no Jew could acquire.

Our conversation was mainly restricted to the few sentences we could exchange while I was on duty. The hospital was a hectic place, with so many sick and so few able-bodied to minister to the needs of the afflicted. With time, I came to understand that Jossl was an exceptional man, not only bright and courageous, but with plenty of smarts. There was no lack of brains, especially in such an abysmal place as Theresienstadt, but Jossl was also kind, generous, selfless and caring. The latter qualities were scarce, indeed almost totally absent in a camp where almost all starved and ailed, and where the harvest of death rose to unimaginable heights.

Step by little step Jossl came to trust me, a feat not readily attainable to a tough, rather distrustful man. He gradually began to confide in me his plans and hopes for the future, should there be one for us. Jossl nursed his beautiful dream of settling in Palestine and building the new Jewish homeland. It would be this new Jewish state that would once and for all bring an end to the persecution of the defenseless Jew, discriminated against by all the nations under the sun.

His anger rose when he described the many affronts staged by the nations of Eastern Europe, which went either unpunished or were only nominally censored by local law enforcement, which made it their practice to come too late when called to quell a pogrom. He almost shook with hatred when he talked about the gun toting SS men, who could kill or maim any Jew they fancied. He could not know that his fury was almost prophetic. It was his dream to survive and build the state which would amend such glaring injustices.

On a more mundane level, Jossl disclosed that he was much impressed by the Czech Jews who were so different from his peers in Ruthenia. Though no inmate was well-dressed, the imprints of an urban, sophisticated environment was not lost on this perceptive man. The relative affluence of the Jews of Bohemia, compared to the grinding penury of the Ruthenian Jews, was easily discernible. It was the poise and gait, the more polished speech, the refined manners, and the broader education, which became evident in any conversation, even a very casual one. This exposed the gap between the West and East of the same state. Jossl partially blamed the prevailing economic chasm for the glaring differences.

In Theresienstadt, he was attracted to the formerly wealthy and more assimilated faction of Jews for their socialization. Jossl unconsciously came into ideological conflict with one of Zionism's tenets, which frowned on higher education and physical comforts. These were deemed frivolous dissipations of energy for the goal oriented, near-fanatical zealots. The physical body was to be cared for and viewed as the vehicle for the vital work of Jewish independence.

The Zionists firmly held that it was imperative to rid Jews of their reverence for higher education, which they believed resulted from the warped values of the Diaspora, which for centuries had denied Jews the normal choices of professions. The Zionists rejected much of the prior pride of Jewish life, the many outstanding intellectuals gracing the nations of Europe, enriching many nations' cultures with art, advanced thinking, business acumen and a myriad other endeavors. The many celebrated Jewish personalities, whose genius enriched the world, were dismissed as pathological outgrowths of the pressured Jewish existence foisted by their unkind and expedient host nations.

Generation after generation of Jews in the Diaspora were forbidden the ownership of land, hence the scarcity of Jewish farmers. The same was true of service in the military; assorted rulers would not admit Jews into their armies, and Jews themselves had little enthusiasm to fight or die for nations that perennially tormented them.

The tenets of Zionism were set to rectify these inequities. The ideology was born in the crucible of Judaic survival and identity, colored by the prevailing political doctrines of the time: Communism, capitalism, nationalism and democracy. The place of the individual in society, his rights, and his duty to his nation, balanced by his self image and cultural and religious heritage, was Zionism's solution to man's social struggles.

Zionists believed, and still do, that by freeing the Jews all mankind becomes freer, and by returning them to their place of origin, Judaism with its important contributions might survive. This seemed compatible, almost across the board with all schools of Jewish belief.

Therefore, the main goal was to return the Jew to perceived normality. Redemption would be achieved by working the soil of the ancient homeland, which the modern day Maccabees would bravely and valiantly defend against any threat or enemy. This course alone would redeem the wounded Jewish psyche and restore the dispersed minority to their rightful place among the family of nations.

With this version of history, the logical conclusion was that a very basic theoretical education was mandatory, and the highest value was placed on the proper training for modern farming, manual labor and courage in battle. The Zionists urged that some traditional Jewish values be turned topsy-turvy, to ready the Jew for his very difficult task of reclaiming the land of Israel. Palestine was much neglected under Ottoman rule and sparsely populated by Arabs, whose methods of agriculture were outdated and harmful to the land.

It was a motto of the Zionists, later popularized by Golda Meir: "People without land returned to land without people." To accomplish this, the Jew had to undergo a major metamorphosis, denouncing most intellectual pursuits and foregoing many physical and trivial luxuries. It was but a logical extension that women were not supposed to use cosmetics; even lipstick was a paltry superficiality, which no "*Chaverah*" would use or own. Jossl bought into that philosophy wholeheartedly, but he could not help liking the softer, less opinionated women, who were never exposed to the harsh indoctrination mandating that women deny themselves all self-indulgences.

Jossl invested the initial weeks of his stay in Theresienstadt in observation of the undercurrents in the camp. He decided that it was too risky to rely solely on the fickle fortune of his job in the bakery. He made up his mind to supplement his camp rations by repairing shoes; his craft was in high demand in a place where no new footwear could be bought, and old shoes quickly fell apart.

The camp's currency was bread and, for some well-appointed inmates, cigarettes, which could be exchanged for almost any desired item. An inmate had to forego several bread rations to have the holes in his shoes patched up and in this way the cobbler was almost guaranteed a steady supply of commodities. Jossl spread the word that he was able and willing to repair shoes, and before long he had more work than he had time or energy for. However, Jossl's good luck did not leave him, not yet anyway. He ran into a man, Armin, who apprenticed with him back in Ruthenia. They agreed to join forces and work together after hours, moonlighting.

Only a few inmates had access to the large "*Kleiderkammer*," the barn, which held all kinds of clothing taken from the newly arriving inmates. Countless pairs of shoes were stored there, as well as piles of garments confiscated from the steadily streaming transports of Jews. Those who had connections or wielded power, "*Protectia*," did not need to seek out Jossl and Armin. Those with access to the "*Kleiderkammer*" could have their pick of garments and footwear, which lay about to be hauled to Germany. However, there were only a handful of those so privileged. Most inmates had no other choice but try to salvage the one and only pair of shoes they owned and wore day in and day out.

Matters were made more difficult by the compulsory daily work attendance. If the holes in the shoes were so large as to let water or snow in, or the tear prevented walking, immediate repair was a necessity, for absence from work was severely punished; after all, "*arbeit macht frei*" ("freedom through work," the mendacious mantra coined by the Nazis). Such crises demanded repair—and payment, which cut deeply into a starving man's food supply. Camp life consisted of uninterrupted trade-offs.

There were no easy or comfortable alternatives, the options hovered between lesser evils. The choice was often between one which would prevent instant death, a second that might delay present woes, and a third to prolong life, if only for a short time.

Jossl and Armin were much sought-after artisans. They repaired shoes, clogs or whatever footwear, as well as possible, anywhere, asking for lower payments than other cobblers in the camp. Even the thinnest slice of bread the prisoner had to do without was potentially fatal. But in the camps, ruled by the laws of the jungle, only the fittest survived; there were few, if any, inmates motivated by humanitarian or charitable considerations. One and all wanted to live, and this usually pitted one inmate against the other. The Germans often forced the inmates into a confrontational stance, turning victims into mutual enemies.

The Germans enjoyed watching their captives' doomsday dance, knowing that all would eventually perish, but the hectic scuffle satisfied some perverted sense. Why, they considered it hilarious that all wanted to live and would do anything to delay the inevitable, final outcome. The Nazis watched and were amused; they knew that they had the last laugh. To themselves they rationalized that they were experimenting with a subhuman species, studying the struggle of the fittest to survive under "controlled" conditions.

Before long, the camp grapevine informed the commandant that there were two master cobblers in the camp plying their trade. The commander was an avaricious man, who smelled an opportunity. He might benefit from their skills, if they were as proficient as hearsay had it.

He ordered Jossl to present himself to the commandery, where he addressed him in a less arrogant tone than customarily used with inmates. He ordered Jossl to make a pair of high, military boots; the kind SS men wore as a part of their uniforms.

Jossl was rather unhappy about the assignment; he knew that any entanglement with the Nazis meant playing with fire. He was given two weeks for the delivery of a perfect pair of boots. The material supplied was of the best and finest quality. Before Jossl was dismissed, the commandant issued a rather blunt warning: "If the boots do not meet the highest standards, you will be sent East with the next transport leaving Theresienstadt." On the other hand, if the final product satisfied the commandant, Jossl would be handsomely rewarded. Other orders would follow suit, and both cobblers could do very well indeed.

The commandant's plan was quite ingenious. The SS men received a generous allowance for their attire. If Jossl could supply the boots for a pittance, the commandant could pocket the money. He would reward the shoemakers with some food, which was of no cost to him.

Jossl hardly underestimated the double-edged jeopardy, inherent in the commandant's proposition. It was a no-win situation. If he were to deliver a shoddy product, the two cobblers would be enrolled in the next transport East. If, in turn, he satisfied the commandant, he would receive some food, but they would be closer to danger. The statutes of the SS stipulated total prohibition of any contact between the Germans and the Jews.

In this new relationship lay the seed of hazard, an incubus. The miserly man would entice the cobblers for a while, satisfy his avarice and then, to cover his hide, would sentence both to death or ship them to an extermination camp. Jossl had no choice. The only course he could follow was to satisfy the Nazi and let events take their own course.

Two weeks later, Jossl presented the commandant with a sample of his craft, which genuinely pleased the Nazi. He immediately ordered more pairs, providing exact measurements, raw materials and a deadline for delivery. The new project was well under way.

For a while, all went well. It almost seemed that Jossl had worried needlessly. Nonetheless, Jossl was filled with foreboding that time was fast running out. Jossl and Armin accumulated a small fortune, not only by concentration camp standards, but by any worldly yardstick. Both men were paid with bread, cigarettes, margarine and sugar, all commodities in high demand in Theresienstadt.

Jossl and Armin exchanged most of it for gold, jewelry and hard currency, always illegally circulating in the camp, which many starvelings readily swapped for foodstuffs. Each master cobbler amassed a considerable nest egg for his new beginning after the war. Armin had faith that he would live to see the end of this misery, whilst Jossl did not believe that the day of liberation would come in his lifetime.

Jossl was a generous and compassionate man who loved to help his less fortunate friends. Nearly all his friends were less well provided for and, since he could help only a few, he carefully chose those he believed to be the worst off, the most in need.

In the course of our talks, I often opened my heart to him, not so much about the fact that I was famished, but for his opinion on how best to barter my bread rations, my only contribution to my ailing family's sustenance. Had I kept all my rations for myself, I still would have been starving.

Nevertheless, I gave up most of my bread, my last resort, to help my ailing sister, then my father, and eventually my mother. All became gravely ill and towards their last days they no longer could consume and digest the horrible gruel distributed in the camp. I was then seventeen years old, and though aged beyond my years, I was no match for Jossl's foxiness and savvy.

While I had no reservations in asking for advice, I still could not beg for handouts. Initially I thought I would die if I were to panhandle. Later, our misery taught me otherwise. When my ill and hungry parents needed something which I could not provide, I swallowed my pride and asked for it, or, worse yet, I offered any service, which would award me with the needed food.

Jossl was considerate enough to stop me in mid-sentence, pressing his index finger gently over my lips, tacitly nodding his consent to supply my needs. On one occasion, I asked him why he was so selflessly kind to me. He flashed his enigmatic smile, pondering a reply. For a long moment, there was a deep silence around us. I fixed my stare at him, never losing eye contact, hoping to force an answer.

Suddenly Jossl looked very young, almost a teenager, though I knew that he was twenty-four years old already. He even blushed, his face radiated innocence and a clean, boyish charm. For a moment the hardened, tough Jossl I knew for so long was nowhere in sight. His guile and craftiness vanished into a new Jossl. It was then that I realized that he was never really young and carefree; he could not even articulate his interest in me, in a boy-girl relationship. He had spent his youth in a dangerous world, surviving by his wits and ability to manage situations to his advantage, never far from danger.

Finally, he answered in a stammering, untutored Czech, the language of a simple man, not well-read or articulate, unaccustomed to the verbal expression of ideas. His slow reply surprised me, to say the least. He mentioned reluctantly that he was aware that in days bygone the two of us belonged to different social classes, but the changed times balanced disparities out.

He than expressed his hope that, given time and opportunity, I might learn to like him, perhaps in a different way than just as a casual friend. He continued in his halting speech, telling me that if he were to survive the war, he would fulfill his dream and emigrate to Palestine, and he would like nothing better than for me to join him and settle in one of the collective settlements with him.

I could hardly believe my ears. Was this a marriage proposal, Jossl style? I did not want to hurt or humiliate him, so I replied with an evasion. I stuttered something about my parents being assimilated, and they would never want to leave the country they considered home, the Czech land. I wanted to turn him down gently, for fear of losing his friendship.

Jossl's enigmatic smile twinkled just for a fraction of a moment as he said that both of us hardly made any sense; only God knew who if anybody will live to see the end of this terrible war. He caressed my hair, said not to worry; he'd love to help my tried parents and me during the dark days of torment.

Jossl and I never broached that subject again, though neither of us ever forgot it. Later, when I was more mature, I understood that Jossl loved me in his unselfish way. His love did not place demands or expect immediate reciprocation. There was great depth to this young man who knew few comforts and by and large was self-educated. He was a devoted and loyal friend, faithful in his attachments and affection to those he called his friends.

The summer of 1944 had begun to recede into fall when ugly rumors hit the camp. Theresienstadt was to be dissolved. The camp buzzed with threats of the general liquidation of all inmates, irrespective of age or physical condition. Jossl kept his cool, pretending to doubt the hearsay. If "class" is, as Hemingway defined it, "composure under duress," Jossl had a great deal of class and style.

Jossl was an invaluable friend. He stood by me in the darkest hours when my parents slowly faded away and, while he could not allay my heartbreak and despair, he was a stalwart comrade whose presence alone provided great support. Initially Jossl shared my hopes that I could avert their demise, and he helped as much as he could.

When the struggle was all but over and all my efforts had proved to be in vain, Jossl stood, backing me in silence. As I could not change or even delay the slipping away of my loved ones into the beyond, Jossl was there. One by one, my family members perished, fading away from an ugly world of indescribable suffering. To us then, it appeared that we had entered the last chapter of this surreal, unbelievable apocalypse.

The latest whisper signaled the oft-floated rumor of the impending liquidation of Theresienstadt, which we often dismissed as a trial balloon aimed at frightening the inmates. However, we all were well aware that Theresienstadt was only a transit and holding camp. Its initial purpose was to facilitate the complex logistics of moving the millions of Jews from their homes throughout Europe to the "Final Solution," death by gas, in the extermination camps to the East.

Jossl and Armin continued working at the bakery and as cobblers for the commandant. Their good luck lasted longer than anyone dared expect. Gradually both became less anxious, accustomed to carrying the double burden, considering themselves lucky beyond their wildest dreams.

As often is the case, when both men felt the least threatened, the axe struck.

The news from the battlefield continued to report uninterrupted victories; only a few believed a word of the thinly veiled lies. It was no secret that the Allies were advancing steadily, gaining ground, and had air superiority in the skies over Germany. Many an SS man began to worry about his fate at war's end, and most decided to clean up their act, to conceal or explain their nefarious deeds, before it was too late. One of the easiest and cheapest ways to redress an image was by ceasing the corruption and black market activities, at the expense of the inmates.

Although Jossl and Armin were well aware that they were blatantly exploited, the deal was also very advantageous to them. However, the commandant, much shaken by the torrent of news of German losses and retreats, felt that he had to terminate his sordid profiteering. The easiest way to silence the two potential witnesses was to remove them from the camp by deportation East.

In 1944, all transports leaving Theresienstadt were directed to Auschwitz, from which return was not likely. There both Jossl and Armin would vanish within the vast multitude of inmates, no longer presenting any danger. Nobody would know them by their Theresienstadt sobriquet "the commandant's cobblers."

The notorious last commandant of Theresienstadt was busy with his plans to slip unobtrusively into civilian life and dissociate himself from his Nazi years. A smarter man would have recognized that it was not only naïve but frankly impossible to disavow his participation in Nazi crimes and slip, like a turncoat, into an invisible existence. He was, after all, a high Nazi official, and his only chance of avoiding apprehension would have been to flee far away from the country where he committed his many crimes. Many chose this route and succeeded in hiding, mainly in countries sympathetic to fascist ideology.

Many a passionate member of the elite SS units hoped that the good fortune they enjoyed in Hitler's heydays might not yet desert them. Did they not luxuriate in a pleasant and profitable niche, while other young Germans, regular soldiers, were fighting on the Russian front? There, in the vast expanse of the Russian plains, they were freezing and dying in swarms; others were wounded, crippled and maimed for life.

The chosen few, appointed to administer Hitler's "Final Solution," spent the war in lucrative, safe positions, overlooking and organizing the wholesale murder of Jews. In addition, most of these Hitler's plenipotentiaries enriched themselves beyond their wildest dreams.

The commandant ordered Jossl and Armin out of Theresienstadt, giving them just a few hours' notice. Jossl was in a hurry as he dropped by to take leave of me. He said there were reasons to believe that the entire camp will be dismantled and he suggested that we should look out for each other in the new camp. In the unlikely case of our survival, we should try to meet in Prague.

He brushed his lips against my cheek and whispered that he had buried a small fortune in gold, jewelry and hard currency in what he believed was a safe place. He hoped to put it to good use in case there was a future in store for us. I did not want to know the location of the hiding place. In case of suspicion, the interrogations were so brutal that even the strongest divulged all they knew.

Jossl seemed disappointed that I refused to listen to his news about the whereabouts of his hiding place, and as time ran out, he took leave of me. He gave me another perfunctory peck on my cheek and left rather abruptly. I followed his quickly disappearing silhouette, soon engulfed in the teeming hive of rushing inmates, all sharing his banishment to the East.

The last leg of his journey through the Nazi mayhem I learned only as hearsay. I pieced it together from information I received from those who were with him after his departure from Theresienstadt.

After the war only one of the "commandant's cobblers" returned from the bowels of hell. Armin by a miracle survived while Jossl, to my grief, perished. Most of what I am about to recount is Armin's narrative, supplemented by a few details from other friends who shared Jossl's last days and witnessed his death.

The loading of the train destined for Auschwitz took place, as usual, behind the "Hamburg" barracks, where the close proximity of the tracks allowed the rapid clearing of the transport. Armin and Jossl climbed into one of the boxcars, where the throng of people was so thick that they had barely enough space to stand. Within an hour people began to faint, more died as the trip progressed, but all had to remain in an upright position; there was no space to lay the lifeless bodies.

In one corner of the car was a pail, the only receptacle for the waste of some 80 people jammed into each car. It goes without saying that even before the train jerked into motion, the bucket overflowed. The air in the tightly sealed car became unfit to breathe. Many were suffering with diarrhea before leaving. Without other sanitation and many unable to reach the pail anyway, people relieved themselves where they stood. Soon most stood ankle-deep in human waste. Few would attempt to get to the pail, having to step on some people, most already at the end of their tether. Only on a few occasions when the train came to a halt, the bolted door was opened, and permission was granted to empty the pail.

The nerves of the deportees were badly frayed, stupefied by the overwhelming stench, body pressed against body, without respite. Few noticed that no food or water was distributed throughout the entire duration of the journey. With every passing hour, the agony in the car increased, and most were convinced and some wished that they would die before arriving at their destination.

Then, suddenly, the moment all prayed for came. The train jerked to a halt and the bolted doors of the cars were wrenched open. Sharp lights flooded the nearly completely dark cars for an instant, blinding people who had traveled for two days and three nights without daylight. The boxcars had no windows only a small, barred opening high up near the ceiling and a few cracks in the walls, which allowed only for a dark murkiness.

The din as the cars were opened was ear shattering. Momentarily blinded, then squinting, they could see heavily armed SS men, some restraining snarling dogs, encircling the entire train. Strange men in striped uniforms ran around shouting at the newly arrived to get out at double time. Bewildered, the people were convinced that they had arrived in hell, when only seconds ago they had been grateful for their release from the cars.

The SS fired warning shots to intimidate and drive home the point that they meant business. If the half-dead people did not hurry up at an acceptable speed, the SS would execute every tardy schlemiel right on the platform. Those who managed to jump out or be pushed were ordered to form columns and advance to the end of the ramp.

Individuals deemed slow were beaten or shot, left to lie on the ground to be collected later. At some point the procession came to a halt, and nearly all were motioned to the right side. A handful only went to the left, but from a distance everything seemed terrifying, bleary and inscrutable.

Armin jumped down first, followed by Jossl. Then in the melee, they lost sight of each other. The column had to advance in an orderly fashion; the Germans had a penchant for "law and order," Nazi style. Armin later recounted how, as he looked back, he saw the pile of dead and dying left behind in the car and caught a glimpse of Jossl who was only steps behind.

In an instant, all became a blur, for Armin was dealt a brutal blow with a stick. Armin's turning around displeased one of the men clad in the striped uniforms. Looking back, talking, turning or waving, all was strictly prohibited and punished severely. They were told to leave their knapsacks in the cars; those would be delivered to them later straight into the new camp. The word "later" meant never.

The column advanced in one direction, passing in front of an officer who separated the arriving Jews into two groups. Most were directed to the right, and a few were sent to the left. Evidently, they were being scrutinized for a selection of some kind, which took place right on the brightly lit "Jewish ramp."

The entire scene was surreal, lifted out of a horror movie. The arriving Jews had little time to ponder the dread unfolding in front of their eyes. The screech of shouted orders and sporadic volleys from shotguns were alarming and deafening. Few regained full composure before approaching the notorious Dr. Mengele, who not only orchestrated this rabid scene, but now went on to perform the selection.

Before confronting the "angel of death of Auschwitz," Armin, and Jossl probably as well, guessed the purpose of this selection. The group sent to right was made up of older men, older women and children. Those appearing unwell were directed to the right. Clearly, this was the wrong place to be. The Germans had little use for Jews who could not work for their war machine or the economy of the "great Reich."

Jossl and Armin, both in their early twenties, looked strong and healthy, obviously good prospects for slave labor. Their time of incarceration in Theresienstadt had not exacted a heavy toll, compliments of their moonlighting. They were chosen for forced labor and directed to the left of the "angel of death." They joined the thousands of slaves exploited, till their dying breath, to advance the German war effort.

What followed was routine, in Auschwitz. The vast majority of the transport was ruled unfit for life; not usable to the Third Reich, they were quickly loaded onto large lorries marked with the calming insignia of the Red Cross. Those too weak or reluctant to climb up into the trucks were beaten savagely by the men in striped uniforms, then lifted and tossed up brutally. At times, they were already, mercifully dead, killed by ferocious blows to their heads or necks. When fully loaded, the lorries sped in the direction of the crematories, where all were pushed into mock showers, which in reality were huge gas chambers.

Auschwitz had the most advanced and modern model of gas chamber in the Third Reich, holding up to 2,000 men, women and children at a time; it was far more efficient than the installations in other extermination camps. Auschwitz could snuff the life out of more then 10,000 people a day. There, squeezed tightly, not leaving space to breath, the inmates were suffocated with Cyclon B, an insecticide.

Those chosen for hard labor, including our two cobblers, were subject to a rough, ignominious initiation to Auschwitz. Orders were screamed, reinforced by vicious blows rained on those deemed too slow, reluctant or disorganized. The pain forced the men to an accelerated pace and immediate compliance.

The first order called for them to undress, suspend their effects on a hanger and then on a specific hook. Then they had to tie their laces leaving the shoes under their clothes. A fast dash to the adjacent shower rooms followed, where their fears of death by gas were washed away with the first drops of fresh water. Their faces moistened, mixed with their tears; even the most hardened men cried freely when they finally trusted that the sprinklers discharged only real water. It was the first moment of relief since they had left Theresienstadt.

Moments before being pushed into the showers, their heads were shaved clean by rough looking men, wielding large, rusty scissors, who with a few deft clips removed all their hair. True, at times they scraped the skin, but in general they acquitted themselves of their task in no time flat.

Following the shower, which nearly scalded their skins one minute and turned them icy the next, they were ordered into the adjoining hall where other inmates tossed their wardrobe at them. It consisted of striped uniforms, most badly soiled and full of holes. None received undergarments, only pants and tunics in various stages of disintegration.

The next step, almost concluding their homecoming to Auschwitz, was to be branded: tattooed with a number on their forearm. This humiliation was the beginning of their full erasure, starting with their names. Henceforth all went by those insolent numbers, marked like cattle. They were no longer addressed by name. They became number so-and-so.

All that completed, the prisoners were ordered into an empty barracks, where they all dropped of, dead tired, on a bare floor. They were exhausted by their ordeal, the journey and shock of their first impressions of hell.

The first night's sleep was fitful, interrupted by unusual noises. The men were so tightly packed, sleeping on the floor, that every time one turned, the rest had to follow suit. Had they not been totally spent by their ordeal, many fights would have broken out in this wretched mass of human desolation.

As on the train a pail was placed in one corner of the hall, entirely out of reach for most. However, an inmate who soiled his clothes was punished by twenty strokes with a club or a Kapo's cane, a penalty few survived. Those men, who could not wait to relieve themselves in the morning, fell into the habit of using their food dish. It sounds repulsive and beyond civilized imagination, but it was the least dangerous solution for this urgent bodily need. Certainly, it was easier to wash the befouled dish than to be beaten to death for soiling one's garb.

They were awakened, while outside the night was still dark, to the piercing sound of a whistle. In Auschwitz reveille was at 4 AM. They were ordered out of the barracks, to stand at attention under the leaden, gray sky of a freezing fall morning. Frost comes early in Poland, and this particular year the winter came earlier than expected.

Armin recounted all this to me after the war; occasionally he was quite emotional, reliving his experiences in a quivering voice, eyes glistening with tears he could not conceal.

During the first roll call, Armin reminisced, he was shivering, hungry and despondent beyond words. Still, he squinted into the darkness, searching for Jossl, the man who was closer to his heart than his own brother. He could not see him, but that did not mean much; in the prevailing darkness he saw only a short distance away, and he could not ask, for talking or moving was strictly forbidden.

Armin looked with dread at the long rows of dead bodies, carried out from the barracks. Many men perished during their first night in Auschwitz. Their bodies were neatly lined up, for they had to be included in the count for an accurate census. This was their last function before being carted off to the crematories.

The first count over, the inmates were lined up for yet another selection, to assign them into working units. Armin was chosen for a detachment destined for Flossenburg, where most inmates toiled in a munitions factory producing bazookas. This production site was known for the incredible speed of work by fast moving chains of inmates, whose tasks were intertwined.

At Flossenburg, inmates worked from six in the morning until seven in the evening, under unimaginable conditions. They drudged, closely supervised by the SS, who shot anyone slowing down or fainting. Even those who dropped dead were shot in the nape of the neck, just to make sure.

The inmates did not get water, the factory was unheated, their clothes were flimsy, and none had a sweater or warm pants, not to mention the unmentionables. If an SS man on duty disliked an inmate, he would accuse him of disobedience. The punishment meted out was 25 lashes, administered by another inmate, a Kapo, who made sure the flogging was cruel and brutal, thus supervising the execution.

Armin had the unfortunate assignment to load the bazookas. The prisoners were ordered to use picric acid, which for any other work detail called for the use of gas masks, but in Flossenburg the Jews did not receive any such amenity; little did the SS care how much lung damage they inflicted. The slaves were dying in droves, but more and more were sent, if requested. Unlike slaves in other times and countries, Jews need not be fed or housed, for they were readily replaced, targeted for elimination and their ranks easily replenished with others. Only death liberated them from the German yoke.

Most German concentration camps, ghettos and jails outdid the horrors of any medieval jail; the best and usually the only liberator was death. To escape the clutches of the ruling sadists, the SS men, the assorted Kapos and Blockaeltestes, was a release from the uneven struggle in which most Jews were doomed to die.

Armin was lucky; he lived through this ordeal and eventually managed to bribe a Kapo and was transferred to another commando, where he was in less jeopardy.

With the advent of the winter, in early 1945, most camps in the threatened Nazi realm received orders to evacuate in the direction of Theresienstadt. Armin and a handful of others survived the death march over the frozen roads of Europe, without food or drink, poorly clothed, suffering from frostbite, diarrhea, and umpteen painful miseries.

When he reached Theresienstadt, Armin was near his end, but a great miracle was also near. Germany was finally brought to her knees, defeated and exposed for the unspeakable crimes perpetrated by the "master race." Many believe that it was that wish to witness the final reckoning of the perpetrators, which prodded many to carry on and continue. The desire to see justice and retribution stimulated the dying to muster the super-human effort, to take another step, one followed by a thousand more similarly excruciating ones, which might allow them to live and bear witness to the Nazi atrocities.

Armin succeeded, but Jossl did not. Jossl ran out of luck, in the final moments of the Jewish apocalypse.

I filled in his missing final days only after the war. As soon as I was physically able to, I embarked upon an intense search for those who might have known, were near or spent time with him after his arrival in Auschwitz.

On that very first morning, when the newly arrived men were sorted out for different working assignments, when Armin was chosen for Flossenburg, Jossl had the rotten luck of being selected for the notorious "Buna" detachment. Little did he know that this was the worst possible commando, even by Auschwitz's standards. Auschwitz, too, had different circles of hell, and Buna was at the bottom of the seemingly endless pit.

Those included in the Buna detachment marched to the freight train and were quickly jostled in. To ensure their compliance, they were brutally beaten by the Kapo. He was a specially wicked beast, cursing and kicking the inmates to an ever-faster speed onto the overflowing wagons. All the Kapos of the Buna commando were vicious and sadistic; all were habitual felons, who enjoyed inflicting pain. They exceeded by leaps and bounds most other Kapos in their eager zest to torture. They were reputed to be the most pitiless and savage of the Nazi cadres.

The journey to Buna took about two hours. When the train came to a halt, the Kapo screamed hysterically, ordering all to get off the train. The inmates were quickly beaten into columns and rushed at an insane speed to the construction site some distance ahead.

Jossl never reached the destination, a work site on a housing project in Buna. Perhaps, as I want to believe, it was a blessing. Few lived to tell the story of the manmade hell of "the Buna detail." Men were shot for perceived inefficient work performance, or they were denounced for the sabotage of orders. Countless men collapsed, dying of exhaustion, on Poland's blood soaked earth.

In spite of all that, I found one man who managed to live and tell the truth about the unimaginable inferno. Zdenek was a handsome youngster from Bohemia who spent a few days in the Buna commando. His handsome, boyish and clean-cut appearance attracted the homosexual Kapo, who released him from this assignment.

Zdenek's unblemished, almost angelic face saved his life, albeit at an enormous price. He had to submit himself to the demands of the Kapo, who kept him as his lover almost to the end of Auschwitz's days, sometime in January 1945. The time spent as the Kapo's lover and servant was hard, but his ordeal was distinctly different than the torment in Buna.

At first Zdenek hesitated to talk about Buna, but then he
grasped that he was my last hope of learning the truth, and I hung
on to every word he uttered. Somehow, that softened his hardened
attitude, and he began his halting narrative.

It was not easy for him to describe what he had to do to
survive Buna; at times his voice trembled with fury, at times tears
rolled down his cheeks as he unraveled the story of his
humiliation, pain and helpless subjugation by a monstrous pervert.
The Kapo was not only a homosexual and a pedophile, but also a
sadist par excellence. The obscenities and lewd acts Zdenek had to
endure to satisfy his sexual needs bordered on super-human
torment. He gnashed his teeth, prevailed and lived to see the day
of freedom.

He remembered Jossl, all right. By sheer co-incidence they
were assigned to the same Buna commando and on their first day
were marched together to the construction site. It was the first and
last day on the Buna detail for both. While Zdenek was noticed
and taken by the pedophile Kapo, who unintentionally and in a
repulsive and horrid way saved his life, Jossl perished. He died a
senseless death even by Auschwitz's standards.

While all slayings, indeed any slaying, is senseless, Jossl's
demise seems, even in retrospect, painfully absurd. Jossl was still
in relatively good shape and perhaps he would have lasted a few
days, during which time he might have arranged a transfer into
another, less dangerous work unit. Jossl had many friends; many
were indebted to him for his generous help in Theresienstadt.
Some might have come through for him; perhaps they were in
position of power in Auschwitz and maybe, just maybe, he might
have lived to the end.

Jossl met his death in a freak accident, the kind that lurked on
every step in that infernal camp. Zdenek, a close acquaintance of
Jossl's from Theresienstadt, vividly recalled the last moments of
Jossl's brief life.

On that fateful day, the column was being marched at a fast
clip, when a man in front of Jossl stumbled and fell. An irate,
crazed Kapo pounced at the offender and began to hit him with his
club. The blows rained on his head and body indiscriminately and
within seconds, blood covered his face, blinding him briefly,

preventing his return to an upright position. The longer the man lay prostrate, the greater the probability that he would be beaten to death. Such were the rough and crude rules of Buna commando. The man writhed with pain, retching, staggered by the ruthless violence.

The SS man accompanying the formation noticed the slow-down and rushed to the site of the trouble. He did not even bother to stop and inquire. Instead, he pulled out his revolver, and took quick aim at the man who still wriggling on the ground, tormented by the irrational violence of the Kapo.

The SS man waved the Kapo aside, aimed at the man on the ground, pulled the trigger and missed. Instead of shooting the man on the ground, his target, he took down the one just behind.

It was Jossl. Jossl was hit in the chest; he tumbled down, mortally wounded by a mad SS man. The German shot from the hip, without as much as stopping, ending the life of a very special man.

It did not end there. The SS man took another aim and this time killed the still groaning, battered man and then, turning back to Jossl, uncertain if he were dead, shot him once more in the abdomen.

Jossl did not suffer long. He lost consciousness almost instantly, bleeding profusely from the wound in his belly. The projectile probably fractured his spleen, causing massive blood loss.

The men of the commando had to carry the lifeless bodies to their workplace, where many more became victims of the pandemonium staged by the crazed Nazis and their helpers the Kapos. Few slaves lasted longer than a few days in the Buna detail.

The death of the two men, the brutality shown and the lust for murder, convinced Zdenek to be grateful for his option to become a lover and pet to the perverted Kapo, who favored him. Though the price for his privileged, sheltered sustenance in Auschwitz was high, it nonetheless offered a lease on life.

At the end of that tragic day, all the bodies had to be carried back to the camp, just to be included in the evening count at roll call. The numbers had to tally, for a precise census was the top priority of the Germans. Once the count was over and matched, the bodies were released and dispatched to the crematories. Later their ashes were scattered around the plains of Auschwitz.

Jossl did not live long enough to witness his dream, the establishment of the state of Israel, come true. He did not see the year 1948, when the United Nations voted for the partition of Palestine, apportioning it between Jews and Arabs. Though the part allotted to the Jews was but a fraction of the original, historical Israel, the country the Zionists hoped to regain and rebuild, it was nevertheless an independent Jewish state. It gave a home, shield, shelter and security to the remainder of the beleaguered, unwanted, homeless and dispossessed Jews.

Although Jossl never saw that glorious day of Jewish revival, I thought of him as I listened to Prague radio, transmitting the final count from the plenary session of the United Nations. I almost sensed his presence in the room; I visualized his happy smile, his joy at a dream come true.

When I immigrated to Israel in 1949, I had a difficult time establishing myself in the poverty-ridden country. But as soon as I managed to save a few pounds, I went to Jerusalem and planted a tree in one of its surrounding forests, to commemorate deceased relatives and friends. I planted one in Jossl's memory, in the city of his dreams, the city of eternal peace.

Although Jerusalem, quite like Jossl, knew little peace, the city was returned and reestablished as the new capital of the free, independent state of Israel. I can imagine and almost visualize Jossl's pride and happiness as his lifelong dream came true.

Although peace is still a distant dream for the land of Jews, the work of Jossl and his peers laid a foundation for the freedom of the much-tried nation. His work was not in vain and though his life was short and turbulent, it helped to usher in a new dawn.

It is my ardent wish that his soul may rest overlooking the Golden City, which once more Jews call their eternal capital.

Wall where prisoners were shot at Auschwitz,
preserved today as a memorial.
Note the floral tributes laid at the foot of the wall.

(Photo courtesy of the author.)

Epilogue

These accounts conclude my writings about actual events that took place during the Holocaust, as I experienced them first-hand and pieced them together with the help of eyewitnesses. I am convinced that many fates of other countless victims might have been even more illuminating and riveting, but their stories have gone unrecorded. They remained anonymous, featureless, drowned in an ocean of blood spilled by the Nazis. I feel that future generations should read the unadorned truth, for it should serve as a warning to those who follow us, of the consequences of unchecked hatred, prejudice and racial intolerance.

I wanted to portray my relatives and friends as they tried to cope. I believe I would have detracted from their martyrdom, had I skipped some aspect of their lives, which was not necessarily flattering to them. Perhaps the reader paused to consider the ways he would have attempted to survive under the conditions described in the preceding pages. The perpetrators forced us all to use means decent people would never consider as options, and we had to live with those consequences for the rest of our days. This, too, was and still is one of the major crimes committed by the Nazis.

If this book does serve as a warning and guide of how to read the signals of impending doom, it will have served its purpose well. Then Cassandra's hoarse voice can find rest; her task will be fulfilled.

Should the following generations choose to ignore the Holocaust and allow its message to collect in the dustbin of history, they will remain vulnerable to a return of the apocalypse. Considering the technological means available for mass murder in the present day, this prospect is too frightening to contemplate.

I would like to close with the wise words of George Santayana, stating: "Nations who choose to forget their past are doomed to relive it."

May God spare us this fate!

Mass graves, Theresienstadt, preserved today
as a memorial to those inmates who died in the camp.
(Photo courtesy of the author.)

Glossary

Blockaelteste—a powerful privileged inmate, responsible for order and smooth functioning of an entire block, consisting of several barracks within a concentration camp. They were chosen by the Nazis and outranked the Kapos. They were infrequently Jews and like the Kapos were often hard core criminals.

Cherchez la femme—look for the woman, humorously suggesting that a woman may be the cause of a problem or a puzzle.

Corpus Delicti—facts constituting or proving a crime, material substance or foundation corroborating a crime.

Council of the Elders—a group of Jewish men handpicked to assist the Elder of the Jews to maintain the ghetto-camp in working order and carry out the orders of the Nazi officials. The Councils were periodically eliminated for knowing too much.

Elder of the Jews—the top dog of the Council, a Jew chosen by the Nazis to administer the ghetto-camp and implement their orders. The Elder was ousted, after some time in office for being privy to a great deal of inside knowledge, and liquidated.

Judenrein—free of Jews, a definition for a place had been emptied of all its Jewish inhabitants.

Kapo—"Kammeradschafts Polizie," police by peers. An oxymoron, for "Kapos" were brutal sadists, appointed to be the inmates' overseers. They were handpicked by the Nazis, usually from the ranks of chronic, violent criminals, and habitual felons. The vast majority had long criminal records. Few were Jews. Their task was to supervise and brutalize the inmates.

Katzetnik—long-term inmates experienced and weather-beaten, tough and hardened, well-versed in the art of surviving against the odds.

Mein Kampf—"My Struggle," a book written by Adolf Hitler summarizing the Nazi ideology and its future goals and methods. It was dictated in the year 1923, taken down and transcribed by his deputy Rudolf Hess, who shared Hitler's imprisonment (after the "Beer Hall Putsch") in the Landsberg prison.

Musselman—an emaciated, starved and rundown inmate, no longer fully alive, wandering aimlessly in search of food.

Weisung—a specific directive attached to the name of an inmate, usually S.B.= *"Sonder Behandlung"* which in Nazi parlance meant death by gassing, immediately upon arrival in Auschwitz.

Index

A

abortion, 15
agency assisting Jewish
  immigrants (Sochnut),
  305
Aliyah (return or ascent to
  Palestine), 301
Alteste, 10
American GI, 57
American GIs during
  relationship, 59
angel of death of
  Auschwitz, 330
annexation of Austria by
  Germany, 68
Anschluss, 68
anti-Semitism, 296
Arabs, 338
arbeit macht frei, 321
Arbeit macht frei, 144,
  227
Argentina
  sheltering SS men, 91
artisans, 322
Aryan supremacy
  Nazi propaganda against
  Jews, 254
Aufbau Kommando, 252
Auschwitz, 48, 86, 102,
  136, 336
  "family camp", 138, 141
  black market, 184

camp orchestra, 219
chimneys of, 49
continuous murder there,
  51
death ever-present, 140
evacuation before
  Russians arrived, 150
gas chambers, 209
happiness, 143
hierarchy of inmates, 224
Jewish ramp (selection),
  179
largest gas chambers, 331
lorries (trucks) with Red
  Cross, 331
Nazis blowing up of part
  of, 190
selection, 214
selection on entry to, 102
selection on ramp, 46
slaves returned to, 144
starvation in, 49
tattooing of inmates, 332
triumph of death, 189
underground resistance at,
  138
unwritten etiquette, 185
Auschwitz industrial
  complex
  Monowitz, 222
Auschwitz-Birkenau, 131,
  134
Australia, 193
Austrian anti-Semite, 69

B

Bar Mitzvah, 299
barracks
  Auschwitz, 217, 332
  Dachau, 49
barracks in Theresienstadt,
  82
Belarus, 282
Belzec, 252
Berlin
  Gestapo headquarters, 38
Black Rose, 307, 313
Blockaelteste, 138, 142,
  220, 345
body weight loss, 59
Bohemia, 12, 18, 249
bribing border guards, 313
British, 307
Buchenwald, 30, 106
Buna, 222, 335

C

cadavers
  pseudo-medical research,
  38
capitalism, 320
carbon monoxide
  execution using, 252
Ceska Lipa, 127, 128, 129
Chalutz (Pioneer), 305
Chamberlain, Neville, 126
Charles University in
  Prague, 119
Chaverah, 320

Cheb, Czechoslovakia,
  115, 121
Christianity
  Jews converting to, 296
Chuppah (canopy), 29
collective punishment
  German policy, 51
commandant's mistress, 89
Communism, 300, 320
Communist party member
  Kapo, 51
concentration camp
  commodities, 323
confiscated valuables of
  Jews, 272
contraband, seized by
  Nazis, 88
corpus delicti, 92
Corpus Delicti, 345
Council of Elders, 19, 84,
  315
Council of the Elders, 179
Covenant, 302
Crystal Night, 69
Curda (betrayer of
  Heydrich's assassins),
  261
Cyclon B, 41, 47, 181,
  220, 331
Czech army, 248
Czech students
  demonstration, 36
Czech Zionist movement,
  76
Czechoslovakia

Ordering *Inferno* in the US

Contact the author's agent, Dr. Michael Schiff.
His address is:
400 East Bay St., #606, Jacksonville, Fl 32202 USA
He can be reached by phone at **904-358-0466** and by email at
DOVMS@aol.com

___ copies at $ 25.00 each (US dollars)   = _____
Shipping & Handling: 1 – 4 books ($4.95)   = _____
                        5 – 9 books ($9.95)   = _____
                        10 – 19 books ($14.95) = _____
                        20 – 29 books ($19.95) = _____
Total check amount enclosed   = _____

Ordering *Inferno* in Canada

Contact the author, Mrs. Vera Schiff. Her address is:
**5 Kenneth Avenue, #507, Toronto, Ontario, Canada
M2N 6M7**
She can be reached by phone at **416-730-0950** and by email
at veraschiff@aol.com

___ copies at $ 30.00 each (Canadian dollars)   = _____
Shipping & Handling: 1 – 4 books ($4.95)   = _____
                        5 – 9 books ($9.95)   = _____
                        10 – 19 books ($14.95) = _____
                        20 – 29 books ($19.95) = _____
Total check amount enclosed   = _____

Printed in the United States
16759LVS00003B/61-69